Veggie Works Vegan Cookbook
by Mark W. Rasmussen

Copyright © 2001 Mark W. Rasmussen

Cover Painting by Kim Rasmussen (circa 1983)

FIRST_EDITION_PRINTING
VERSION 2 - RELEASE 7
ISBN 0-9709966-1-6

Published by Veggie Works, Inc.,
817 Belmar Plaza, Belmar, NJ 07719
www.veggieworksworld.com

Designed by Luther G. Brossa
52 Belshaw Avenue, Eatontown, NJ 07724
<lgbrossa@hotmail.com>

Printed by Wolf Press, Inc.
1138 Pine Brook Road, Tinton Falls, NJ 07724
732.544.8881 / www.wolfpress.com

DEDICATION

This book is dedicated to all of those individuals whose lives have reached a crossroad. Individuals whose logic and knowledge have outpaced their habits and actions. To the people who realize the universal benefit of adopting a vegan diet, for the betterment of themselves and the world, but have found the path difficult and the resources lacking. And also to those yet unconvinced, I present you with recipes that challenge anything that you can muster from your world of animal products.

Finally, I dedicate this book to the entire animal kingdom, whose suffering and enslavement for the purposes of human consumption, has gone on far too long.

Table of Contents

Contents

Contents

Contents

Soup Making & Other Basics

Contents

From the Grill

Contents

Sautés

Contents

Breads & Doughs

Contents

Vegan Meats

Contents

Desserts

Contents

Contents

Glossary

Appendix

Resource Directory

Homespun Recipes

Index

Credits

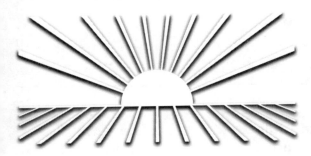

I would like to take time here to thank all of those who helped make the Veggie Works Vegetarian Restaurant a successful, thriving enterprise. If not for these people, this book would never have been written. From the relatives and friends who helped finance its start, to those who helped maintain its daily functions, I thank you all!

Foremost, I thank my lovely wife - and business partner - Elif (aka "Liz"), who shared the struggles and joys with me, from the moment we decided to open a vegetarian restaurant. Through the toughest of times - as with the best of days - we've shared everything. Her spirit, stamina, and skills, have inspired me to persevere through all obstacles. Without her, none of this would have been possible.

My second greatest inspiration has been my young son, Erik, who's been vegan from birth. Erik was raised on the recipes found in this book and is living testament to the power behind this diet. I would also like to thank my two adult daughters Maegan and Temperance who contributed their talents in the first year to help us get started, and whose wisdom and intelligence helped to guide me.

Next are the relatives and friends who contributed financially to our original business start-up, and have been there in times of need. The list begins with my wife's father Dr. Ates Basatemur and my mother, Victoria Rasmussen whose contributions have been greatest. It continues with my deceased father, William Rasmussen and deceased stepfather Richard Lombardi.

The use of this cookbook is easily mastered. First, decide what you want to cook. This can be done through the Table of Contents, Index, Meal Planner & Themes chapter, or, random browsing of the book's contents!. All recipes are listed alphabetically in their respective chapters. So it's up to you, start at the beginning and read through the chapters, or go right to a recipe and start cooking. Every effort was expended in making your use of the Vegan Cookbook as efficient as possible.

Why Vegan?

Why should I adopt a vegan diet? If you have purchased this book you have probably contemplated this question already. Perhaps you already know the reasons or maybe you are still searching for the reasons. Perhaps you understand why you should be vegan but don't believe that you can, realistically.

This book was composed with the intent of making it easier for people to become vegan in a world predicated on the systematic consumption of animal products. A world with very little to offer towards the development of a life-style independent of products made from or with animal products.

America has become a socioeconomic system that promotes it's livestock factory farming industries to support an infrastructure of jobs and businesses dependent on the success of those industries. A chain of supply and demand that is staggering in its scope and influence. When it is said that every part of the animal is used, they aren't kidding. Not just for food consumption, these animals furnish all the leather used to make shoes, belts and other clothing accessories. Animal body substances are used in pharmaceuticals and cosmetics sold world wide. The billion pets that live in America depend on the livestock by-products that make up the bulk of their pet food. The rendering plants need bodies for the products they produce and the waste they reduce.

Unfortunately, the demands of our world on these products have created a beleaguered environment that is collapsing under the strain of increasing abuse. With globalism as top priority on the agendas of politicians and international corporations, the prospects of improving these conditions are dismal. The interests of these groups include the marketing of these principals, products and industries to the underdeveloped countries of the world. We are reassured that these "experts" know what is best for everyone and everything, spending billions of dollars annually in public relations to convince us.

What politicians and those with vested interests in the production of animal goods don't care to mention are the negative consequences of their actions. Human health has deteriorated with increased obesity, arterial and coronary dis-

Preface

eases, cancer, auto-immune diseases, bacterial poisoning, diabetes and other strange and new diseases. America leads the world in these diseases when compared to underdeveloped countries whose cultures have supported a mostly vegetable based diet, with flesh consumption minimal. Factory farming interests want these countries to adopt the American diet, with its fast food hamburgers and chicken. With its well marbled beef for the wealthy, cheap meat for the poor, and all its inherent diseases.

America is rapidly being drained of its fresh water supply by billions of thirsty animals earmarked for our future consumption. One beef cow can consume as much as 250,000 gallons of water in its short lifetime. Factory farmed chickens and pigs use millions of gallons of water in their operations annually. Factory farming creates more than two thirds of our nation's runoff pollution, dumping tons of nitrates and bacteria into our waterways and destroying the natural ecology and poisoning fish.

Our land is over grazed and over farmed for livestock feed. About 90% of America's farmland is dedicated to producing feed for livestock. A cow is a ruminant animal with four stomachs designed to break down high concentrations of cellulose in wild grasses while creating proteins through enzymatic action by fixing nitrogen. A cow never needs to eat wheat, corn or soybeans unless you need to fatten them up a for short life and a high yield at the slaughterhouse. It is the force feeding of these grains that contribute to the high fat content of the meat, rendering it even more dangerous to your health when you eat it.

In countries where grain and soybean feed is not abundantly available, the insidious and life threatening disease - bovine spongiform encephalopathy (BSE) - commonly referred to as "Mad Cow", is the result of feeding these unfortunate animals processed by-products of their own slaughtered species! It's now been confirmed that humans can acquire variant Creutzfeldt-Jakob disease (vCJD) from BSE contaminated meat products. The response of those who risk losses in the marketplace, is to promise better screening of diseased animals, and the eventual development of drugs to combat the spread of BSE. What you must always ask yourself, are the promises of meat producers' to be trusted now and in the future, or would it not be more a intelligent to simply forgo meat as a dietary option?

Millions of acres of natural forests worldwide have been decimated for the production cattle, pigs and chickens in just a few short decades. Millions of oxygen producing and carbon dioxide consuming trees, bushes and grasses have been cleared in the Amazon rain forest to graze cattle. These cattle spend a short youth consuming natural grasses before they are sent to America's feedlots to be fattened on grains and soybeans. This worldwide system of clearing land, farming feed, grazing, transporting, manufacturing, packaging and retailing beef consumes a thousand times more energy to produce a pound of flesh than is required to produce a pound of grain.

The agony of factory farmed livestock and the cruelty inflicted upon them by their human tormentors is beyond belief. The modern meat producing factory farm is not the classic country farm, where the friendly farmer knows every animal by name, and every beast lives a decent life before its sudden and unexpected death. At the factory farm, from birth until death the relentless hell of their existence is a life that no man would ever consciously wish upon another creature. Yet we thoughtlessly accept this torture, as long as it is neither seen nor heard. The rational for this chain of 'necessary' evil behavior is to produce a clean packaged product we can buy at the local supermarket, feed our hungry bodies and go on with our life.

Becoming a true vegetarian, or vegan, is a personal stand against the forces of worldwide ecological destruction. It is an intent to bring an end to the exploitation of animals. It is taking control of one's health and of one's life. It is opposing the automatic generation of evil with the willful generation of goodness. It is stepping forward on the evolutionary path.

Some of the greatest people who have ever lived on this planet have been vegetarian. Geniuses such as Plato, Martin Luther, Benjamin Franklin, Isaac Newton, Albert Einstein, Thomas Edison and Ghandi were vegetarian. These people, and many more, were strong believers in the benefits of vegetarianism and wrote profusely on the subject.

These famous vegetarians were not alone in their time. Most people are not aware of the common practice of vegetarianism by social and religious groups throughout history. From King Tut's family empire in ancient Egypt, to the Essene Jews of the Dead Sea, to the Hindu culture of India, the Hunzas of the Himalayas, the Buddhists of Southeast Asia, China and Japan, the Albigensians and Cathors of Medieval Europe, the Seventh Day Adventists of America... entire societies thriving for decades or centuries, some of which were entirely vegan. The Albigensians/Cathars, for example, were a society of Gnostic Christian intellectuals, artists, mathematicians and craftsmen whose extended families comprised a population of millions, all of whom were entirely vegan. This group thrived for nearly 500 years until they were exterminated by the Inquisition in the middle ages.

Preface

This book was written with the intent of planting a seed in the fertile soil of evolutionary progress. We hope to establish a set of fundamentals, principals and guidelines for families to start living a vegan life-style. It is our desire that the information in this book be used like a toolbox to repair your diet. Every tool you'll require is in the box, complete with instructions. Every aspect of vegan world cuisine is covered in this book. From breakfast through dinner, from soups to desserts, from simple side dishes to vegan banquets... it is all covered here. Every recipe, method and procedure detailed is designed to teach you the basics and inspire new creations.

Life begins daily with the mundane activities ahead. Let those activities be accomplished through positive action. Allow yourself to do the good you were intended for. Respect the world you were created in. Go Vegan!

Mark W. Rasmussen
Author and Chef

Final Thought...

As I was finishing up the final touches on this book, I kept coming back to the actual cover, never quite feeling satisfied with its look. Then I came across an oil painting that the author's sister, Kim, painted in 1983. Kim passed away at a very young age, from breast cancer. When you look at this painting, know that she would have wanted us all to cherish this planet's natural bounty, and never take life for granted.

Luther G. Brossa
Designer <lgbrossa@hotmail.com>

Getting Started

Introduction

The following represents a complete list of all the ingredients, materials and tools to make all the recipes in this cookbook. It is not intended to suggest that you need to accumulate everything listed before you can start cooking the recipes in this book. You will, however, want to ensure that you do have the most fundamental materials, tools and ingredients before starting.

In addition, every recipe lists all of the materials needed to successfully complete it. Until you're familiar with the process, it helps to start with the simplest of recipes, as a means of building confidence in your cooking skills.

Using the recipes in this book requires the assembly of some basic materials including dry goods, herbs and spices, produce, kitchen equipment and miscellaneous items.

Cleaning Produce

Prior to all produce preparation, wash all hard-surfaced fruits and vegetables using a (dedicated) vegetable scrub brush. In many instances, you may not be able to procure organic produce. In such cases, you may want to soak produce in a ten to one (10:1) solution of water to white vinegar. That means, you'd take 9 cups of cold water and mix one cup of white vinegar to create an extremely effective - yet very inexpensive - solution for removing surface toxins from produce. Depending on the actual produce's surface characteristics, the soaking time would more or less change in duration. A leafy produce (such as spinach) could be 15 minutes or less, and hard surfaced foods (such as cranberries) could require 2 to 4 hours of soaking. You can extend soaking process, but always remember, you also risk imparting a vinegar-like flavor to the soaked produce itself! At the conclusion of the soaking process, soaked produce must be completely immersed in rinsing water, to remove all traces of soaking solution.

Hygiene

Always wash your hands well, before you start preparing food. This means, keeping a separate bar of soap and finger-nail scrub brush available at the wash station. It has been determined, that the hands are the primary vector (carrier) of pathogens! Periodic disinfection of all hand contacted surfaces (equipment controls, utensils, cabinet door knobs, cutting boards, and so forth) is extremely important, to ensure a healthy kitchen environment...for everyone. A good chef knows the importance of cleanliness. As food is - obviously - ingested by us all, your attitude and expectations, should be one of demanding professionalism.

Kitchen Safety

A top priority of every chef, must be safety! Basic rules for the safe handling of cutting instruments, must be observed. Where possible, avoid unnecessary contact with food stuffs. Any hint of spoilage, merits immediate disposal of questionable foods! Always have hot pads or mittens around, to prevent painful burns. Use caution when pouring away boiling solutions! Keep the floors clean of spills and slippery materials. Food timers and thermometers are a necessity, and attentiveness to range, oven, grill and broiler temperatures is imperative. Fire is useful...but dangerous, and must always be respected. A first-aid kit, complete with burn medication, antiseptics and bandaging should be accessible to all family members and kitchen personnel, and must always be kept well stocked.

Suggested Equipment

The following is a comprehensive list of stock items of various categories, starting with basic kitchen equipment:

Chef's Knife	Citrus Squeezer
Wire Whisk	Cooking Pots & Pans
Rubber Spatulas	Rolling Pin
Tongs	Knife Sharpener
Oven and Range	Blender
Baking Dishes	Muffin Pan
Food Processor	Cutting Board
Vegetable Peeler	Cooking Spoons
Mixing Bowls	Metal Spatulas

Getting Started

Spaghetti Strainer
Food Timer
Vegetable Juicer

Pastry Cutter
Pastry Brushes
Loaf/Bread Pans

Notes: Stainless steel, cast iron or anodized non-stick pots and pans are recommended. Stainless steel utensils and mixing bowls are also highly recommended.

A sharp knife is a must. An electric sharpener produces a great edge but using it too often will take too much steel off the blade, eventually reducing its usefulness. Regular use of a traditional hand held steel sharpener is best as long as the knife is new or in great condition.

Grains & Flours

brown rice
quinoa
vital wheat gluten
cornstarch
soy flour
barley
unbleached pastry flour

bulgar wheat
whole wheat flour
corn meal
bread crumbs
millet
basmati rice
unbleached white flour

Spices & Herbs

thyme
coriander
marjoram
salt
dill
cardamom
rosemary
onion powder
asafetida

oregano
basil
bay leaves
curry powder
black pepper
mustard
sage
chili powder
cumin

fenugreek
vanilla
cinnamon
mace
habenero
savory
tarragon
anise clove
ginger root & powder
garlic powder
caraway seeds

cajun spice blend
allspice
lavender
file powder
paprika
cayenne
cilantro
horseradish
clove
parsley
celery seeds

Pasta

linguini
lasagna
ziti
ditilini pasta

penne
orzo
couscous
large shells

Condiments & Sweeteners

balsamic vinegar
soy sauce
dijon mustard
raw sugar
apple cider vinegar
brown rice syrup
xanthum gum
Sucanat

peanut butter
louisiana hot sauce
molasses
vegetable bouillon
sesame tahini
xylitol
non-dairy chocolate chips
agar agar

miso paste

Soy Products

silken & firm tofu
TVP beef style
TVP poultry style
soy mozzarella cheese

tempeh
TVP burger blend
soy milk
soy cheddar cheese

Beans, Seeds, Nuts

pinto beans
black beans
cantilini beans
sesame seeds
lima beans

kidney beans
great northern beans
beans
sunflower seeds
walnuts

peanuts

Oils & Spreads

olive oil
roasted sesame oil
flax seed oil

soy oil
soy margarine
canola oil

Wraps & Flatbreads

tortillas	taco shells - soft
taco shells - hard	spring roll wraps
whole wheat pita bread	

Produce

broccoli	onion
mesclum mix	endive
fennel	mushrooms
turnip	asparagus
string beans	leeks
mustard greens	escarole
bean sprouts	summer squash
butternut squash	cauliflower
red onion	carrots
garlic clove	portabella mushrooms
rutabaga	bok choy
spinach	nappa
colored bell pepper	jalapeno peppers
acorn squash	chickpeas (canned)
cucumbers	lemons
yams	celery
parsnip	peas
kale	potatoes
snow peas	zucchini
corn (white & yellow)	oranges
sweet potatoes	fresh tomato,
pineapple	sundried & canned

Salads, Dressings & Dips

Introduction

The chilled, prepared salad recipes found in this chapter add variety and nutrition to any meal. They can be served as appetizers, refrigerated for several days and can provide great side dishes to lunch or dinner courses.

In this chapter you will learn that simple raw vegetables, green salads, nuts, beans and grains can be transformed into unique dishes by combining them in different ways with different sauces and dressings.

You will also discover how to create prepared Dressings, Dips and condiments that other recipes in this book rely on and that provide the foundations for new creations.

Included in this chapter as well are recipes for fruit salad dressings. These easily blended raw dressings add color and flavor to mixed fruit combinations.

Babaganouj

This pureed eggplant salad has Middle Eastern origins; each region with its own variation. This Turkish version is the way we make it at Veggie Works.

MEASURE	INGREDIENT
2 large	eggplants
1/2 cup	sesame tahini
1/4 tsp	cumin
1	garlic clove
(to taste)	salt

Place whole, unpeeled eggplants in a baking dish and bake at 400°F for about 40 minutes or until completely soft. Remove from oven and cool. Cut eggplants in half, then, using a spoon, scrape the seed row out and discard. Be careful not to waste the juices. Remove the flesh from the skins.

Add all other ingredients together with eggplant and juices. Place in a food processor and puree. Pulsing the food processor will create a pulpier version. Makes a great dip for chips, crudites or pita wedges. [4-8 PORTIONS]

Coleslaw

This salad combines our vegan mayonnaise recipe, also listed in this chapter, with healthful raw cabbage and caraway seeds.

MEASURE	INGREDIENT
1/2 head	white cabbage - shredded
1	carrot - grated
3/4 cup	*Mayonnaise*
1 tsp	apple cider vinegar
1 tsp	caraway seeds
(to taste)	salt & black pepper

Shred cabbage by slicing thin strips off head. Grate carrot. Mix all ingredients and chill until serving. [4-8 PORTIONS]

Cold Broccoli Salad

This basic garlic and olive oil method can be used for broccoli or a variety of vegetables.

MEASURE	INGREDIENT
2 heads	broccoli
3 Tbsps	olive oil
2	garlic cloves - diced
1/4 cup	water
(to taste)	salt & black pepper

Salads, Dressings & Dips

Remove buds with small stems from broccoli head; and set large stalk aside.

Heat a frying or sauce pan. Add oil to pan. Add garlic to oil and turn flame down. Slowly and lightly brown garlic, then, quickly pour water into pan. Add broccoli to pan and cover. Steam broccoli in garlic and oil mixture until tender. Season with salt and pepper. Remove from heat and refrigerate.
[4-6 PORTIONS]

Eggless Egg Salad
A delicious vegan version with healthy tofu -- instead of the cholesterol balls we're all so familiar with.

MEASURE	INGREDIENT
1 lb package	firm tofu - crumbled
2 cups	*Vegetable Stock*
1/2 cup	*Mayonnaise*
1/2 tsp	onion powder
1/4 tsp	garlic powder
2 Tbsps	nutritional yeast
(to taste)	salt & black pepper

In a mixing bowl, drain and crumble tofu with your hands. Heat vegetable stock in a small sauce pan and add the crumbled tofu. Boil tofu for 3-5 minutes to alter the texture to a more egg-like product. Allow to cool, drain off excess liquid then add remaining ingredients and mix gently but thoroughly. Chill before using.
[4-8 PORTIONS]

Elbow Macaroni Salad

Great summer picnic or barbecue salad. Use a good brand of elbow pasta for best results.

MEASURE	INGREDIENT
2 cups	elbow macaroni
1 Tbsp	salt
1 medium	fresh tomato - chopped
1	green bell pepper - chopped
1 cup	*Mayonnaise*
(to taste)	salt & black pepper

Boil elbow macaroni in four or more cups of water with a tablespoon of salt. Boil 8-10 minutes then rinse with cold water until noodles have cooled. Chop up tomato and bell pepper and add together with noodles and mayonnaise. Salt and pepper to taste. [4-8 PORTIONS]

Fruit & Nut Salad

This simple, yet festive, side adds color to any holiday table. Great snack for the kids, too.

MEASURE	INGREDIENT
1 cup	xylitol
1/4 cup	water
1	orange - peeled & sectioned
1	apple - cored & wedge sliced
1	banana - thin round sliced
1 cup	pineapple - course chunked
1 cup	mixed nuts (unsalted - raw)

Heat a small skillet or frying pan and add the xylitol and water. Begin cooking this down, reducing the water out of the sugar, forming a syrup.

Meanwhile, peel the orange and isolate each section. Peel, core and slice the apple into small wedges. Peel and slice banana into thin rounds. Drain pineapple chunks.

When syrup thickens considerably, toss in the fruit and stir fry a minute to coat the fruit sections. Remove the sugar glazed fruit from the pan and combine with the nuts in a bowl. Mix well together and serve. [2-4 PORTIONS]

Garden Pasta Salad

Easy pasta salad that everyone loves. Use your choice of pasta. Good use for fresh veggies.

MEASURE	INGREDIENT
2 cups	pasta - uncooked
1	yellow bell pepper - chopped
1 large	cucumber - sliced
3 large	mushrooms - sliced
1 large	fresh tomato - wedge cut
1 head	broccoli
1/4 cup	olive oil
2 Tbsps	apple cider vinegar
1 tsp	basil - dry
(to taste)	salt & black pepper

Boil the pasta 8-12 minutes, drain, rinse well and set aside. Chop peppers, slice cucumber and mushrooms, then cut tomato into wedges. Cut flowerets from broccoli and steam for three minutes or until bright green. Remove broccoli and plunge into cold water. This retards any further cooking and preserves its crisp green color.

Place prepared veggies and cooled pasta together in a mixing bowl, mix in oil, vinegar and seasonings. Chill well before serving. [4-8 PORTIONS]

German Potato Salad

Vegan variation of German recipe with vegan-style Canadian bacon. Tasty...and hearty.

MEASURE	INGREDIENT
6 large	idaho potatoes - peeled & chunked
1 medium	onion - chopped
2 large	celery stalks - chopped
1/4 cup	soy oil
1 package	vegan-style canadian bacon
1	romaine lettuce heart
2-3 Tbsps	apple cider vinegar
(to taste)	salt & black pepper

Wash potatoes, stripe peel potatoes, and cut into large chunks. Place potatoes in pot of water and boil on medium heat until potatoes are almost done. While still firm (test with a fork) drain off water and let potatoes rest while cooling. Turn over potatoes once or twice to insure that they cool evenly.

Chop up onions and celery. Heat a skillet or frying pan and pour in oil. Sauté onions, celery and chopped Canadian bacon until tender. Chop up romaine lettuce heart and mix with cooling potatoes Pour entire contents of skillet over potatoes. Add vinegar, salt, pepper and mix well. Chill well. [4-8 PORTIONS]

Grilled Portabella Orzo Salad

Delicious salad, with distinctive grilled flavor. An excellent example of the versatility of Portabella mushrooms.

MEASURE	INGREDIENT
4 large	portabella mushroom caps - sliced
2	green bell peppers
2	red bell peppers
1/2 cup	*Grill Goddess Sauce*

Salads, Dressings & Dips

MEASURE	INGREDIENT
1/2 lb	orzo - uncooked
1 pt	cherry tomatoes

Slice portabella mushroom caps into thin pieces. Remove seeds and stem, then quarter peppers. Par boil peppers. In a large mixing bowl, pour in prepared sauce and add peppers and mushrooms. Allow a few minutes to marinate.

 Meanwhile, cook orzo according to package directions. When orzo is completely soft, remove from heat and rinse with cold water. Set aside.

Have a hot grill ready. Turn grill flame down and put marinated mushrooms, tomatoes and peppers on grill. Baste with some of the remaining prepared sauce then flip and baste again. Place grilled veggies in mixing bowl with remainder of the prepared sauce. Add in orzo and chill, then serve.
[4-8 PORTIONS]

Japanese Sesame Kale with Miso
An interesting and delicious way to eat those greens.
Great side dish or lunch salad.

MEASURE	INGREDIENT
1 lb	kale - fresh
1/4 cup	sesame seeds - raw
2 Tbsps	miso paste
1/4 cup	water
1 Tbsp	soy sauce
1 Tbsp	apple cider vinegar
2 Tbsps	roasted sesame oil

Wash kale well and strip leaves from each stalk. Steam leaves - at least 5 minutes - in about 1 cup water on a low flame. Drain off liquid. You can save this nutritious liquid by adding to your **Vegetable Stock**.

Heat up a skillet or non-stick fry pan until very hot. Turn flame to low and add raw sesame seeds. Stirring or flipping often, roast seeds to a golden brown. Keep an eye on this, as seeds burn up fast, when unattended.

Mix miso paste well with 1/4 cup water or cooking liquid, in a medium sized bowl. Add in soy sauce, vinegar, and roasted sesame oil. Put cooled kale into bowl, add sesame seeds and mix well. Chill before serving. [4-8 PORTIONS]

Leek Salad
This is an old Turkish recipe variation and an excellent way to enjoy leeks.

MEASURE	INGREDIENT
4 large	leeks
1	onion - chopped
2 large	carrots - sliced diagonally
1/4 cup	olive oil
1 Tbsp	allspice
1 tsp	salt
1 cup	*Brown Rice* - cooked
1 bunch	dill - fresh

Leeks are notoriously dirty. Discard wilted outer leaves and cross cut eighth inch rounds using crisp white stalk and tender outer green leaves. Place cut leek rounds in pot of cold water to soak dirt off. Chop onion and slice up carrot diagonally. Heat olive oil in small sauce pot. Put onions in pot and turn heat to medium. Cook onions a few minutes then add drained leeks and carrot pieces.

Stir vegetables, add allspice and salt, put lid on pot and slow cook until soft and tender. Rinse cooked rice briefly to remove excess starch and add to mixture. Also add chopped fresh dill. Turn off heat and to cool. Refrigerate until ready to serve. [4-8 PORTIONS]

Mediterranean CousCous Salad
One from the Near East. Couscous is quick to make and compliments this tasty ethnic salad.

MEASURE	INGREDIENT
1 cup	couscous - uncooked
1 cup	water - boiling
1 cup	cauliflowerettes
1 cup	carrots - chopped
1/2 cup	sundried tomatoes
1	green bell pepper - chopped
1/2	red onion - chopped
1/4 cup	black olives - chopped
1 tsp	cumin
1/2 tsp	allspice
1/3 cup	chickpeas - cooked & rinsed
2	lemons - juiced
1/4 cup	olive oil
2 pinches	salt

Pour in couscous into boiling cup of water, then turn off flame. Cover and let set for 5 minutes. Fluff up with fork.

In a pot or skillet, steam cauliflower and carrots until firm, but not over done.

Separately prepare sun-dried tomatoes by covering with water and simmering for 5 minutes in a pot or skillet. Cool and then chop into large pieces. Chop up peppers, onions, then mix with sliced olives, spices, chickpeas, tomatoes, cauliflower and carrots in a large bowl. Add in lemon juice, olive oil, and salt.

Dump cooked couscous into strainer or colander and rinse with cold water to remove starch. Add couscous to veggie mix and stir up well. Refrigerate until ready to serve. [4-8 PORTIONS]

Mediterranean Potato Salad

Another excellent potato salad. Goes well with just about anything. A winner at picnics.

MEASURE	INGREDIENT
12 medium	red potatoes - course chopped
1/2	red onion - chopped
1	celery stalk - chopped
1	red bell pepper - chopped
1 Tbsp	salt
1/2 tsp	black pepper
1/4 cup	soy oil
3 Tbsps	apple cider vinegar

Wash and strip-peel potatoes and chop into larger pieces. Put into pot of salted water and boil until firm and almost done. Drain off water and dump potatoes in a bowl.

Chop up vegetables and combine with the potatoes, salt, pepper, oil and vinegar. Chill and serve. [4-8 PORTIONS]

Mexican Corn & Bean Salad

High protein salad with fresh Mexican flavors. Great summer side dish.

MEASURE	INGREDIENT
1 cup	pinto beans - cooked
1 cup	kidney beans - cooked
1	green bell pepper
1	red bell pepper
1 small bunch	cilantro
2	garlic cloves - crushed
1 cup	fresh corn - cut

Salads, Dressings & Dips

MEASURE	INGREDIENT
1/4 tsp	cumin
1	lemon - juiced
1/4 cup	soy oil
(to taste)	salt & black pepper
1	jalapeno pepper - diced (optional)

Rinse home-cooked or canned beans and put into large mixing bowl. Chop up peppers and cilantro and add all remaining ingredients into bowl and mix well. For added flavor, you can also mix in a diced jalapeno pepper. Chill and serve. [2-4 PORTIONS]

Mock Chicken Salad

**Recipe tastes like the original...but better. High protein.
Great for quick sandwiches and fresh green salads.**

MEASURE	INGREDIENT
2 cups	*Vegetable Stock*
1 cup	TVP poultry style - chunks
2	celery stalks - chopped
1/2 cup	*Mayonnaise*
1 tsp	apple cider vinegar
(to taste)	salt & black pepper

In a sauce pot, bring vegetable stock to a boil. Add dehydrated TVP to boiling stock. Turn down flame and simmer for 5 minutes covered. Remove from stove and strain off remaining liquid back into stock pot and save. Set TVP aside to cool. Chop up celery and add to mixing bowl with TVP chunks and all remaining ingredients. Mix well, then chill before serving. [2-4 PORTIONS]

Oriental Lo Mein Salad
Here is a simple noodle salad with veggies and Oriental flavorings. Makes a good lunch.

MEASURE	INGREDIENT
1 lb	lo mein noodle (or suitable replacement)
3 Tbsps	roasted sesame oil
1	carrot- julienne cut
1	red bell pepper - sliced
4	bok choy stalks - sliced
3 large	mushrooms - sliced
1 head	broccoli
1/4 cup	water (for boiling)
2 Tbsps	soy sauce
3 Tbsps	sesame seeds - roasted
2 Tbsps	apple cider vinegar

Cook noodles according to directions on package. Rice stick noodles work as well as linguini, spaghetti or any other long noodle. Rinse well and drain. Put noodles in a mixing bowl, add 1 tablespoon roasted sesame oil to noodles. This keeps them loose and prevents them from sticking to each other.

Julienne cut carrot, slice pepper, bok choy and mushrooms, then remove broccoli buds from stalk. Set the stalk aside and save for use in your vegetable stock.

Heat up a skillet, add water with sliced veggies, then boil for 2 minutes. When adequately boiled, remove veggies and rinse with cold water to retain crispness.

Combine all noodles, prepared veggies, soy sauce, roasted sesame seeds, vinegar and remaining oil inside a bowl and mix well. Served chilled.
[4-8 PORTIONS]

Pasta Salad with Fresh Basil

**Enjoy the flavor of fresh basil in this salad that features
large pasta types and fresh tomatoes.**

MEASURE	INGREDIENT
1 lb	pasta shells - medium size
2 large	fresh tomatoes - wedge cut
2	celery stalks - thin cut
1 large bunch	basil - fresh
5	garlic cloves - chopped
1/4 cup	olive oil
2 Tbsps	balsamic vinegar
(to taste)	salt & black pepper

Cook pasta according to package directions. Drain, rinse and set aside. Cut tomatoes into wedges, celery into thin rounds. Wash basil, strip leaves from stalks and discard stems.

Chop up garlic and brown lightly in the oil. Retard browning by adding in the balsamic vinegar and remove from heat. Put pasta, tomatoes, celery and basil in a mixing bowl and pour oil, garlic, and vinegar over everything. Add salt, pepper and mix well, then refrigerate. [4-8 PORTIONS]

String Bean Salad

**Similar to the broccoli salad and a good way
to illustrate the garlic and oil method.**

MEASURE	INGREDIENT
1 lb	string beans - fresh
5	garlic cloves
1/4 cup	olive oil
1/3 cup	water
(to taste)	salt & black pepper

Wash beans and snap or cut ends off. Lightly brown garlic in olive oil then add water, beans, salt and pepper. Cover and steam beans about 5 minutes. Remove from heat slightly under cooked. Allow to cool before using. Refrigerate.
[4-8 PORTIONS]

Tabouli
Tabouli is a traditional Mediterranean bulgar wheat salad with diced raw veggies and parsley. It's one of the best known salads in standard Vegetarian cuisine.

MEASURE	INGREDIENT
1/2 cup	bulgar wheat
1 cup	water
1 large bunch	parsley - diced
1/2	red onion - diced
1	green bell pepper - diced
1 large	fresh tomato - diced
1	lemon
2 Tbsps	olive oil
(to taste)	salt

Combine the bulgar and water in a small saucepan and bring to a boil. Reduce heat and simmer for 3-5 minutes. Turn off heat and allow to stand, covered for another 20 minutes.

Dice up parsley, onion, pepper and tomato. Combine bulgar with veggies, add juice from lemon, olive oil salt and mix well. Chill before serving.
[4-6 PORTIONS]

Three Bean Salad
Traditional summer salad with a garlic and olive oil twist.

MEASURE	INGREDIENT
1 lb	string beans
1 lb	chickpeas - cooked
1 lb	kidney beans - cooked
3 Tbsps	olive oil
5	garlic cloves - diced
4 Tbsps	apple cider vinegar
(to taste)	salt & black pepper

Steam string beans and rinse with cold water to retain green crispness. Rinse cooked chickpeas and kidney beans and add all beans to a mixing bowl. Heat a skillet and pour in the olive oil and diced garlic. Lightly brown garlic and remove heat. Pour oil and garlic over beans. Add vinegar, salt and pepper and mix well. Chill well. [4-8 PORTIONS]

Tofu Nappa Salad
Ever wonder what to do with Chinese nappa cabbage? This recipe combines raw tofu and nappa in a delightful way.

MEASURE	INGREDIENT
1 large head	nappa cabbage - chunk chopped
1 lb package	firm tofu - cubed
1/4 cup	roasted sesame oil
1/4 cup	sesame seeds - roasted
4 Tbsps	soy sauce
2 Tbsps	apple cider vinegar
1/4 cup	cilantro - chopped

Cut off base and chop nappa leaves and stalks into large chunks. Chop tofu into 1/2 inch cubes. Combine all ingredients, toss well and serve. [6-8 PORTIONS]

Dressings

Salad Dressings are to raw vegetable salads what sauces are to sautés. A good salad dressing will effectively set the tone of the salad without masking the natural flavors of the raw vegetables. The following recipes reflect these principals while possessing unique and delicious flavors.

Creamy Cucumber Dressing
This tasty dressing presents the fresh taste of cucumbers in a creamy, soy-based body.

MEASURE	INGREDIENT
1 12-oz package	silken-firm tofu
1	cucumber - peeled & seeded
1 cup	soy milk
2 Tbsps	onion powder
1 Tbsp	garlic powder
1 tsp	salt
few sprigs	parsley
1/2 cup	soy oil (for dribbling)

Blend all ingredients - except soy oil - in food blender. After suitable period, slowly dribble oil while blending, until smooth yet thick. Keep refrigerated. [10-12 PORTIONS]

Creamy Garlic Dressing
A simple yet flavorful dressing used in green salads, falafel, or as a sandwich spread.

MEASURE	INGREDIENT
1 cup	*Sour Cream*
3	garlic cloves
1 Tbsp	water
(to taste)	salt

Mix ingredients thoroughly in a blender. Keep refrigerated. [4-8 PORTIONS]

Creamy Ranch Dressing
A robust flavored green salad dressing with a rich buttermilk taste. A Veggie Works staple.

MEASURE	INGREDIENT
1 12-oz package	silken-firm tofu
1 cup	soy milk
2 Tbsps	onion powder
1 Tbsp	garlic powder
1 tsp	salt
few sprigs	parsley
1/2 cup	soy oil

Blend all ingredients - except soy oil - in food blender. After suitable period, slowly dribble oil while blending, until smooth yet thick. Keep refrigerated. [6-10 PORTIONS]

Euro-Asian Vinaigrette

This deep flavored green salad dressing combines a blend of ingredients from the Far East, as well as southern Europe.

MEASURE	INGREDIENT
1/3 cup	soy oil
1/3 cup	virgin olive oil
1/4 cup	apple cider vinegar
1/4 cup	balsamic vinegar
1/3 cup	water
1/3 cup	soy sauce
6-8	garlic cloves - finely diced
1 tsp	cajun spice blend
1 level Tbsp each:	thyme, oregano, marjoram & basil

Mix all ingredients thoroughly. Store refrigerated. [6-10 PORTIONS]

French Dressing

A basic French dressing that's naturally vegan, and great with green salads.

MEASURE	INGREDIENT
1 cup	soy oil
1/4 cup	apple cider vinegar
2 Tbsps	lemon juice
1/2 cup	*Ketchup*
1 tsp	mustard powder
1 tsp	paprika
1 tsp	salt
1 tsp	tarragon leaves

Salads, Dressings & Dips

MEASURE	INGREDIENT
1 tsp	cayenne pepper
1/3 cup	raw sugar

Mix all ingredients thoroughly. Store refrigerated. [4-6 PORTIONS]

Fresh Fruit Salad Dressing
Turn any simple fruit salad into exotic ambrosia.

MEASURE	INGREDIENT
2 cups	fresh fruit - chopped
1-2	avocados - ripe
2-3 Tbsps	olive oil
2 Tbsps	lemon juice

Blend (or process with food processor) all ingredients. Use immediately.
[4-8 PORTIONS]

Herbed Vinaigrette Dressing
**Here's another every day green salad dressing.
Lots of herbs with a fresh light taste.**

MEASURE	INGREDIENT
1/3 cup	soy oil
1/4 cup	olive oil
1/4 cup	apple cider vinegar
3 Tbsps	water
1/2 tsp each:	basil, oregano, thyme, marjoram & tarragon
1 Tbsp	salt

Mix all ingredients well and use. Refrigerate and shake well before using.
[4-6 PORTIONS]

Lemon Herb Dressing
A tasty herb dressing without vinegar.

MEASURE	INGREDIENT
1/2 cup	olive oil
1	lemon - juiced
1/4 cup	water
1 tsp	salt
1 pinch each:	tarragon, thyme, oregano, basil, marjoram & black pepper

Mix everything well and serve. Chill and mix before serving. [2-4 PORTIONS]

Mayonnaise
Many recipes in this book depend on the use of this excellent vegan mayonnaise.

MEASURE	INGREDIENT
1 12-oz package	silken-firm tofu
1/4 cup	apple cider vinegar
2 Tbsps	salt
3 Tbsps	raw sugar (or xylitol)
1/2 cup	soy oil

Put all ingredients - except soy oil - in blender (or food processor). Begin blending until mass is thickened. Pour in oil slowly while continuing to blend. Mixture should be creamy thick. Mayonnaise will keep refrigerated for weeks.
[4-6 PORTIONS]

Oriental Sesame Dressing
This is our most popular green salad dressing.
A dressing that makes one grade-A salad.

MEASURE	INGREDIENT
1/2 cup	soy oil
1/4 cup	roasted sesame oil
1/3 cup	apple cider vinegar
1/4 cup	soy sauce
1/4 cup	sesame seeds - roasted
4	garlic cloves - mashed
4 Tbsps	raw sugar (or xylitol, or brown rice syrup) mixed with 1/4 cup water
1/2 cup	water

Mix all ingredients thoroughly. Store refrigerated. [4-8 PORTIONS]

Spicy Avocado Dressing
If you like avocado, you'll love this green salad dressing.

MEASURE	INGREDIENT
2 large	avocados - ripe
1	lemon - juiced
1/4 cup	olive oil
1	jalapeno pepper - finely diced
1/3 cup	water
1 tsp	cajun spice blend
1 tsp	salt

Choose avocados that are firm but ripe with a nice green color. Scoop meat out and discard shell. Add avocado and all ingredients to blender and blend well. Chill before serving. [4-8 PORTIONS]

Sunrise Seed Sauce

A alternative fruit or green salad dressing, high in protein with great flavor. This recipe can be varied by using different nuts and seeds.

MEASURE	INGREDIENT
1 cup	sunflower seeds - raw
3 cups	water - cold
1	avocado - ripe
1/4 cup	olive oil
1	lemon - juiced
2 Tbsps	soy sauce
1 tsp	cajun spice blend

Soak seeds overnight in the water. Do not soak longer than 12 hours unrefrigerated. Combine soaked seeds, water and all other ingredients in a blender or food processor. Blend until texture is creamy. [3-6 PORTIONS]

Tahini Vinaigrette

An excellent salad dressing featuring prepared tahini.

MEASURE	INGREDIENT
1/2 cup	soy oil
1/3 cup	apple cider vinegar
1 Tbsp	marjoram
1 Tbsp	salt
1 cup	*Tahini Sauce*

Mix everything together and apply to green salads. Save refrigerated.
[4-8 PORTIONS]

Dips

This is entirely left up to you. Just use the vegan sour cream recipe, add onion powder for onion dip or diced jalapeno and a pinch of cumin for a spicy Mexican dip. Use your imagination and have fun!

Chutney

Chutney is a cooked fruit and vegetable relish.
Served to accompany Indian cuisine.

MEASURE	INGREDIENT
1	mango - peeled & chopped
1	papaya - peeled & chopped
1	green tomato - diced
1	onion - diced
2	green apples - diced
1/2 cup	raw sugar (or xylitol)
1/2 cup	apple cider vinegar
1/2 tsp	salt
1 tsp	ginger root - minced
1/2 tsp	cinnamon
1 pinch	clove
1 tsp	turmeric

Use a mango and papaya that are almost ripe, but still firm. Peel and chop up the flesh of these fruits and place in a mixing bowl. Dice up the green tomato and add this and the other ingredients to the bowl.

Transfer the contents of the mixing bowl to a sauce pot and bring this to a boil. Reduce heat and simmer for 10 minutes. Remove from heat and chill before serving. [4-8 PORTIONS]

NOTE: There are numerous recipes for chutney recorded in thousands of cookbooks, all indicating the variety of creative possibilities this condiment offers. This recipe represents a typical Indian chutney.

Guacamole

A popular Mexican avocado dip for tortilla chips or as ingredient for many Mexican dishes.

MEASURE	INGREDIENT
2	avocados - ripe
1/2	lemon - juiced
1/2 small	fresh tomato
1/2 small	onion
1	garlic clove
1/4 tsp	cumin
1/4 tsp	cajun spice blend
	(or cayenne pepper)
1/2 tsp	salt

Mix all ingredients in a blender (or food processor). Keep chilled.
[4-8 PORTIONS]

Hummus

Popular Middle Eastern paté. Great dip or sandwich spread. A high energy health food, too!

MEASURE	INGREDIENT
5-6	garlic cloves
2 16-oz cans	chickpeas
1/2 cup	*Tahini Sauce*
1-2	lemons - juiced
1 tsp	salt

Using a food processor, start with pulsing the garlic until it is chopped fine. Add remaining ingredients to food processor and blend. Refrigerate.
[8-12 PORTIONS]

36

Ketchup

**America's number one condiment; ketchup
is both easy and fun to make.**

MEASURE	INGREDIENT
1 4-oz can	tomato paste
1/4 cup	raw sugar (or xylitol)
1/2 cup	mustard - prepared
1/4 cup	soy oil
1 Tbsp	apple cider vinegar
1 Tbsp	salt
1/4 cup	water
1 Tbsp	onion powder
1 tsp	garlic powder

Simply blend all ingredients together. Keep refrigerated. [20+ PORTIONS]

Raw Food Paté

**Easily digestible and packed with nutrients. Use as a
dip, lettuce leaf stuffing or cracker topping.**

MEASURE	INGREDIENT
1 head	romaine lettuce
6 ozs	field greens
1/4 cup	sunflower seeds - raw
1/4 cup	nuts
1	avocado - ripe
1	lemon - juiced
1	carrot - grated
1	celery stalk - chopped

MEASURE	INGREDIENT
4 Tbsps	olive oil
1/2 tsp	cajun spice blend
1/4 tsp	thyme - powdered
(to taste)	salt & black pepper

Wash lettuce and discard inferior leaves. Remove best inner large crisp leaves and set aside. Put other ingredients into a food processor and process into coarse paté. Stuff saved romaine leaves with paté and serve as hor d'oeuvres. [4-8 PORTIONS]

Salsa

It's great to make your own salsa. It's fresh, and you can adjust it to your liking. The following is a good basic version.

MEASURE	INGREDIENT
3 large	fresh tomatoes - chopped
1 Tbsp	tomato paste
1 small	jalapeno pepper - seeded
1 Tbsp	apple cider vinegar
2 pinches	cumin
1 Tbsp	salt
2	garlic cloves
1/2	onion - chopped
1	colored bell pepper - seeded
1/4 cup	cilantro - chopped

Put fresh tomatoes, tomato paste, jalapeno pepper, vinegar, cumin and salt together into a food processor and pulse until mixed but not liquefied, then set aside. Process garlic, then add onion, bell pepper and pulse. Combine all contents, then mix in cilantro. Salsa is ready to serve. [4-8 PORTIONS]

Sesame Tahini Sauce

A staple Middle Eastern cold sauce used in dressings salads, falafel and other sandwiches. High in protein, seed oils and energy.

MEASURE	INGREDIENT
8 ozs	sesame tahini
10 ozs	water
2	lemons - juiced
1 Tbsp	salt

Blend everything thoroughly in a blender and refrigerate. Add more salt, or water, to adjust taste and consistency. [4-6 PORTIONS]

Sour Cream

Vegan sour cream is used in many other recipes throughout this book. This one's a substitute for the animal-based dairy version.

MEASURE	INGREDIENT
1 12-oz package	silken-firm tofu
2 Tbsps	apple cider vinegar
1 Tbsp	salt

Use a food processor to blend ingredients into a thick creamy mixture. Store refrigerated. [8-12 PORTIONS]

Tamari

What is tamari? Is it soy sauce? If not, how is it different? Here's our interpretation.

MEASURE	INGREDIENT
1 cup	soy sauce
2	garlic cloves - crushed
3 Tbsps	apple cider vinegar
2 Tbsps	water
2 Tbsps	roasted sesame oil
1 slice	ginger root

Combine all ingredients, and allow to steep for several days. [20+ PORTIONS]

Soup Making & Other Basics

Introduction

This is a very important chapter. Not only will you learn how to become a master soup maker, with dozens of recipes, but you'll learn fundamentals that will improve your skills as a chef. Instructions on how to cook dry beans, rice and pastas are also included in this chapter.

Soup making can be a great joy as long as you are guided by a firm understanding of materials. Having a good knowledge of herbs, spices, flavors of vegetables, starchy vegetables, beans, grains, pastas and condiments will help you to become a better soup chef. Knowing methods, techniques and cooking times of ingredients is essential. Every recipe in this chapter is designed to walk you through the necessary steps to help ensure a fine end product! Note: These recipes are reproduced from a restaurant production environment, so feel free to proportionally reduce ingredient measures to suit your needs.

Autumn Moon Soup
This recipe captures the baked goodness of squash, pumpkin or yam. Great seasonal flavors.

MEASURE	INGREDIENT
5 large	yams (or sweet potatoes, or 1 medium pumpkin, or 4 butternut squash, or 5 acorn squash)
2 qts	*Vegetable Stock*
1 tsp	salt
2 Tbsps	soy oil

Bake any set of the above squashes and tubers, or combine some of them maintaining roughly the same volume, at 400°F for 45 to 60 minutes. If squash or tuber is very soft, it is done. Allow to cool then cut in half and dig out pulp, discarding the skin or shell. Put meat in soup pot and add vegetable stock, salt and oil.

Using a blender or a hand held inversion blender, blend mixture until smooth. Return to heat and bring to boil. Remove from heat and serve. [8-12 PORTIONS]

American White Bean Soup
Hearty cool weather soup, mixed beans create a delicious white bean soup. Lots of aminos...a brain food!

MEASURE	INGREDIENT
1 lb	navy beans - dry
1 lb	cantilini beans - dry
1 lb	great northern beans - dry
3 qts	water
3 qts	*Vegetable Stock*
2	bay leaves
1/4 cup	soy oil
2 medium	onions - chopped
1 small bunch	celery stalks - chopped
4 medium	carrots - chopped
1 Tbsp	thyme leaf
1 Tbsp	marjoram
1 tsp	salt

Soak beans overnight. Drain and rinse beans. Alternatively, use the quick soak method described in the section on cooking beans, if you find it easier. Put rinsed beans in large soup pot, add three quarts of water, three quarts of stock, bay leaves and bring beans to a boil, then reduce heat and simmer for about 45 minutes or until done.

In another sauce pot, heat up oil and sauté chopped onions, celery, carrots, with herbs. Cover and simmer until soft.

Soup Making & Other Basics

Pour sautéed veggies into cooking beans. Soup is finished when beans are done. [20+ PORTIONS]

Baked Butternut Soup
This soup calls for butternut squash but acorn squash works just as well. A very easy soup that's great for winter.

MEASURE	INGREDIENT
5-6	butternut squash - prebaked
2 qts	*Vegetable Stock*
2 Tbsps	soy oil (or soy margarine)
1 qt	water
1 tsp	powdered thyme
1 Tbsp	salt

Bake whole squash in 450°F oven for one hour. Remove cooked, softened squash and allow to cool, about 10 minutes. Slice squash in half, scoop out meat. Add squash meat and other ingredients to soup pot and bring to a boil. Remove from heat, blend and serve. [12-16 PORTIONS]

Cabbage Potato Rice Soup
A hearty, cold weather soup from Eastern Europe. It utilizes cold storage ingredients, such as cabbage, onions, carrots and rice.

MEASURE	INGREDIENT
1 large head	cabbage - chopped
2	onions - chopped
4	potatoes - peeled & chunked
1 large	carrot - thin sliced
4 Tbsps	soy oil
1 Tbsp	salt
1 pinch	black pepper

MEASURE	INGREDIENT
1 tsp	powdered thyme
1 Tbsp	paprika
2 qts	**Vegetable Stock**
1/2 cup	**Brown Rice** - uncooked
1 qt	water

Core and chop up cabbage. Chop onions, peel and chunk potatoes, and slice carrot into thin rounds. In a large soup pot, heat oil and start sautéing onions. After a few minutes, add in cabbage, salt, pepper and spices, cover and slowly sauté until cabbage cooks down to half its original volume.

Pour vegetable stock, water, rice and potatoes into soup pot. Simmer until potatoes are done. Note: If using uncooked rice, first pre-cook rice in quart of water, before mixing with other ingredients. [12-16 PORTIONS]

Chili

This is our award winning chili! With beans, spices, and soy burger, this recipe is a perennial favorite.

MEASURE	INGREDIENT
1 lb	TVP burger blend - dry mix
3 & 1/2 cups	ice cold water
2 large	onions - chopped
6-8	celery stalks - chopped
2	green bell peppers - chopped
1 large	red bell pepper - chopped
2	jalapeno peppers - diced
4	garlic cloves - diced
2	bay leaves
1 tsp	cumin
2 Tbsps	oregano
1 Tbsp	salt

MEASURE	INGREDIENT
3 qts	whole peeled tomatoes
2 Tbsps	chili powder
1 Tbsp	cajun spice blend
1	habenero pepper (optional)
3 cups	kidney beans - precooked
3 cups	pinto beans - precooked

Mix the burger blend with the cold water, then refrigerate for at least 30 minutes, or more.

Wash and chop up onions, celery, peppers, then dice jalapeno pepper and garlic. In a large soup pot (preferably stainless steel), start sautéing onions with the bay leaf, cumin, oregano and salt. When onions are translucent, add other vegetables, garlic and jalapeno to sauté, then cook until half done. Add in burger, being careful not to crumble it too much. Cover and cook on low heat until meat and veggies are done (about 10 minutes).

Chop up cooking meat a little with cooking spoon. Break up whole tomatoes with your hands in a large mixing bowl. Add tomatoes, chili powder, cajun spice blend and habenero pepper (for extra hot flavor) to Chile sauté, and slowly bring to a boil, stirring occasionally.

Stir in cooked beans and cook until everything is sufficiently heated (160°F or more). Chile is ready to serve. Refrigerate and/or freeze for later use. [20+ PORTIONS]

Chinese Noodle Soup
A tangy and robust soup with oriental flavors.

MEASURE	INGREDIENT
1 lb	spaghetti - large (or lo mein noodles)
2 Tbsps	roasted sesame oil
2 qts	water
1/2 tsp	cayenne pepper
3 Tbsps	apple cider vinegar

MEASURE	INGREDIENT
6 ozs	hoisin paste
1/4 cup	soy sauce
1/2 cup	miso paste
4 Tbsps	cornstarch - dissolved in
	1/4 cup cold water
1 bunch	scallions - chopped

Cook off noodles according to package directions, rinse with cold water and sprinkle with 2 tablespoons of roasted sesame oil. Set aside.

In a large soup pot heat 2 quarts of water, with the cayenne pepper and vinegar. Take out two cups of this hot liquid and mix in hoisen paste, soy sauce and miso paste. Add this to the soup pot and bring to a boil. Mix cornstarch slurry into heated soup. Reduce heat, add noodles and scallions. Serve hot.
[8-12 PORTIONS]

Corn Chowder
Everyone loves corn chowder. This is as good a corn chowder recipe as you'll find anywhere.

MEASURE	INGREDIENT
1/4 cup	soy oil
1 large	onion - chopped
3	garlic cloves - diced
1	green bell pepper - chopped
1	red bell pepper - chopped
4	celery stalks - chopped
4 medium	potatoes - peeled & cubed
2 medium	zucchini - chopped
1 Tbsp	thyme leaf
2 Tbsps	salt
1 Tbsp	cajun spice blend
6 cups	fresh corn - cut

Soup Making & Other Basics

MEASURE	INGREDIENT
2 qts	*Vegetable Stock*
2 cups	soy milk

Peel and cube potatoes, then chop up vegetables. Heat up oil in soup pot. Start sautéing onions, then garlic, peppers and celery. After a few minutes, add in potatoes, zucchini, herbs, salt and spices. Cover and allow to cook on medium heat for about ten minutes, then add corn - juice and all.

Sauté mixture another 5 minutes then pour in vegetable stock. Bring soup to a boil, then simmer until potatoes are completely done. Stir and scoop out one quarter of the soup mixture and set aside. With an inversion blender, blend the remaining three quarters while adding the soy milk. Mix the unblended soup with the blended soup. Reheat and it's ready to serve. [12-16 PORTIONS]

Country Lentil Soup
This is our most popular lentil soup, with a deep basic flavor that everyone loves.

MEASURE	INGREDIENT
2 lbs	lentils - dry
4 qts	*Vegetable Stock*
1 qt	water
2	bay leaves
2 large	onions - chopped
1 bunch	celery stalks - chopped
5-6	carrots - chopped
1 Tbsp	thyme leaf
1 Tbsp	marjoram
1/2 tsp	salt
1/2 tsp	black pepper
1/4 cup	soy oil
1/4 cup	soy sauce

Start cooking lentils in vegetable stock and water, with bay leaves in large soup pot. In another pot sauté chopped veggies, thyme, marjoram, salt and pepper with oil. Sauté for 15 minutes on low-medium heat then add to pot with cooking lentils. Pour in soy sauce and simmer until lentils are done. [20+ PORTIONS]

Cream of Broccoli Soup

A vegan version of a popular creamed vegetable soup. These soups are usually based on one particular vegetable, such as mushrooms, celery or asparagus.

MEASURE	INGREDIENT
4 bunches	broccoli
2 qts	*Vegetable Stock*
1 large	onion - chopped
1/4 cup	soy oil
1 tsp	salt
1 pinch	black pepper
1 pinch	thyme
1/4 cup	whole wheat flour
2 cups	soy milk

In a soup pot, cook broccoli in vegetable stock, until soft and done. Remove two cups of this cooked broccoli and set aside. In another pot, sauté onions in oil, with salt, pepper and thyme. Add whole wheat flour to sautéing onions, stirring and cooking a few more minutes.

Pour the broccoli and stock into onion mixture and bring to a boil. Simmer 3 minutes and remove from heat. Add the soy milk and blend with an inversion blender. Mix in the earlier set aside broccoli pieces, and the soup is complete. [8-12 PORTIONS]

Cream of Mushroom Soup

Another vegan creamed soup featuring a single vegetable. This recipe illustrates the general method for making creamed vegetable soups.

MEASURE	INGREDIENT
1/4 cup	soy oil
1 large	onion - chopped
3 lbs	mushrooms - sliced
1/4 cup	whole wheat flour
2 qts	*Vegetable Stock*
2 cups	soy milk

Heat up oil in a soup pot. Chop up onions and sauté in soup pot. Cook onions until translucent, then add whole wheat flour and cook a few more minutes.

Pour in sliced mushrooms and cover. Cook down covered mushrooms, on medium low heat for about 10 minutes. Pour in vegetable stock, bring to a boil and simmer another ten minutes.

Stir and remove 2 cups of mushrooms from soup. Blend remainder of soup and soy milk with a hand-held inversion blender. Add back in the mushrooms previously removed, and soup is ready. [12-16 PORTIONS]

Cream of Tomato Soup

Easy and simple creamed soup that tastes like Mom used to make. Excellent for soup-and-sandwich combo.

MEASURE	INGREDIENT
2 qts	tomato juice (or V8)
2 Tbsps	soy margarine
1 Tbsp	onion powder
1 qt	*Vegetable Stock*

MEASURE	INGREDIENT
1 cup	soy milk
(to taste)	salt

Heat up everything together; mix thoroughly and serve. [16-20 PORTIONS]

Curried Lentil Soup
A flavorful lentil soup, with a taste from Northern India.

MEASURE	INGREDIENT
1/4 cup	soy oil
2 large	onions - chopped
2	yams (or sweet potatoes) - chopped
4	parsnips - chopped
4	carrots - chopped
2 lbs	lentils - dry
1 tsp	salt
1 Tbsp	curry powder
3 qts	*Vegetable Stock*
2	bay leaves

Heat a soup pot and add soy oil. Chop up onions, yams, parsnips and carrots, then sauté - covered - on medium low heat for about five minutes. Combine the lentils, salt, and curry powder with the sautéing mixture. Continue cooking - covered - for five more minutes, stirring occasionally.

Pour in vegetable stock, bay leaves and bring to a boil. Turn down heat and simmer - approximately 30 minutes - until lentils are done. [16-20 PORTIONS]

Curried Spinach Potato Soup

A popular soup at Veggie Works. A good opportunity to try curry, and an excellent way to enjoy spinach.

MEASURE	INGREDIENT
2	onions - chopped
1 Tbsp	salt
1/4 cup	soy oil
2 Tbsps	curry powder
6	potatoes - chunked
3 lbs	spinach
3 qts	***Vegetable Stock***
1 qt	water

In a large soup pot, sauté chopped onions with salt, in the soy oil. Add in curry powder and cook five minutes more. Wash and peel (or leave unpeeled) potatoes, cut into chunks and mix into sauté. Cover and cook for another ten minutes then add the washed spinach. Pour in vegetable stock and water, then simmer until potatoes are soft. [12-16 PORTIONS]

Curried Root Soup

This interesting recipe explores the flavor of root vegetables in a curried soup.

MEASURE	INGREDIENT
1 large	rhutabaga - peeled & chopped
5-6	parsnips - peeled & chopped
5-6	yams (or sweet potatoes) - peeled & chopped
5-8	carrots - peeled & chopped
6-8 medium sized	turnips - peeled & chopped
5	white potatoes - peeled & chopped
2 Tbsps	soy oil

MEASURE	INGREDIENT
2	onions - course chopped
1 Tbsp	salt
2-3 Tbsps	curry powder
3 qts	*Vegetable Stock*
1 qt	water

Peel all vegetables and chop into half inch by three inch rounds. Chop onions in large chunks. Note: You don't need be too exact, as we are only interested in having all the vegetables to cook evenly together.

Heat a soup pot on the stove and add the oil. Add onions, salt and curry powder, stir and reduce heat to caramelize onions 10 minutes. Next add the chopped vegetables, vegetable stock, and water. Bring this to a boil, reduce heat and simmer until all the root vegetables are soft. Blend contents with an inversion blender until smooth. Serve immediately, or refrigerate for future use.
[16-20 PORTIONS]

Daikon Radish Soup

Normally pickled in the Far East, Daikon's pungency is mellowed when cooked, producing a flavor all its own. Invigorating and medicinal.

MEASURE	INGREDIENT
4-8 large	daikon radishes - grated
3 qts	*Vegetable Stock*
1 qt	water
1/4 cup	soy sauce
2	anise cloves
3 Tbsps	apple cider vinegar
1/2 lb	small red beans - precooked
3 Tbsps	cornstarch - dissolved in
	1/4 cup cold water
1 lb block	tofu - diced
1 bunch	scallions - diced

Wash the radishes and grate them through a food processor. Put the vegetable stock, water, soy sauce, star anise and vinegar into a large soup pot. Add in grated daikon and cooked beans.

Bring to a boil, lower heat and simmer until radish is translucent and tender. Add cornstarch slurry to soup, to thicken slightly. Add diced tofu and scallions. Soup is ready to serve. [16-20 PORTIONS]

Egyptian Carrot Yam Soup
A carrot flavored soup tempered with sweet yam and mild Near Eastern spices. Lots of beta carotene.

MEASURE	INGREDIENT
1 lb	carrots - course chopped
3	yams (or sweet potatoes) - course chopped
2 qts	**Vegetable Stock**
1 qt	water
1 large	onion - chopped
1 Tbsp	salt
1 tsp	coriander
1/2 tsp	cumin
1 tsp	cardamom
2 Tbsps	soy oil

Peel and chop carrots and yams in large chunks. Place carrots, yams, vegetable stock and water into a large soup pot. Bring contents to a boil, then simmer until carrots and yams are very soft.

Meanwhile, in a frying pan, sauté onion, salt and spices with the oil. When onions are translucent, add this mixture to the simmering carrots and yams.

When everything is done, remove soup from heat and blend entire mixture. Serve with pita wedges and side of **Sour Cream**. [12-16 PORTIONS]

Escarole & Bean Soup

A traditional Italian soup that's high in calcium, vitamins and magnesium.

MEASURE	INGREDIENT
2	onions - chopped
6	garlic cloves - diced
2 Tbsps	oregano
1 Tbsp	salt
1/2 tsp	black pepper
1/4 cup	olive oil
5 heads	escarole - chopped
2 qts	***Vegetable Stock***
3 qts	water
1 lb	cantilini beans - precooked

In a large soup pot sauté onions, garlic and spices in the olive oil. Wash escarole very well and chop up into large pieces. Add chopped escarole to sauté and cover. Simmer on medium low heat until mass is reduce to half its original size. Pour in vegetable stock, water and beans, then simmer until escarole is tender. [18-24 PORTIONS]

French Onion Soup

The ever popular Continental soup, usually topped with bread, cheese and oven baked.

MEASURE	INGREDIENT
4 large	spanish onions - special cut
2 Tbsps	soy oil
1/4 cup	white wine
1 Tbsp	mustard - prepared
1/2 tsp	salt

Soup Making & Other Basics

MEASURE	INGREDIENT
1 Tbsp	apple cider vinegar
3 qts	*Vegetable Stock*

Cut onions in half and remove hearts. Turn onion halves on their sides and cut into thin slices. Heat up a sauce pot, add oil and onion slices. Turn down heat and slow cook onions until translucent and caramelized. Add wine and remaining ingredients and bring to a boil. Serve. [16-20 PORTIONS]

Gazpacho Soup

Our version of the popular cold, raw summer soup.
With fresh veggies, lots of vitamins and enzymes.

MEASURE	INGREDIENT
4	ripe fresh tomatoes - diced
1 large	green bell pepper - diced
2	cucumbers - peeled & diced
1/2 large	red onion - diced
1 small bunch	parsley - diced
2 qts	tomato juice (or V8)
2 qts	*Vegetable Stock*
1 tsp	salt
1 tsp each:	oregano, marjoram, basil, thyme, & tarragon

Dice up tomatoes, pepper, cucumbers, onion and parsley, then mix together very well in a bowl. Note: Set aside one cup of these well-mixed veggies.

In a cold storage container (or bucket), mix tomato juice, vegetable stock, salt and herbs. Add the mixed veggies (minus the cup that's set aside) to liquid base.

Using a blender, mix all contents thoroughly. Now, finally add the remaining cup of mixed veggies. Chill well before serving. [16-20 PORTIONS]

Grilled Portabella Leek Soup
A wonderful grilled 'steak' flavor is created by the combination of ingredients in this soup.

MEASURE	INGREDIENT
4 bunches	leeks
8	portabella mushroom caps - thin sliced
1 cup	*Grill Goddess Sauce*
4 qts	*Vegetable Stock*
1 cup	*Brown Rice* - cooked
3 Tbsps	cornstarch - dissolved in
	1/4 cup cold water

Have your grill (or hibachi) hot and ready. Rinse leeks well. Cut root end off leeks then cut into long strips. Soak leeks in cold water, making sure all dirt is removed.

Put leeks and thin sliced portabella caps in large mixing bowl with one cup Grill Goddess Sauce. Marinate for a few minutes then start grilling portabella caps on a medium heat, covered, and flip and baste occasionally, until soft. Set mushrooms aside in another mixing bowl.

Make sure grill is hot, then place mass of leek leaves on grill. Reduce heat a little and continuously move leeks to prevent burning. Baste often with remaining Grill Goddess Sauce. When well grilled, chop up leeks and remove to bowl with grilled portabella mushrooms.

In a soup pot, combine portabellas, leeks, remaining sauce and stock. Bring to a boil, add rice and simmer thirty minutes. Mix cornstarch slurry into soup. Stir soup for one minute and serve. [16-20 PORTIONS]

Holiday Pumpkin Soup
**Great tasting and nutritious soup, that goes
with the winter holiday season.**

MEASURE	INGREDIENT
1 medium	pumpkin - fleshed & cubed
3 qts	*Vegetable Stock*
2 cups	soy milk
2 Tbsps	soy margarine
2 tsps	cinnamon
1 tsp	allspice
2 tsps	salt
1/2 tsp	ginger powder
1 Tbsp	molasses
1-2 Tbsps	raw sugar (Sucanat or xylitol)

Cut pumpkin in half, top to bottom. Remove seeds and stringy seed net and discard. Now, score lines on the interior of the pumpkin halves with a small knife 2 inches apart. Next, score lines 2 inches apart perpendicular to the first set of lines. Finally, take a large spoon and scoop out the flesh from the tough outer skin. The result should be enough cube-like pieces of pumpkin to make this soup.

Place the cubed pumpkin flesh into a soup pot, add the vegetable stock and other ingredients and heat to a boil. Reduce heat and simmer until pumpkin cubes become soft. Remove from heat and blend soup with an hand held inversion blender. Serve immediately or store refrigerated for later use.
[12-16 PORTIONS]

Island Blend Soup

The distinctive flavors of the Caribbean, and the creaminess of coconut make this spicy soup a delight.

MEASURE	INGREDIENT
6 large	yams (or sweet potatoes) peeled & chunked
6 large	carrots - peeled & course chopped
2 qts	**Vegetable Stock**
2 qts	water
1 tsp	cumin
1 tsp	allspice
1 tsp	cinnamon
1/2 tsp	nutmeg
1/2 tsp	ginger powder
2 Tbsps	garlic powder
1/2 cup	molasses
1 Tbsp	salt
1 small	habenero pepper (optional)
8-12 ozs	coconut milk

Peel and chunk yams. Peel and chop carrots. When ready, boil yams and carrots in vegetable stock and water. Add in spices, molasses, salt and cook until yams and carrots are very soft. Note: For a spicier version, add a small habernero pepper.

With an inversion blender, blend up soup while adding coconut milk. Garnish with chives and serve. [16-20 PORTIONS]

Mexican Pinto Bean Soup

Interesting, nutritious bean soup with mild Mexican spices. Yams influence the flavor.

MEASURE	INGREDIENT
1 lb	pinto beans
3-4	yams (or sweet potatoes) - chopped
2	onions - diced
1 each:	green bell pepper - diced
	red bell pepper - diced
	yellow bell pepper - diced
3 Tbsps	soy oil
4	garlic cloves - diced
1/2 tsp	cumin
1 Tbsp	oregano
2 qts	**Vegetable Stock**
2 qts	water
1 cup	fresh corn - cut

Cook off beans, rinse and set aside. Chop and dice up the vegetables, then sauté them in oil with garlic and seasonings. Combine vegetable stock, water, pre-cooked beans and corn with the sauté, and bring to a boil.

Turn heat down and simmer until vegetables are soft. Stir and serve.
[16-20 PORTIONS]

Minestrone Soup

**This minestrone is one of the most nutritious -
and delicious - soups in the world.**

MEASURE	INGREDIENT
3 heads	escarole - chopped
1/2 head	white cabbage - chopped
2 medium	zucchini - chopped
3	carrots - chopped
4	celery stalks - chopped
6	broccoli stalks - skinned & cubed
1/4 cup	olive oil
1	onion
1 Tbsp	thyme
1 Tbsp	oregano
6	garlic cloves
1 & 1/2 cups	kidney beans - cooked
1 & 1/2 cups	cantilini beans - cooked
1 Tbsp	salt
1/2 tsp	black pepper
2 cups	*Stewed Tomatoes*
2 qts	*Vegetable Stock*
1 qt	water

Wash three heads of escarole thoroughly, then cut off bottoms and chop up leaves. Chop up cabbage, zucchini, carrots and celery. Cut outer skin off broccoli stalks and cube marrow.

Heat oil in a soup pot and sauté onions, herbs and garlic. Stir to avoid burning.

Add chopped escarole and cabbage to sauté, then cover. Reduce heat to low and simmer until escarole reduces. Add chopped zucchini, broccoli marrow, beans, salt and pepper to sauté. Break up tomatoes and add to sauté. Cook 5 more minutes, then add vegetable stock, water. Simmer another 20 minutes.
 [12-16 PORTIONS]

Miso Soup

This ancient Japanese soup is largely responsible for introducing seaweed, tofu, and miso paste, into the Western diet.

MEASURE	INGREDIENT
3 qts	water
2	carrots - strip cut
4	bok choy stalks - strip cut
1 bunch	scallions - small cut
1/4 cup	dulse seaweed - dry
1/2 cup	wakame seaweed - fresh
1/2 cup	miso paste
2 Tbsps	soy sauce
1 cup	tofu - cubed
1 cup	mushrooms - sliced
1 Tbsp	roasted sesame oil

In a soup pot, heat water. Cut carrots and bok choy into strips and scallions into small rounds. Place dry dulse seaweed in hot water and soak 5 minutes. Rinse wakame (packaged fresh; packed in salt) and chop it up.

Remove about 3 cups of hot water from soup pot into a bowl, then whisk miso paste in until it becomes a slurry.

When water boils, toss in cut veggies (except scallions), seaweed, soy sauce, tofu, mushrooms and sesame oil. Simmer 3 minutes, remove from heat and then pour miso slurry - though a seive or strainer - into soup. Stir up soup, then finally add scallions, as soup is done. [12-16 PORTIONS]

Mock Chicken Noodle Soup

If you love old fashioned chicken noodle soup, you'll love this recipe. Healthier for you...and the chicken too!

MEASURE	INGREDIENT
1 lb	spaghetti
1 lb	tofu - half inch cubed
1 lb	*Perfect Gluten Flank Steak* - cubed
2 Tbsps	soy oil
2	onions
1 bunch	celery stalk
3	carrots
3 Tbsps	soy oil
3 qts	*Vegetable Stock*
3 qts	water
1 tsp	powdered thyme
1 tsp	powdered savory
1 Tbsp	turmeric
1 Tbsp	salt
1 tsp	black pepper
3 Tbsps	nutritional yeast
3 Tbsps	cornstarch - dissolved in 1/4 cup cold water

Break spaghetti into 2 inch pieces, cook off, rinse and set aside. Cube tofu and gluten steak into half inch pieces. In a skillet, fry gluten steak, in 2 tablespoons of soy oil, for 30-45 seconds and set aside. Chop up onions, celery, celery and carrots.

Sauté these chopped veggies in a large soup pot with the 3 tablespoons of soy oil. Stir and sauté 10 minutes then add vegetable stock, water, tofu, herbs, spices and yeast. Bring to a boil. Mix cornstarch slurry into soup, while stirring. Lower heat and simmer twenty minutes. Combine pasta and gluten steak with soup mixture. Simmer a few more minutes, then soup is done.
 [20-30 PORTIONS]

Moonlight Sonata Soup

**Its appearance resembles the moon through trees.
The flavor and nutritional value is incredible.**

MEASURE	INGREDIENT
4 large	yams (or sweet potatoes) - peeled & chopped
3 lbs	fresh spinach - chopped
2	onions - chopped
4 Tbsps	olive oil
1 Tbsp	salt
2 tsps	powdered thyme
3 qts	*Vegetable Stock*
2 qts	water
2 Tbsps	cornstarch - dissolved in
	with 1/4 cup cold water

Peel and chop yams into small cubes. Wash and chop spinach. Chop up onions then begin sautéing them in a soup pot with the olive oil. After a few minutes add the yam cubes, chopped spinach, salt and thyme. Cover, lower heat, and cook ten minutes, stirring occasionally. Add the vegetable stock and water, then simmer twenty minutes more. Stir in the cornstarch slurry to thicken soup and serve. [20+ PORTIONS]

MultiBean Soup

The combined flavors of various beans is the magic within this soup. Loaded with amino acids and delicious, too.

MEASURE	INGREDIENT
1/2 cup each: (combined)	lentils, kidney beans, navy beans, black beans, pinto beans, red beans chickpeas, cantilini beans lima beans, split peas & great northern beans
3 qts	***Vegetable Stock***
2 qts	water
2	onions - chopped
1 bunch	celery stalks - chopped
5	carrots - chopped
4	garlic cloves - diced
2 Tbsps	thyme leaf
2 Tbsps	marjoram leaf
2 Tbsps	salt
1/4 cup	soy oil

Soak beans together overnight [or use quick soak by bringing beans to a boil in 3 quarts of water, turning off flame and cover for 1 hour]. Drain soaking water off after soak period and combine these prepared beans with 3 quarts of vegetable stock and 2 quarts of water. Bring this to a boil, reduce heat and simmer for 1 hour.

Chop up vegetables. Using another pot, sauté onions, celery, carrots, garlic, herbs and salt in the oil, covered and on medium low heat for 15-20 minutes. Next pour sautéed vegetable mixture into the cooking beans. Simmer this mixture until hardest beans are very soft. Soup is finished and ready to serve!
 [20+ PORTIONS]

Mushroom Barley Soup

**A well liked, traditional barley soup, and completely vegan.
You'll love its hearty flavor.**

MEASURE	INGREDIENT
1 lb	barley
2 qts	water
1 & 1/4 cups	soy oil
2	onions - chopped
1 Tbsp	thyme leaf
1 Tbsp	salt
1 Tbsp	soy sauce
3 lbs	mushrooms - sliced
1/4 cup	white wine
3 qts	**Vegetable Stock**

Rinse barley with cold water. In a soup pot put 2 quarts water and barley and bring to a boil. Lower heat and simmer.

Using another pot, heat oil and begin sautéing chopped onions, thyme, salt and soy sauce. When onions are translucent, add mushrooms to sauté. Sauté mixture covered, stirring occasionally, for 15 minutes on low heat.

Pour wine into sauté and turn up heat. Stir mixture and combine with cooking barley and water. Pour in vegetable stock and bring mixture to a boil. Lower heat and cook - covered - for about 1 hour.
[20-25 PORTIONS]

New World Lima Bean Soup

**Unlike the flash frozen variety, the dry lima bean's
in this recipe offer a rich, unique flavor.**

MEASURE	INGREDIENT
2 lbs	jumbo lima beans - dry
2 qts	**Vegetable Stock**
2 qts	water
1 Tbsp	salt
2	bay leaves
3 Tbsps	olive oil
2	onions - chopped
5-6	carrots -chopped
1 bunch	celery stalks (with leaves) - chopped
5	garlic cloves - crushed
2 Tbsps	thyme leaf
2 Tbsps	marjoram
1/2 tsp	black pepper

Soak beans overnight in 1 gallon of water or use quick soak method. Rinse beans and put them in a large soup pot with the vegetable stock, water, salt and bay leaf. Bring this to boil, lower heat and simmer, covered.

In another pot or large skillet, heat the oil. Sauté chopped onions, carrots, celery, garlic, herbs, and black pepper, on medium heat, covered.

Stir sauté mixture occasionally and cook ten minutes. Add sauté mixture to lima beans and liquid. Simmer soup on low heat, covered, until beans are very tender. [16-20 PORTIONS]

Old Fashioned Black Bean Soup
Delivers basic home-spun goodness.
A good introduction to black beans.

MEASURE	INGREDIENT
2 lbs	black beans - dry
3 qts	*Vegetable Stock*
3 qts	water
1 Tbsp	salt
1	bay leaves
2	onions - diced
4	carrots - diced
2	green bell peppers - diced
1	red bell pepper - diced
3 Tbsps	soy oil
2 Tbsps	thyme leaf
1 Tbsp	marjoram

Rinse the beans, then cook them in the vegetable stock and water with salt and the bay leaf. No need to soak black beans as they will cook in about 1 hour.

Dice up the vegetables, then sauté them in a skillet with the oil and herbs. Cover and simmer on low, stirring occasionally.

Sauté mixture 15 minutes then add to cooking beans. Continue cooking soup until beans and carrots are soft. [20+ PORTIONS]

Old World Leek Soup

Experience the wonderful goodness of leeks.
You won't believe the great flavor...

MEASURE	INGREDIENT
4 large bunches	leeks - cross cut
2	onions - chopped
1/4 cup	olive oil
6	potatoes - chunked
4 large	carrots - peeled & slant cut
3 qts	*Vegetable Stock*
1 qt	water
2 Tbsps	thyme leaf
1 Tbsp	salt
1 tsp	black pepper

Wash leeks well, cut off root end and remove some of the inferior looking outer leaves. Cross cut 1/4 inch rounds and put into pot of cold water to soak. Leeks are the dirtiest of vegetables and this method works well.

Heat oil in a large soup pot. Chop up onions and sauté them in the oil. Drain leeks well and add them to the onions. Peel or just wash potatoes, then cut into soup chunks. Peel and slice carrots into diagonal rounds.

Combine all remaining ingredients with vegetable stock and water, then bring to a boil. Lower heat and simmer soup until potatoes are done. [12-16 PORTIONS]

Pasta Fagioli Soup

A traditional Italian soup often found as an appetizer in Italian restaurants. This is the 'red' version, using left-over marinara as the sauté constituent.

MEASURE	INGREDIENT
2 cups	ditilini pasta - cooked
1 lb	cantilini beans - dry
2 qts	*Vegetable Stock*
1 qt	water
2 cups	*Marinara Sauce*

Cook off the ditilini pasta, rinse and set aside. Soak beans overnight or use quick soak method and rinse off soak water. Cook beans in vegetable stock and water, until done (about 45 minutes).

When beans are done and tender, combine all ingredients with beans and cooking liquid. Simmer a few minutes and serve. [12-16 PORTIONS]

Portabella Orzo Soup

Another tasty use of the portabella mushroom. Combine this with the flavor of roasted peppers and wonderful orzo pasta. It makes an outrageous soup!

MEASURE	INGREDIENT
8	portabella mushroom caps - sliced
1/4 cup	olive oil
6	garlic cloves - diced
1/4 cup	balsamic vinegar
1 tsp	salt
1 Tbsp	thyme leaf
2 whole	red bell peppers - roasted - peeled & diced
2 whole	green bell peppers - roasted - peeled & diced

MEASURE	INGREDIENT
2 qts	**_Vegetable Stock_**
1 qt	water
2 cups	orzo - cooked
3 Tbsps	cornstarch - dissolved in
	1/4 cup cold water

Slice up portabella mushroom caps into thin slices. Mix oil, diced garlic, vinegar, salt and thyme in a bowl. Place mushrooms in same bowl and marinate a few minutes.

Have grill hot and ready. Remove mushrooms with a slotted spatula or spoon and place on grill. Baste with remaining marinade, turning once, and grill until done. Set aside in original bowl with remaining juice.

In a 400°F oven, bake peppers in a baking dish until soft, about twenty minutes. Remove from oven and put peppers in a paper bag to cool for 15 minutes.

Remove peppers from bag and peel off skin. Dice peeled roasted peppers and add them to grilled portabellas. In a soup pot, combine vegetable stock, water and contents of mixing bowl and bring to a boil. Add precooked orzo and cornstarch slurry. Stir and serve. [12-16 PORTIONS]

Split Pea Soup
No chapter on soups should be without a version of split pea. This is our basic recipe.

MEASURE	INGREDIENT
2 lbs	split peas - dry (green or yellow)
3 qts	**_Vegetable Stock_**
3 qts	water
2	onions - chopped
5	carrots - chopped
5	celery stalks - chopped

Soup Making & Other Basics

MEASURE	INGREDIENT
4 large	potatoes - peeled & small cubed
1 tsp	salt
1 Tbsp	powdered thyme
1/4 cup	soy oil
1 cup	soy milk

Cook split peas in vegetable stock and water, on low heat - covered - for about one hour. Chop up onion, carrots and celery. Peel and cube potatoes into small pieces. Sauté veggies with salt and herbs in oil for about 15 minutes, or until tender.

Combine sauté and split peas and simmer until peas are very tender. Remove from heat. With a small sauce pot remove about one quarter of the soup. Using an inversion blender, blend remaining three quarters of soup with soy milk. Add saved soup to blended mixture, stir and serve. [20+ PORTIONS]

Sonoran Black Bean Soup

A spicy black bean soup with deep southwestern flavors. Spicy-hot like the great Sonoran desert.

MEASURE	INGREDIENT
2 lbs	black beans - dry
2 qts	*Vegetable Stock*
3 qts	water
1 Tbsp	salt
1 whole	habenero pepper
1/4 cup	tomato paste
1/4 cup	soy oil
2	onions - diced
2	green bell peppers - diced
2	red bell peppers - diced
5	garlic cloves - diced

MEASURE	INGREDIENT
2 Tbsps	cajun spice blend
1 tsp	salt

Combine beans, vegetable stock, water and 1 tablespoon of salt in a soup pot and bring to a boil. Throw in 1 whole habenero pepper, add tomato paste, turn heat down, cover pot and simmer.

Meanwhile, in another pot or skillet, heat oil and sauté diced onions, peppers and garlic with the Cajun spice and 1 teaspoon of salt. Stir often and sauté 15 minutes. Combine sauté with cooking beans, and simmer soup until beans are done. Stir and serve. [20+ PORTIONS]

Thai Sweet Potato Soup

Another in our line of blended sweet potato soups. This version is spicy, creamed with coconut and South East Asian flavors.

MEASURE	INGREDIENT
8 large	yams (or sweet potatoes) - peeled & course chopped
2 qts	*Vegetable Stock*
2 qts	water
1 Tbsp	salt
1 tsp	cinnamon
1 tsp	allspice
1 tsp	lemon zest
1/2 tsp	powdered ginger
1 tsp	garlic powder
4 Tbsps	roasted sesame oil
1/4 cup	molasses
1 cup	coconut milk
1/2 cup	cilantro - chopped

Soup Making & Other Basics

Peel, rinse and chop yams into large pieces. Dump yams into soup pot with vegetable stock, water, salt, spices, sesame oil and molasses. Heat this to a boil then reduce to a simmer.

When yams are soft, remove from heat source and add coconut milk. Using an inversion blender, blend soup until smooth. Serve topped with chopped cilantro. [16-20 PORTIONS]

Vegetable Barley Soup
A hearty vegetable soup...enjoyed by everyone.

MEASURE	INGREDIENT
1 lb	barley - hulled
2 qts	**Vegetable Stock**
2 qts	water
1 tsp	salt
1/4 cup	olive oil
4	garlic cloves - diced
1	onion - chopped
1 cup	fresh tomatoes - chopped
4	celery stalks - chopped
3	carrots - thin chopped
2 medium	zucchini - chopped
1	green bell pepper - chopped
1	red bell pepper - chopped
1 lb	string beans - chopped
1 lb	mushrooms - sliced
1 tsp	marjoram leaf
1 tsp	thyme leaf
1 tsp	salt
2 cups	spinach - chopped

Rinse barley and cook with vegetable stock, water and 1 teaspoon salt until tender, about 45 minutes.

Meanwhile, in another pot, heat oil then sauté diced garlic, chopped onions, tomatoes, celery, carrots, zucchini, peppers, string beans, sliced mushrooms, herbs and 1 teaspoon salt. Continue sautéing for about 15 minutes.

Combine barley - with its cooking liquid - to sauté mix, then add chopped spinach and cook 5 more minutes. Stir and serve. [12-16 PORTIONS]

Vegetable Noodle Soup
A familiar staple everyone loves, because it's such a great way to enjoy vegetables and pasta together!

MEASURE	INGREDIENT
1	onion - chopped
1/2 head	white cabbage - chopped
2	celery stalks - chopped
3	carrots - chopped
2 cups	string beans - chopped
2	zucchini - chopped
2	summer squash - chopped
2 cups	mushrooms - sliced
1/4 cup	olive oil
1 Tbsp	thyme
1 Tbsp	basil
1 Tbsp	marjoram
1 Tbsp	salt
2 cups	chickpeas - precooked
2 cups	*Stewed Tomatoes* - crushed
2 qts	*Vegetable Stock*
1 qt	water
2	bay leaves

Soup Making & Other Basics

MEASURE	INGREDIENT
2 cups	elbow macaroni, shell, penne (or similar pasta) - cooked

Chop up onions, cabbage, celery, carrots, string beans, zucchini, squash, then slice up mushrooms. In a heated pot, add oil, then pour in prepared veggies, herbs, salt, and precooked chickpeas. Sauté this mixture - stirring occasionally - on low heat. After 15 minutes, stir crushed tomatoes into this sauté mixture, then simmer an 5 more minutes.

Pour in vegetable stock, water and bay leaves, then bring to a boil. Add cooked noodles, lower heat, then simmer 20 more minutes and soup is done.
[12-16 PORTIONS]

Vegetable Stock
The importance of a good vegetable stock is the cornerstone of excellent vegetarian cooking. Most cuisines throughout the world, find stock to be a fundamental ingredient.

Unlike meat based stocks, which do include a small amount of vegetables and herbs, vegan based stock simply rely on flavors from concentrated amounts of vegetables and vegetable sourced foods.

At Veggie Works, we maintain a 'living stock'; one which depends on the nutricious juices of cooked off beans and vegetables, often dirived from other preparations. Soy sauce, concentrated vegetable paste, nutritional yeast, textured and hydrolyzed soy proteins, herb and vegetable powders also play a role.

The following is a good home model to work with. Experiment, as most veggies work well. Some vegetables have very distinctive flavors, which can modify - or even over power - the taste, and should be used with caution until you're familiar with their results. Note: Never use onion skins! Contrary to popular belief, most vegetable skins or casings will ruin the stock.

MEASURE	INGREDIENT
3	potatoes - peeled & chopped
3 small	yams (or sweet potatoes) - peeled & chopped

MEASURE	INGREDIENT
1/4 cup	soy oil
2 large	onions - chopped
1 bunch	celery stalks - chopped
4	portabella mushrooms - chopped
1-2 bunches	leeks - well rinsed & chopped
6	garlic cloves - crushed
1 lb	carrots - shredded
1 lb	turnips - shredded
3 medium	zucchini - shredded
1 Tbsp	salt
1/4 cup	soy sauce
1/2 cup	nutritional yeast
1 lb	spinach - chopped
1 Tbsp	thyme powder
4 Tbsps	tomato paste
10-12 qts	filtered water - with vegetable bouillon or paste (as optional booster)

Wash all vegetables thoroughly. Peel and chop potatoes and yams, then set aside. In a large stock pot, heat oil then add chopped onions. Turn down flame and caramelize onions. Chop up celery, portabella mushrooms, leeks, and add these - with the crushed garlic - to cooking onions. Shred carrots, turnips and zucchini in a food processor, then add these vegetables with the salt, soy sauce and nutritional yeast to the cooking mixture. Cover and sauté about 10 more minutes until mixture is cooked down.

Pour filtered water into sauté mix, then add all remaining ingredients. Bring to a hard boil then reduce heat to simmer contents - covered - for about an hour. Allow mixture to cool. Using a small sauce pot, scoop out stock and pour liquid and vegetables through a large wire strainer into one or more containers.

You may want to freeze some of the stock and save some refrigerated.
 [30+ PORTIONS - depending on applications]

Soup Making & Other Basics

Note: Allow to cool and remove congealed oil from surface of stock, making broth virtually fat-free.

Vichyssoise

This completely vegan version of the chilled blend of leek and potato soup features great flavor...in the French tradition!

MEASURE	INGREDIENT
1 gal	*Old World Leek Soup*
2 cups	soy milk

Simply blend pre-made Old World Leek potato soup with soy milk, then return mix to refrigerator. Serve chilled, with a sprig of fresh thyme, or spoonful of *Sour Cream*. [16-20 PORTIONS]

Zucchini Rice Soup

Too many zucchini in your garden, this summer? Here's one way to make good use of them.

MEASURE	INGREDIENT
1 large	onion - chopped
5	garlic cloves - minced
1/4 cup	olive oil
6-10	zucchini - chopped or sliced
1 Tbsp	salt
1 Tbsp	thyme leaf
1 Tbsp	marjoram leaf
3 qts	*Vegetable Stock*
2 qts	water
2 cups	*Brown Rice* - cooked

Chop up onions and sauté them with minced garlic, in the olive oil, for 5 minutes. Chop up (or slice) the zucchini then add them with salt and herbs, to the sauté. Cover the pot and let the zucchini steam down - on low medium heat - for 10-15 minutes.

Remove cover and add the vegetable stock and water. Bring this to a boil, reduce heat and simmer 30-40 minutes. Add the cooked rice and simmer another 15 minutes. Soup is now ready to serve. [16-20 PORTIONS]

* If you want to use uncooked rice, just add it to the sauté early on and finish the soup in the same manner as described above. Let the cooking rice indicate when the soup is done.

Burgers & Sandwiches

Introduction

Burgers and sandwiches seem to be America's contribution to the world's cuisine. Although other countries have their forms of convenience foods, the burger and sandwich, is a truly American expression. Traditional burgers and sandwiches have animal-based meat as the main ingredient. This chapter will show you the endless possibilities for good vegan sandwiches and burgers, by providing a variety of recipes from the lunch menu at Veggie Works.

We'll discover how prepared vegetables make great sandwiches. Grilled or baked vegetable melts are described here using soy cheeses, great for flavor, nutrition and satisfaction. Quesadillas, a wonderful Meso-American 'sandwich', are explored here as well.

The sandwiches, burgers and quesadillas listed in this chapter are the same as those that are enjoyed by thousands of happy patrons, at the Veggie Works Restaurant. These recipes, and all of the recipes included in this book have been successfully tested on numerous subjects with purely positive results. Not only do these sandwiches stand alone as great meals, they are also intended to establish a foundation, in each category, from which the advanced vegan chef can experiment.

Avocado & Hummus Sandwich
**Another great avocado sandwich; this combination
is a lunch favorite at Veggie Works.**

MEASURE	INGREDIENT
1/2	firm ripe avocado - scooped & strip sliced
1	whole wheat *Pita Bread*
	(or 2 slices whole grain bread)

MEASURE	INGREDIENT
4 Tbsps	**Hummus**
3 leaves	romaine lettuce - shredded
2 slices	ripe fresh tomato
2 rings	red onion - sliced
3 slices	cucumber - thin sliced
(as needed)	alfalfa sprouts
1/2 tsp	cajun spice blend

Use an avocado that is slightly soft, yet still firm, with a bright green appearance. Slice up one half, and save the other half for use in another recipe.

Heat the pita and slice it open by cutting around the seam. Layer on the hummus, shredded lettuce, sliced avocado, tomatoes, onions, cucumber, sprouts and lightly sprinkled cajun spice.

Avocado & Soy Cheese Sandwich
A nice fresh sandwich, with a good balance of protein, fat, carbohydrates, enzymes and vitamins.

MEASURE	INGREDIENT
1/2	firm ripe avocado - scooped & strip sliced
1	whole wheat **Pita Bread**
	(or 2 slices whole grain bread)
1 Tbsp	**Mayonnaise**
1/2 cup	salad greens - shredded
2 pinches	cajun spice blend
2-3 slices	soy cheese
2 slices	ripe fresh tomato
(as needed)	alfalfa sprouts

Use an avocado that is slightly soft, yet still firm, with a bright green appearance. Slice up one half, and save the other half for use in another recipe.

Burgers & Sandwiches

If using a pita, heat it up in an oven or toaster (lowest setting) then slice around the edge to open it up. Spread mayonnaise over the bread. Next, layer, from bottom up, the shredded salad greens, sliced avocado, cajun spice, cheese slices, sliced tomatoes and sprouts.

Bacon Lettuce & Tomato Sandwich
This vegan version of the all American classic, makes a great sandwich with authentic flavors. Healthier too!

MEASURE	INGREDIENT
3 Tbsps	soy oil (for skillet or griddle)
5 slices	vegan-style bacon
	(or 5 *Tempeh Bacon Strips*)
2-4 Tbsps	*Mayonnaise*
1	kaiser roll (or *Pita Bread*,
	or 2 slices whole grain bread)
1/2 cup	lettuce - shredded
2-3 slices	ripe fresh tomato

Heat a skillet and pour in oil, add vegan-style 'bacon' (or tempeh bacon strips) and brown on both sides. Remove and drain well on paper towels. Note: You can marinate the tempeh before frying, or add marinade after frying (see chapter on *Vegan Meats*).

Spread the mayonnaise on both sides of a roll (or bread). Layer, starting with the lettuce, then bacon and finally tomato.

Baked Tofu Turkey Sandwich

This sandwich rivals the flavor and nutrition of any 'real' turkey sandwich, without the karma...

MEASURE	INGREDIENT
1 lb package	firm tofu - thin sliced
1 cup	*Mock Poultry Marinade*
1/4 cup	water
2 slices	whole grain bread
1/4 cup	*Brown Gravy* (if serving hot)
2 Tbsps	*Mayonnaise* (if serving cold)
1/2 cup	lettuce - shredded (")
2-3 slices	ripe fresh tomato (")

Slice tofu into four thin slices of the widest possible size. Marinate the tofu slices for and hour or more, in marinade. Grease a baking dish or pan and pour in tofu and marinade. Add 1/4 cup water and place in 450°F oven. Bake 30 minutes turning tofu slices once or twice.

If serving sandwich hot, heat up gravy in another pan on the stove, adding remaining juice from marinade. Serve open face, pouring gravy on top.

If serving sandwich cold, use mayonnaise, lettuce and tomato on sandwich.

Basic Bean Burger

This recipe presents a good basic bean burger. Any combination of cooked beans, works well with this recipe.

MEASURE	INGREDIENT
1/4 cup	beans - cooked & mashed
1/4	onion - diced
1	carrot - shredded
1	garlic clove - diced

Burgers & Sandwiches

MEASURE	INGREDIENT
2-3 Tbsps	whole wheat flour
2-3 Tbsps	bread crumbs
1	zucchini - shredded (optional)
2 pinches	salt

Mash up the cooked beans a little, but don't puree. In a mixing bowl, combine all ingredients using your hands to knead mixture. Form into a ball, then press into a patty. Pan fry on both sides, until done. [1 PORTION - LARGE]

Black Bean Burger

An excellent Mexican flavored burger, with lots of nutrition; which is also a wonderful example of how great - meatless - burgers can be!

MEASURE	INGREDIENT
1/4 cup	black beans - cooked & mashed (fresh cooked preferred or canned)
1/4	onion - diced
1/4	colored bell pepper - diced
1	garlic clove - diced
1 Tbsp	whole wheat flour
1 small	carrot - shredded
2 Tbsps	bread crumbs
2 pinches	chili powder
2 pinches	cajun spice blend
3 Tbsps	soy oil (for skillet or griddle)

Mash up the cooked beans a little, but don't puree. Dice the onions, peppers and garlic. With the exception of the frying oil, combine all ingredients into a mixing bowl; then using your hands to knead ingredients, mix well. Form resulting burger 'meat' into a ball, then press into a patty.

Have a griddle or skillet hot, pour in some oil for frying, then set burger on top. Cover burger and lower heat to medium low setting. After 4-5 minutes, flip the burger and continue cooking - uncovered - another 4-5 minutes. Serve on a roll (or pita bread, or two slices of whole grain bread). For a deluxe version, melt a slice of soy cheese during final cooking phase, then top with **Salsa** when placed on roll.

Chicken Fried Gluten Sandwich
Southern style cooking provides the inspiration for this chicken fried gluten steak sandwich.

MEASURE	INGREDIENT
1	**Perfect Gluten Flank Steak**
2 pinches	cajun spice blend
2 pinches	powdered thyme
2 pinches	salt
1/4 cup	whole wheat flour
1/4 cup	soy milk
1/4 cup	bread crumbs
1/4 cup	soy oil (for frying)
1/4 cup	**Brown Gravy** (if serving hot)
2 Tbsps	**Mayonnaise** (if serving cold)
2 leafs	lettuce (")
2-3 slices	ripe fresh tomato (")

Cut gluten steak in half. Sprinkle the spice, herb and salt on both sides of the steaks. Next, coat steaks with flour. Dip the flour coated steak into a bowl with soy milk and then into the bread crumbs. You can re-dip again into soy milk and the bread crumbs for a thicker breading.

Heat the oil in a skillet or fryolator. If using a fryolator, drop the breaded steaks in and fry until they begins to float, then remove and drain. If using a skillet, fry the steaks on one side for 2-3 minutes, flip and fry the other side. Remove and drain.

If eating the sandwich hot, simply put fried steak on a roll (pita or two slices of whole wheat bread) then pour gravy over same. If having it cold, use the mayonnaise, lettuce, tomato. This recipe makes two hearty sandwiches.

Chicken Fried Tofu Sandwich
**If you like old fashioned home cooking, this one's for you.
Hot or cold, this is a very satisfying sandwich.**

MEASURE	INGREDIENT
1/4 lb package	firm tofu - thin sliced
2 pinches	cajun spice blend
2 pinches	powdered thyme
2 pinches	salt
1/4 cup	whole wheat flour
1/4 cup	soy milk
1/4 cup	bread crumbs
1/4 cup	soy oil (for frying)
1/4 cup	*Brown Gravy* (if serving hot)
3 Tbsps	*Mayonnaise* (if serving cold)
2 leafs	lettuce (if serving cold)
2 slices	fresh tomato (if serving cold)

Cut a block of firm tofu into 4 thin slices, of the widest possible size. Sprinkle the spice, herb and salt over tofu slabs. Next, coat the tofu with flour. Dip the flour coated tofu into a bowl with soy milk and then into the bread crumbs. You can re-dip again into the soy milk and bread crumbs for a thicker breading.

Heat the oil in a skillet or fryolator. If using a fryolator, drop the breaded tofu in and fry until it begins to float then remove and drain. If using a skillet, fry the tofu on one side for 2-3 minutes, flip and fry the other side. Remove and drain.

If eating the sandwich hot, simply put fried tofu on a roll (pita or 2 slices of whole wheat bread), then pour gravy over same. If having it cold, use the mayonnaise, lettuce, tomato. [4 PORTIONS]

Chinese Cabbage Spring Roll
Traditional Pacific Rim style spring rolls, make great appetizers!
Simple, tasty...and impressive.

MEASURE	INGREDIENT
1/2 head	nappa cabbage - shredded
1 large	carrot - shredded
1	daikon radish - shredded (optional)
2 Tbsps	roasted sesame oil
2 Tbsps	soy sauce
1 Tbsp	apple cider vinegar
4-5	spring roll wraps

This recipe makes about 4 large spring rolls. With the exception of the spring roll wraps, mix all other ingredients and allow to marinate for a few minutes...to several days. When desired, remove a handful of marinated mix - squeezing off excess liquid - and place in middle of an open wrap. Fold bottom corner over, towards top corner. Wet three remaining sides and fold the left and right sides towards the center. Roll the mass upwards and seal the edges.

If using a fryolator, heat oil to 350°F and lower springs rolls into oil. You may need to hold down roll with slotted spoon for a few seconds, until it sets up. Fry until spring roll begins to float, then remove and drain on paper towels.

If using a frying pan, heat oil until it begins to smoke, lower heat to medium setting and fry spring roll on both sides. Serve with Duck Sauce or Tamari, for dipping.

Falafel
**Traditional Middle Eastern 'fritter'
sandwich, stuffed inside a pita.**

MEASURE	INGREDIENT
1 cup	chickpeas - cooked
1/2 cup	*Bulgar Wheat* - cooked
1 tsp	salt
2	garlic cloves - minced
1/2	onion - diced
1 bunch	parsley - diced
1 tsp	cumin
1 tsp	coriander
1 tsp	cajun spice blend
1/4 cup	whole wheat flour
(as needed)	soy oil (for frying)
1	whole wheat *Pita Bread*
1 cup combined:	lettuce - shredded, red onion, tomato, bell peppers - diced
2-4 Tbsps	*Tahini Sauce*

Using a food processor, coarsely puree chick peas. Combine coursely pureed chick peas, prepared bulgar, salt, minced garlic, diced onions, diced parsley, spices and whole wheat flour in a bowl, then mix well.

Heat oil in fryolator or skillet to 350°F. Form falafel mix into small balls (or barrels) and fry until done, about 5 minutes. Note: Always make up one ball and fry it before making up entire batch. If single falafel ball begins to disintegrate, mix in additional flour.

Heat pita and slice off a 1 inch piece from pita's edge. Open pita from cut section and start to stuff, alternating shredded lettuce and diced veggies with falafel balls and sauce. [4-6 PORTIONS]

Grilled Portabella Sandwich

Featuring grilled Portabella mushrooms, sweet peppers and eggplant, basted with 'Grill Goddess Sauce'.

MEASURE	INGREDIENT
2	portabella mushroom caps - thin sliced
1	red bell pepper - seeded, boiled & julienne cut
1	green bell pepper - seeded, boiled & julienne cut
2 slices	eggplant - thin diagonal cut
1/4 cup	*Grill Goddess Sauce*
	whole grain bread or *Pita Bread*

This recipe makes 2-3 sandwiches. Have grill hot and ready. Slice mushroom caps into thin pieces. Quarter peppers and remove seeds and stem. Cut two thin slices of eggplant by cross cutting on a diagonal.

Boil pepper pieces until green peppers begin to change color. Remove peppers and plunge in cold water to stop the cooking process.

Using a pastry (or grill basting) brush, spread vegetables on grilling surface, then baste them with the sauce. When veggies develop defined grill lines, turn them over with a metal spatula. When well grilled, remove veggies to bowl or container and pour in remaining sauce. Finally, slice all boiled peppers with a julienne cut. Vegetables are now ready to assemble into sandwiches. Serve fresh off the grill on whole wheat pitas, or stuff tortillas to make a great veggie wrap. You may want to top with soy cheese and bake a few minutes in a hot oven to create your own portabella melt.

Grilled Vegetable Melt Sandwich

Similar to the Grilled Portabella Sandwich, this recipe features a wider assortment of veggies, layered with cheese.

MEASURE	INGREDIENT
1	red bell pepper - seeded, boiled & julienne cut
1	green bell pepper - seeded, boiled & julienne cut
4 slices	zucchini
4 slices	yellow squash
1	onion - sliced
2-4 slices	eggplant - thin diagonal cut
2-4 slices	ripe fresh tomato
(as needed)	other vegetables - parboiled (optional)
1/4 cup	*Grill Goddess Sauce*
1/3 cup	soy cheese - grated

Boil pepper pieces until green peppers begin to change color. Remove peppers and plunge in cold water to stop the cooking process.

Note: All other vegetable slices can be grilled without par-boiling. If using the optional vegetables -- thin sliced carrots, yams, potatoes, cauliflower, broccoli -- they will require parboiling before grilling.

Using a pastry (or grill basting) brush, spread vegetables on grilling surface, then baste them with the sauce. When veggies develop defined grill lines, turn them over with a metal spatula. When well grilled, remove veggies to bowl or container and pour in remaining sauce. Finally, slice all boiled peppers with a julienne cut.

In a small baking pan, layer grilled vegetables with soy cheese in between and bake until cheese melts. Use a spatula to remove to sandwich bread or Pita.
[2 PORTIONS]

Harvest Burger

Our most popular burger. Made with Texturized Vegetable Protein burger mix; high in protein and fiber, without the saturated fats and cholesterol.

MEASURE	INGREDIENT
1 cup	TVP burger blend - dry mix
1 & 2/3 cups	ice cold water
2 Tbsps	soy oil

Add TVP dry mix to water and stir well, then refrigerate for 15 minutes or more before use. Moisten hands with water and form balls of desired size and weight. With wet hands, flatten balls to form burgers.

Have a hot skillet, frying pan, griddle or grill ready. Pour in 1 tablespoon of oil. Place burger over oil and cover. Cook on medium heat 3-5 minutes, turn then cook same time on other side. If using grill, paint burger and grill grates with oil before putting burger on. [2-4 PORTIONS]

Mexican Quesadilla

This recipe is our version of a popular Mexican dish. An excellent appetizer for *The Maximilian* dinner.

MEASURE	INGREDIENT
1 large	tortilla
1 Tbsp	*Mexican Sauce*
2 ozs	vegetables - diced
2 ozs	black beans - cooked
2 ozs	*Guacamole*
2 ozs	soy cheese - grated
2 ozs	*Salsa* (for dipping)

Have a hot oven ready (500°F) and a hot grill. This recipe can be completed using only an oven, or only a grill, but it's easier is both are available.

Put tortilla in oven for about one minute to make it pliable. Spread the Mexican Sauce over one side. Start layering veggies (diced onion, peppers, tomatoes), and beans on one half of the side, and the guacamole on the other half. Sprinkle the cheese over the veggies and fold over the side with guacamole.

Put the folded quesadilla on a baking sheet or pizza screen and oven bake for 4-5 minutes. Remove quesadilla from oven and place on hot grill. Wait 5-10 seconds then turn quesadilla 90 degrees. Grill another 5-10 seconds and flip. Repeat process. Remove, cut into four pieces and serve with salsa for dipping.

Philly Cheese Steak Sandwich

A delicious and popular sandwich. Our version has all the flavor and body of the traditional version...without the negative side effects.

MEASURE	INGREDIENT
2-4 ozs	**Perfect Gluten Flank Steak** - thinly sliced
1/2	onion - thin sliced
1/2	green bell pepper - thin sliced
1/2	red bell pepper - thin sliced
1 & 1/2 Tbsps	soy oil
1/3 cup	soy cheese - grated
(as needed)	whole grain bread

Thinly slice gluten steak, onions and peppers. Heat up a frying pan or cast iron skillet. Pour in oil and start sautéing onions and peppers. Lower heat, cover, cook 5 minutes.

Toss in gluten strips and continue to sauté another 5 minutes on medium heat/ stirring occasionally. Add grated soy cheese, cover and lower heat. After 2-3 minutes cheese should be melted. It is best when a skin develops on the bottom.

Use a metal spatula to carefully flip over Philly. It should look and behave like an omelet. Lift mass out of pan and place on bread, roll or pita.

Pizza

Pizza is much easier to make than most people realize. Use the recipe for Pizza dough in this book, vegan cheese and toppings to make a great meal.

MEASURE	INGREDIENT
(as needed)	unbleached white flour (for rolling dough)
fist-sized ball	*Pizza Dough*
1/2 cup	*Marinara Sauce*
1/2 cup	soy mozzarella cheese - shredded
(as needed)	toppings: sliced colored bell peppers,
(")	onions, mushrooms, olives,
(")	steamed broccoli, vegan-style
	pepperoni, fried TVP burger blend
	(...possibilities are endless!)

Sprinkle a little flour on cutting board, flatten dough ball and roll it into a circle half the size and twice the thickness desired. Pick up dough crust and, if you can't toss it, put it over your fist and stretch the sides gently. Work it this way carefully until it is desired size. Place dough crust on pizza screen or greased tin and oven bake at 450°F - 500°F until it begins to puff and firm up.

Spread marinara over crust leaving the edges exposed. Put on cheese and toppings, then bake until cheese melts. Brush oil on crust 2-3 minutes before removing from oven.

Portabella Mushroom Burger
There are several Portabella burgers on the market. Most contain eggwhites and lack flavor. Our version is entirely vegan and flavorful!

MEASURE	INGREDIENT
1	onion - diced
3 Tbsps	olive oil
1 Tbsp	thyme leaf
1 Tbsp	salt
5	garlic cloves - diced
4	portabella mushroom caps - sliced
1/4 cup	whole wheat flour

Sauté diced onions with oil in a pot or large skillet. Add thyme and salt and fry on medium for 3-5 minutes. Next add diced garlic and sauté another 3 minutes. Finally, dump sliced portabella mushrooms over sauté, lower heat and cover.

After a few minutes have passed, uncover and mix contents thoroughly. Cover and simmer, stirring occasionally until mushrooms are well cooked, which is usually about ten minutes.

Allow sauté mixture to cool then put it into a food processor. Add flour and pulse mix until it is coarsely blended. Form patties with your hands and fry on both sides using medium heat, with a hot skillet or griddle. Serve on pita, sandwich bread or dinner rolls. [2-4 PORTIONS]

Sloppy Joe
Ever had a Sloppy Joe sandwich and loved it?
This version is fantastic...and it's vegan!

MEASURE	INGREDIENT
1 cup	TVP burger blend - dry mix
1 & 2/3 cups	ice cold water
1 small	onion - chopped
1/2	green bell pepper - chopped
1/4 cup	soy oil
1 tsp	salt
1 tsp	thyme leaf
1/2 cup	mushrooms - chopped
1/2 cup	*Basic Barbecue Sauce*
3 Tbsps	raw sugar
1/4 cup	water

Mix the burger blend with the cold water, then refrigerate for at least 30 minutes, or more.

Chop onions and peppers and sauté in the oil with the salt and thyme on medium heat for 5 minutes. Add the prepared burger and mushrooms to the sauté and chop it up a little. Cover and cook on low for 5 minutes. Uncover, stir and chop up some more, cover and cook another 3 minutes.

Pour in barbecue sauce, raw sugar, water and cook down, covered, 10 minutes until mix is thick and chunky, yet saucy. Serve over sandwich bread, pita or dinner roll. Store leftovers refrigerated. [4-8 PORTIONS]

Soy Ham & Turkey Melt Sandwich

This recipe works with every type of vegan cold cut, and can serve as a general method for sandwich grilling.

MEASURE	INGREDIENT
2 Tbsps	soy margarine
2 slices	**Whole Wheat Bread**
3 slices	vegan-style canadian bacon
3-4 slices	soy cheese
3 slices	**Baked Tofu Turkey**
(as needed)	fresh tomato slices (optional)

Heat up a frying pan, skillet or griddle. Spread half of the margarine on one piece of bread. On other piece of bread layer vegan-style canadian bacon, cheese, tofu turkey, more cheese and tomato. Put buttered piece of bread on top and flip over sandwich. Put sandwich in skillet and spread margarine over top piece of bread. Cover, lower heat and cook until underside has browned. Flip sandwich over and brown other side. Sandwich is ready.

Spinach Quesadilla

Here is another great quesadilla from Veggie Works. Whether you love or hate spinach, this is a tasty way to eat it.

MEASURE	INGREDIENT
1 large	tortilla
2 ozs	**Mexican Sauce**
1/4 cup	spinach - cooked
2 ozs	soy mozzarella cheese - shredded

Paint tortilla shell with the Mexican sauce then layer the spinach and cheese on half the tortilla. Fold over the quesadilla and bake 5 minutes in a hot oven.

Remove to a hot grill and rapidly grill on both sides. Slice into 3-4 pieces and serve with **Salsa**.

Tofu Burger

Another great use of Tofu, this recipe reflects the versatility of this food product, in the form of a burger.

MEASURE	INGREDIENT
1/2 lb package	firm tofu - hand crumbled
2 Tbsps	onions - diced
2 Tbsps	mushrooms - diced
1 Tbsp	tomato paste
2 Tbsps	whole wheat flour
2 Tbsps	bread crumbs
2 pinches	thyme leaf
1 tsp	salt
1 pinch	black pepper
2 Tbsps	soy oil

In a mixing bowl, crumble tofu with your hands. The better crumbled the tofu, the better the burger will hold together. An alternative method is to pulse tofu in food processor using chopper blade.

Combine all other ingredients with the crumbled tofu - except the oil - in the mixing bowl. This recipe make 2 large or 3 small burgers, so separate the mixture evenly and form round balls using wet hands. Flatten balls with hands while smoothing the edges.

Have a hot skillet (or griddle) ready, then put in 1 tablespoon of oil and place the burger patties into skillet. Lower heat and cover, then cook patties on medium for about 5 minutes. When ready, uncover, add the other tablespoon of oil, flip over patties, then cook, uncovered, for another 5 minutes. Serve on bun or pita.

Veggie Burger

Unlike other veggie burgers on the market which contain eggwhites as their main ingredient, our version uses walnuts and lentils as protein constituents, and flour as a binder.

MEASURE	INGREDIENT
1 cup	lentils - cooked
1/2 cup	walnuts - ground
2	carrots - grated
1/2	onion - diced
4	mushrooms - diced
1/4 cup	whole wheat flour
1/4 cup	bread crumbs
1 tsp	salt
1 pinch	black pepper
1 tsp	thyme leaf

Combine all above ingredients and mix well. Form into seven ounce patties (makes 4-6 burgers). You can freeze patties or cook immediately. Use a hot griddle or skillet with little or no oil. Cook, covered, about 4 minutes on one side.

Cook uncovered about 4 minutes on other side. Serve on dinner roll or pita with lettuce, tomato and your favorite condiment.

Veggie Melt Sandwich

Simple raw and steamed vegetables make up this sandwich. Easy to make, tastes good and is very nutritious.

MEASURE	INGREDIENT
1	whole wheat **Pita Bread** (or whole grain bread)
2 Tbsps	red onions - diced
2 Tbsps	sweet peppers - diced
2 Tbsps	cucumber - diced
2-3 ozs	soy cheese - grated
2 Tbsps	mushrooms - sliced
2 Tbsps	fresh tomato - sliced
2 Tbsps	broccoli - steamed
2 Tbsps	carrots - steamed

Heat pita and slice open. First layer the diced veggies then half the cheese on the open pita. Layer more sliced vegetables, then the steamed vegetables and top with the rest of the cheese. Close sandwich and oven bake until cheese melts.

An alternative method is to pan fry. [see **Soy Ham & Turkey Melt Sandwich**]

Sauces & Gravies

Introduction

In this chapter you will discover the power of sauces and gravies, and their role in transforming food into art. You'll see how they add flavor, nutrition and personality to meals; that a handful of simple vegetables, veggie meats, beans and grain or pasta can be rendered into hundreds of distinctly different and sophisticated dishes with sauces.

The ability to create and use great sauces and gravies distinguishes the great chef from the mediocre one. Having saucemaking instructions in a separate chapter help to make more readable the recipes in other chapters which depend on these preparations. This approach is also designed to encourage the creativity of the reader, by using these sauces in entirely original dishes.

So whether you intend to combine one of the sauces with its designated meal as described in other recipes, or wish to use one in your own creation, you'll surely find this chapter of great value!

Alfredo Sauce

Here is our simple vegan rendition of a classic high cholesterol sauce. Has the body and flavor, without cholesterol or saturated fats.

MEASURE	INGREDIENT
1 qt	soy milk
6 ozs	soy parmesan cheese
1/4 cup	soy margarine
1-2 tsps	salt

Heat soy milk in sauce pot over medium low flame, then stir in parmesan cheese, margarine and salt. Allow the mixture to heat up to a low boil. Reduce heat and simmer 5 more minutes to thicken sauce. Serve with pasta or sautés.
[8-10 PORTIONS]

Bangkok Black Bean Sauce
Great with stir fried vegetables or original sautés, this sauce lends a unique flavor to any dish.

MEASURE	INGREDIENT
1 cup	black beans - dry
3 cups	*Vegetable Stock*
1 tsp	salt
2 Tbsps	roasted sesame oil
1/2 tsp	ginger root - diced
1/2 tsp	garlic clove - crushed
1/2 tsp	cayenne pepper
2 Tbsps	soy sauce
2 Tbsps	cornstarch - dissolved in 1/4 cup cold water

Cook the beans until tender in the vegetable stock with salt. Strain off the liquid and set aside.

In another sauce pot, heat oil and lightly brown ginger and garlic; then add cayenne pepper, soy sauce, bean liquid and 1/2 cup black beans. Bring to liquid to hard boil, then stir in cornstarch slurry mixture to thicken. Add the remaining half-cup of beans, then refrigerate. [2-4 PORTIONS]

Basic Barbecue Sauce

Although there are plenty of commercial brand barbecue sauces available, here's a simple sauce that you can create.

MEASURE	INGREDIENT
1/2 cup	water - cold
3 Tbsps	cornstarch
1/3 cup	apple cider vinegar
3 lbs	tomato paste
1/2 cup	mustard - prepared (or 3 Tbsps dry mustard powder)
1/4 cup	molasses
1/2 cup	malt syrup
2 Tbsps	raw sugar
1 tsp	salt
1/2 tsp	black pepper
1 tsp	garlic powder
1 Tbsp	onion powder
1 tsp	Liquid Smoke (optional)

Mix all ingredients in a sauce pot. Heat pot to a boil while stirring. Turn off heat and allow to cool. Great for grill glaze or condiment. [MAKES 2-1/2 CUPS]

Brown Gravy

This is great stuff. It can be used as a hearty gravy in all-American cuisine, or, as a thickener and flavor enhancer in customized recipes.

MEASURE	INGREDIENT
1/3 cup	soy oil
1/4 cup	whole wheat flour

MEASURE	INGREDIENT
1/4 cup	unbleached white flour (organic)
1 qt	**Vegetable Stock**

Heat up a sauce pot and pour in oil. Mix flours and add to the hot oil. Whisk for about two minutes. Pour in vegetable stock and whisk until gravy boils and thickens. If gravy is too thick add more stock. If too thin, whisk more flour in while cooking. [MAKES 1 QT]

Buffalo Hot Sauce
Traditional hot dipping sauce great for tofu or gluten buffalo wings.

MEASURE	INGREDIENT
1 stick	soy margarine
1 cup	louisiana hot sauce

Place stick of margarine in a frying pan or skillet and heat slowly until completely melted. Add hot sauce and mix thoroughly. Can be stored in refrigerator, but should be served at room temperature.

Cheese Sauce
This sauce is wonderful for vegetable side dishes, baked pasta, or to spruce-up stuffed-pockets and wraps.

MEASURE	INGREDIENT
1 cup	**White Sauce**
1/4 cup	soy cheese - grated

While slowly stirring, heat up white sauce; then add grated soy cheese and continue stirring in, until throughly melted.

Cranberry Sauce

**A traditional holiday side dish, with its sweet and tart flavor.
Harvested from the lakes and bogs of North America,
cranberries are an autumn treat.**

MEASURE	INGREDIENT
3 cups	water
1 & 1/2 cups	raw sugar (Sucanat or xylitol)
1/2 cup	dark brown sugar
1 qt	fresh cranberries - well rinsed

Bring water to a hard boil, then stir in sugars. Add the cranberries and boil just a couple of minutes, until the skins on the berries begin to split. Remove from the heat and chill several hours before serving. [10-20 PORTIONS]

Creamed Curry Sauce

**This delicious vegan sauce is great for sautés and grilled
or roasted veggie meats. With its mild and
creamy exotic flavor, it compliments
Indian or Malaysian cuisine.**

MEASURE	INGREDIENT
1 cup	*Vegetable Stock*
2 Tbsps	curry powder
1/2 cup	*Sour Cream*
1 tsp	soy oil
2 Tbsps	arrowroot powder (or cornstarch) - dissolved in 1/4 cup cold water

Heat up vegetable stock in a sauce pot on stove. Stir in curry powder, sour cream and oil. Bring to a boil.

Mix the arrowroot (or cornstarch) with cold water, then add this slurry to boiling liquid. Continue stirring until mixture returns to a boil, then remove immediately and use, or refrigerate. [4-8 PORTIONS]

Creole Sauce

Another sauce recipe with a rue base. Perks up any sauté, soup or casserole with authentic Cajun flavors.

MEASURE	INGREDIENT
1/4 cup	soy oil
1/3 cup	whole wheat flour
2 Tbsps	cajun spice blend
1 Tbsp	onion powder
1 qt	*Vegetable Stock*
3 Tbsps	louisiana hot sauce
1/4 cup	white wine

Heat a sauce pot and add oil. Stir in whole wheat flour, cajun spice, and onion powder. Lower heat and cook rue while whisking or stirring for 2 to 5 minutes. Turn up heat and pour in vegetable stock, hot sauce and wine. Stir mixture until it boils and thickens. [8 PORTIONS]

Dijon Wine Sauce

A French provincial sauce for sautés, veggie meats and side dishes.

MEASURE	INGREDIENT
1/4 cup	*Vegetable Stock*
1/2 cup	white wine
2 Tbsps	soy margarine - melted
1/4 cup	dijon mustard
1 Tbsp	tarragon leaf

Sauces & Gravies

MEASURE	INGREDIENT
1/2 tsp	powdered thyme
1/2 tsp	salt
2 Tbsps	cornstarch - dissolved in 1/4 cup cold water

Heat up all ingredients to a boil, then mix the cornstarch slurry into it. Allow to thicken, then remove from flame. Use in custom sautés and other preparations. Keep refrigerated. [4 PORTIONS]

Enchilada Sauce
The world's best enchilada sauce is simpler to make, than you might think. Here's the secret:

MEASURE	INGREDIENT
1 qt	***Vegetable Stock***
1/4 cup	chili powder
1 Tbsp	garlic powder
1 tsp	cajun spice blend
1/4 cup	soy oil
1/4 cup	whole wheat flour

Heat the vegetable stock, mixed with chili powder, garlic powder and cajun spice in a sauce pot. Bring to a boil, then lower heat and simmer for 5 minutes.

Pour the seasoned stock through a fine mesh strainer into another container and discard the pulp. In another pot, heat the oil and stir in the flour, making a rue. Stir the rue for a few minutes then add the strained stock.

Bring mixture to a boil, reduce heat and simmer a minute to thicken sauce. Use in Mexican cooking. Refrigerate. [8-12 PORTIONS]

Etruscan Sauce

This sauce was developed for *The Etruscan* dinner. With the deep flavors of sundried tomatoes and balsamic vinegar, it goes especially well with pasta.

MEASURE	INGREDIENT
1 cup	sundried tomatoes
2 cups	***Vegetable Stock***
1/4 cup	white wine
1/4 cup	balsamic vinegar
1 Tbsp	basil - dry
1 tsp	salt
1/4 cup	olive oil
8	garlic cloves - diced
2 Tbsps	cornstarch - dissolved in 1/2 cup cold water

Combine sun-dried tomatoes and vegetable stock in a sauce pot and bring to a boil. Lower heat and simmer 5 minutes. Add wine, balsamic vinegar, basil and salt and continue to simmer.

Heat olive oil in a small pan, then add diced garlic. Lower heat and stir garlic until it begins to brown. Ladle small amount of simmering liquid from other pot into browning garlic to retard browning and to deglaze pan. When garlic is browned, add the garlic mixture to simmering sauce.

After simmering another five minutes, remove from heat and blend entire mixture using an infusion blender or conventional blender.

Reheat sauce to a boil, then stir in cornstarch slurry. Bring sauce to a boil again, then remove from heat. Refrigerate. [18-24 PORTIONS]

Fricassee Sauce

**Familiar continental sauce traditionally used with poultry.
It's great with meat analogs, tempeh or tofu
dominated sautés, sides and casseroles.**

MEASURE	INGREDIENT
1/4 cup	soy oil
1/4 cup	unbleached white flour (organic)
2 cups	*Vegetable Stock*
1 tsp	salt
2/3 cup	*Sour Cream*

Heat oil in a sauce pot and stir in flour, making a rue. Pour in vegetable stock
and salt and bring mixture to a boil. Reduce heat, then stir in sour cream.
[6-12 PORTIONS]

Garlic and Oil

**This simple basic recipe provides the foundation to many great
tasting sauces. Excellent for steaming vegetables,
or for hot or cold pasta dishes.**

MEASURE	INGREDIENT
6	garlic cloves - thin sliced
1/4 cup	olive oil
1/2 tsp	salt
1-2 Tbsps	parsley leaves (optional)
1/4 cup	water (or *Vegetable Stock*)

Brown thinly sliced garlic in oil, with salt and parsley. Slowly add water (or vegetable stock) to retard browning, then simmer 3 minutes. [3-4 PORTIONS]

Garlic Sesame Sauce

With the nutty-flavor of roasted sesame oil and garlic, this sauce is great for sautés, or pasta side dishes.

MEASURE	INGREDIENT
1/4 cup	roasted sesame oil
1/4 cup	garlic cloves - crushed
1 qt	**Vegetable Stock**
1/4 cup	soy sauce
2 Tbsps	apple cider vinegar
1/2 tsp	cayenne pepper
1/4 cup	sesame seeds - roasted
3 Tbsps	cornstarch - dissolved in
	1/4 cup cold water

Heat oil in a sauce pot. Add garlic, reduce heat and stir until garlic begins to brown evenly. Next add in vegetable stock, soy sauce, vinegar and cayenne pepper. Bring mixture to a boil, then reduce heat and simmer.

If you can't buy roasted sesame seeds do the following: Heat a skillet or frying pan very hot. Pour in raw sesame seeds and lower heat. Stir or flip pan frequently until seeds are evenly browned.

Slowly combine the cornstarch slurry with the simmering sauce, then stir in sesame seeds. When sauce thickens, remove from heat. Sauce can be stored refrigerated. [20-35 PORTIONS]

Grill Goddess Sauce

This sauce uplifts grilled vegetables, tofu, tempeh, gluten or seitan steaks. It possesses just the right flavor for grilling portabella mushrooms. Great in soup, salads and sautés, too!

MEASURE	INGREDIENT
1/3 cup	xylitol (or brown rice syrup)
1/3 cup	water
1/2 cup	soy sauce
1/2 cup	apple cider vinegar
1/2 cup	soy oil
1/4 cup	garlic cloves - crushed
2 Tbsps	cornstarch - mixed with
	1/4 cup water (optional)

Mix the xylitol and water, then boil in a small pan until mixture becomes syrup-like. Combine this syrup with the other ingredients, and mix well. No need to refrigerate. Use to marinate foods and/or grill baste foods with a brush. Can also be thickened with the optional cornstarch slurry to form a glaze, for grilling and other applications. [MAKES 2-1/2 CUPS - USE SPARINGLY FOR BASTING]

Hollandaise Sauce

Traditionally a rich French sauce with butter and eggs, this recipe uses healthy tofu and is entirely vegan.

MEASURE	INGREDIENT
1 12-oz package	silken tofu
2 Tbsps	lemon juice
2 Tbsps	nutritional yeast
2 Tbsps	soy margarine - melted
1 tsp	salt
1 tsp	turmeric

MEASURE	INGREDIENT
1 pinch	cayenne pepper
1 Tbsp	cornstarch - dissolved in 3 Tbsps cold water

Blend tofu, lemon juice, yeast, melted margarine, salt and spices, then pour into a sauce pot. Heat slowly, while stirring, until mixture begins to boil. Slowly stir in cornstarch slurry, until sauce thickens. [MAKES 1 CUP]

Jamaican Jerk Sauce

Another Jamaican sauce with a molasses base. This concoction uses raspberry juice for a unique, authentic flavor. Use it to grill, baste, broil or sauté!

MEASURE	INGREDIENT
1/2 cup	orange juice
1/2 cup	raspberry juice*
1/2 cup	molasses
1/4 cup	louisiana hot sauce
1 tsp	salt
1 tsp	garlic powder
1 tsp	allspice
1/2 tsp	ginger powder
2 Tbsps	cornstarch - dissolved in 1/4 cup cold water

Combine all ingredients - except cornstarch slurry - into a sauce pot and heat to a boil. Reduce heat to a simmer, then slowly stir in cornstarch slurry into simmering sauce. Allow to thicken and remove from heat. Refrigerate.
[MAKES 1-1/2 CUPS - USE SPARINGLY]

*Raspberry juice may be difficult to obtain. A trick is to buy a bag or frozen berries and let them thaw in a bowl. Pour off the juice (should be about half a cup). Use left-over raspberries in a dessert or fruit smoothie.

Jamaican Jungle Sauce
A unique sauté sauce; for glazing, broiling and grilling...with great island flavor.

MEASURE	INGREDIENT
2 cups	orange juice
1 cup	coconut milk
1 cup	molasses
1 tsp	cumin
1 tsp	garlic powder
1 tsp	allspice
1/2 tsp	nutmeg
1/2 tsp	ginger powder
1 tsp	cinnamon
1/2 tsp	cayenne pepper (for medium heat (optional))
1/2 tsp	habenero pepper (for very hot (optional))
3 Tbsps	cornstarch - dissolved in 1/4 cup cold water

Combine all ingredients - except cornstarch slurry - then heat mixture to a boil. Reduce heat to a simmer, then slowly stir in cornstarch slurry into simmering sauce. Sauce will thicken immediately. Remove from flame. Refrigerate for storage. [16-24 PORTIONS]

Lemon Herb Sauce

A great sauce, unthickened, to marinate, or for roasting, grilling, or broiling. Thickened, it is wonderful for stir frys, sautés or as a grill glaze.

MEASURE	INGREDIENT
1 cup	*Vegetable Stock*
1/4 cup	lemon juice
1/4 cup	soy oil
1 tsp	salt
1 tsp each:	thyme, oregano, marjoram, basil, & tarragon
2 Tbsps	cornstarch - dissolved in 1/4 cup cold water

Mix ingredients - except cornstarch slurry - then allow to stand several minutes so the herbs can infuse their flavor. Refrigerate.

To thicken, heat mix to a simmering boil, then slowly stir in cornstarch slurry. Mix and cool. [8-10 PORTIONS]

Marinara Sauce

Marinara is a passionate thing. Everyone is familiar with tomato sauce and many of us have personal recipes that we are proud of. This is our basic version.

MEASURE	INGREDIENT
1 large	onion - diced
1/4 cup	garlic clove - crushed
1-2	bay leaves
2 Tbsps	salt
1 tsp	black pepper
3 Tbsps	oregano

Sauces & Gravies

MEASURE	INGREDIENT
1/4 cup	olive oil
2 cups	tomatoes - crushed
2 cups	**Stewed Tomatoes**
1/4 cup	basil
1/4 cup	red wine

Sauté onions, garlic, bay leaves, one tablespoon salt and black pepper with one tablespoon of oregano, in the olive oil. Continue sautéing until onions are translucent and garlic slightly caramelized.

Pour in the crushed tomatoes. Break up the stewed tomatoes with your hands and add them to the cooking sauce. Add the basil, wine, remaining salt and oregano, then stir well. Simmer another half hour, to an hour, while stirring occasionally. [MAKES 1/2 GAL]

Mexican Sauce

All purpose sauce for fajitas, quesadillas and other special Mexican dishes. Two versions are listed here: one with tomatoes, and one without.

MEASURE	INGREDIENT
1 cup	**Vegetable Stock**
1 Tbsp	onion powder
1 tsp	garlic powder
1 Tbsp	chili powder
1/2 tsp	cumin
2 Tbsps	soy oil
1 Tbsp	cornstarch - dissolved in 1/4 cup cold water
1/2 cup	tomato puree (optional)

Combine all ingredients - except cornstarch slurry - in a sauce pot, then bring to a boil. Reduce heat to a simmer for 5 minutes, then slowly add cornstarch slurry to thicken. To make the red version, simply add the optional tomato puree before thickening sauce. [MAKES 1 CUP]

Mock Poultry Marinade
An effective 'medium' for imparting poultry like flavor to foods.

MEASURE	INGREDIENT
3 cups	*Vegetable Stock*
1/2 cup	orange juice
2 Tbsps	nutritional yeast
1/2 tsp	powdered thyme
1/2 tsp	powdered sage
1 Tbsp	soy sauce
2 Tbsps	soy oil
1 tsp	sea salt
2 Tbsps	arrowroot powder (or cornstarch)

Mix all ingredients thoroughly. Use this sauce to marinate foods - such tofu, seitan and gluten meats. You can optionally thicken the sauce base with an arrowroot powder (or cornstarch), to make a grill glaze. [MAKES 3-1/2 CUPS]

Olympian Sauce
A mild - yet flavorful - sauce. Excellent for sautés, or for broiling and grilling.

MEASURE	INGREDIENT
2 cups	*Vegetable Stock*
1/2 tsp	salt
1/2 tsp	savory
1/2 tsp	powdered thyme
1	orange - juiced

Sauces & Gravies

MEASURE	INGREDIENT
1/2	lemon - juiced
3 Tbsps	cornstarch - dissolved in 1/4 cup cold water

Heat stock to a boil, then add salt, savory and thyme. Squeeze the juice from the orange and lemon, then add this to the boiling stock. Lower heat and simmer five minutes.

Bring simmering mixture back to a boil, then slowly stir in cornstarch slurry to thicken. Once thickened, remove from heat. [12-16 PORTIONS]

Pepper Steak Sauce
This is our version of Chinese Pepper Steak Sauce. Due to its robust flavor, this sauce lends itself to a variety of meals.

MEASURE	INGREDIENT
2 cups	**Vegetable Stock**
2 Tbsps	apple cider vinegar
1/2 cup	soy sauce
2 Tbsps	roasted sesame oil
1 tsp	garlic powder
2 pinches	cayenne pepper
3 Tbsps	cornstarch - dissolved in 1/4 cup cold water
1 pinch	habenero pepper (for very hot (optional))

Heat the vegetable stock to a boil, then add other ingredients - except cornstarch slurry - to boiling stock. Reduce heat to a simmer, then slowly stir in cornstarch slurry into simmering sauce. Stir for an additional half minute - to mix and thicken sauce - then remove from heat. [8-10 PORTIONS]

Note: This sauce responds well with spice heat, so feel free to adjust the volume according to your taste by adding more cayenne. If not hot enough, add pinches of ground habenero pepper..

Pesto Sauce

Wonderful vegan rendition of a popular Italian green sauce, with nuts and dried cheese. This sauce is good with cold or hot meals.

MEASURE	INGREDIENT
4 cups	basil leaves - fresh
2 cups	parsley - fresh
1/2 cup	pignoli nuts
1/2 cup	walnuts
1/2 cup	soy parmesan cheese
1/2 cup	virgin olive oil
1 tsp	salt

Make sure the basil and parsley are well rinsed then place the leaves in a food processor with chopper blade. Pulse mass down to reduce size in half, then remove to a bowl.

Put the nuts in the cleaned processor and grind well. Add the pulsed greens back to the processor with the nuts. Add the parmesan cheese and pulse while dribbling the oil. Increase the pulsing speed and pour in the rest of the oil and salt. The result should be a well blended, yet coarse sauce with an outrageous flavor. [MAKES 4 CUPS]

Polynesian Sauce
Southeast Asian ginger, citrus juices, and coconut milk, highlight this indigenous tasting sauce.

MEASURE	INGREDIENT
2 cups	pineapple juice
1 cup	orange juice
1/2 cup	coconut milk
1/4 cup	soy sauce
2 Tbsps	apple cider vinegar
2 Tbsps	molasses
3 slices	ginger root
1 Tbsp	garlic powder
3 Tbsps	cornstarch - dissolved in
	1/4 cup cold water

Heat up all ingredients - except cornstarch slurry - to a boil. Reduce heat and simmer for about five minutes. Increase heat, then slowly stir in cornstarch slurry into simmering sauce, until it thickens. Refrigerate. [12-16 PORTIONS]

Seafood Sauce
This sauce imparts mild seafood flavor to dishes. Great with tofu crabcakes, tofu 'fish' fillets, or vegetables.

MEASURE	INGREDIENT
2 cups	*Vegetable Stock*
1	orange - juiced
1	lemon - juiced
1 tsp	salt
1 pinch	black pepper
2 tsps	tarragon leaf
1 Tbsp	Old Bay Seasoning

MEASURE	INGREDIENT
3 Tbsps	cornstarch - dissolved in 1/4 cup cold water

Heat vegetable stock to a boil, then add orange juice, lemon juice, salt, pepper, tarragon and seasoning and bring to a boil. Reduce heat to a simmer, then slowly stir in cornstarch slurry until it thickens. Remove from heat. [8-10 PORTIONS]

Singapore Sunset Sauce
Another great Asian Pacific sauce made with common ingredients. Simple, yet one of the most satisfying sauces in its class.

MEASURE	INGREDIENT
1/4 cup	roasted sesame oil
1/4 cup	garlic cloves - crushed
2 cups	pineapple juice
1 cup	orange juice - fresh
1/4 cup	louisiana hot sauce
1/2 cup	soy sauce
2 Tbsps	apple cider vinegar
3 Tbsps	cornstarch - dissolved in 1/4 cup cold water

Heat up a sauce pot and add the sesame oil. Wait a few seconds, then stir in garlic. Allow garlic to brown lightly while stirring.

Combine pineapple juice, orange juice, hot sauce, soy sauce and vinegar with the browning garlic. Bring this to a boil, reduce heat and simmer five minutes. Strain off and discard garlic.

Return sauce to heating pan, increase heat to boil liquid. Slowly stir in cornstarch into boiling sauce. Stir until sauce thickens, then remove from heat. Refrigerate for storage. [12-16 PORTIONS]

Sweet & Sour Sauce

Here is a great all world sauce that goes well with a variety of vegetable dishes. This sauce is unique because it really takes on the ethnicity of the subject.

MEASURE	INGREDIENT
3 Tbsps	soy oil
3 Tbsps	unbleached white flour (organic)
1 cup	*Vegetable Stock*
1/4 cup	apple cider vinegar
2-3 Tbsps	raw sugar (or brown rice syrup)
1/2 tsp	salt
2 pinches	black pepper

Heat oil and slowly add flour to make a rue. Add all other ingredients to heated rue, then bring to a boil to thicken sauce. Remove from heat. [4-6 PORTIONS]

Swedish Meatball Gravy

A specialized sauce - traditionally used with meatballs - is included here to accompany our vegan rendition of *Swedish Meatballs*.

MEASURE	INGREDIENT
2 cups	*Brown Gravy*
1/2 cup	*Vegetable Stock*
1/2 cup	*Sour Cream*
1/2 tsp	nutmeg

Heat gravy with vegetable stock and whisk smooth. Whisk in sour cream, then add nutmeg and...voila! [MAKES 3 CUPS]

Tahini Sauce

This sesame seed butter sauce is a staple in the Middle East and Eastern Mediterranean. Popular with falafel, in salad dressings, or in hot sauces.

MEASURE	INGREDIENT
1 cup	sesame tahini
2 cups	water - cold
2	lemons - juiced
1 scant Tbsp	salt

Simply blend all ingredients and store refrigerated. [18-24 PORTIONS]

Teriyaki Sauce

Great for grilling vegetables or vegetable-based meats, in sautés or pasta dishes.

MEASURE	INGREDIENT
1 cup	pineapple juice
1/4 cup	apple cider vinegar
1 cup	soy sauce
1/4 cup	molasses
4-5 slices	ginger root
5	garlic cloves - whole
1/2-1 tsp	cayenne pepper
3 Tbsps	cornstarch - dissolved in 1/4 cup water

Heat pineapple juice, vinegar, soy sauce and molasses together in a sauce pot. Toss in ginger slices, whole garlic cloves and cayenne pepper and bring sauce to a boil. Reduce heat and simmer for five minutes.

Sauces & Gravies

Remove ginger and garlic and discard. Slowly stir in the cornstarch slurry, with simmering liquid, increase heat and continue stirring until sauce thickens. Remove and store refrigerated. [4-8 PORTIONS]

Thai Peanut Sauce

A popular sauce from southeast Asia. This sauce is great with steamed vegetables, pasta, or raw crudite. So good, you'll find a host of uses for it.

MEASURE	INGREDIENT
1 cup	peanut butter (natural) - drain off oil, then mix
1 cup	orange juice
1 cup	coconut milk
1	lime - juiced
2 Tbsps	raw sugar (or brown rice syrup, or xylitol)
1/2 tsp	cayenne pepper
2 Tbsps	soy sauce
1-2 Tbsps	roasted sesame oil
1-2 Tbsps	cornstarch - dissolved in
	1 cup cold water

Pour off settled oil from natural peanut butter, before thoroughly mixing into a butter consistency. Remove 1 cup of peanut butter from jar, then place it in a sauce pot.

Mix all other ingredients - except cornstarch slurry - with peanut butter. Begin heating mixture while whisking smooth. When sauce comes to a boil, slowly stir in cornstarch slurry and allow to thicken. Remove from heat and refrigerate. [8-12 PORTIONS]

Verde Sauce

Our version of the ancient Eurasian sauce. It combines fresh local greens, scallions, garlic, olive oil, capers and olives, for a fresh - slightly pungent - flavor.

MEASURE	INGREDIENT
3-4	garlic cloves
1/4 cup	capers
1/2 cup	green olives
1 qt	field greens - fresh
1 cup	parsley leaves
2 Tbsps	balsamic vinegar
1 tsp	salt
1 cup	olive oil

In a food processor, start chopping garlic, capers and olives. Next add a handful of greens, parsley leaves, vinegar and salt. Pulse while adding olive oil slowly. Add more greens and oil until all contents are reduced to a smooth paste. [6-8 PORTIONS]

Walnut Gravy

Interesting and tasty sauce, created for specialty dishes, such as rolades, puff pastry or filo pastry pies.

MEASURE	INGREDIENT
1/4 cup	soy oil
1/4 cup	whole wheat flour
2 cups	*Vegetable Stock*
1 cup	soy milk
2 pinches	allspice
1 cup	walnuts - course chopped

Sauces & Gravies

Heat oil in a sauce pot, add flour and stir to make a rue. Pour in vegetable stock, soy milk, allspice and coarsely chopped walnuts into heated rue. Reduce heat to a simmer, then allow gravy to thicken. Remove from heat and refridgerate. [MAKES 3 CUPS]

White Sauce

A vegan version of multi purpose white sauce. Can serve as a base for other sauces; such as cheese sauce, or, as a thickening - creaming agent in blended soups.

MEASURE	INGREDIENT
1/4 cup	soy oil
1/4 cup	unbleached white flour (organic)
2 cups	soy milk
1 tsp	salt

Heat oil and stir in flour. If using white flour, be sure to use good organic, unbleached flour. Stir flour and oil rue on low heat for about one minute. Pour in soy milk and salt. Raise the heat and bring to a boil, while constantly stirring. When sauce thickens remove from heat. Store refrigerated. [MAKES 2 CUPS]

Grains, Beans & Side Dishes

Introduction

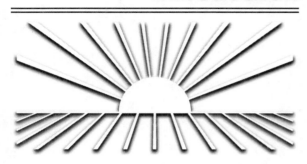

Hot side dishes, with vegetables, grains and beans, add color and diversity to meals. For multi course dinners or feasts, good side dishes are a must. Knowledge in preparing an interesting variety of side dishes is an asset to any good cook.

Knowing how to cook off grains, beans and pastas is integral to preparing great meals. Although directions are usually on the box, these staples are often stored in kitchen canisters, so recipes are included in this chapter for your convenience.

In this chapter you will learn how to prepare a variety of different complementary foods. Many of these simple preparations play an important role in the successful production of more complex, Multi-course meals. These side dish recipes provide a variety of complementary accompaniments for any sized meal.

Hopefully the recipes in this chapter will kindle the spark of creativity in anyone interested learning these fundamentals. A great artist needs to know his paints and brushes. Any good chef needs to know the basics of his or her trade as well. Understanding your craft is the key to freedom.

Au Gratin Vegetables
Makes a hearty side dish or the basis for a casserole such as scalloped potatoes.

MEASURE	INGREDIENT
2 cups	vegetables - steamed
1/2 cup	soy cheese - shredded
2 pinches	cajun spice blend
1 pinch	salt
1 cup	**White Sauce**

Using a small baking dish, soup crock or similar baking vessel, layer (or stack) steamed vegetables in with shredded cheese, cajun seasoning and salt. Heat up white sauce, then pour over vegetables and bake in a 400°F oven for 15 minutes. [4 PORTIONS]

Artichokes Italian Style
Tasty hot or cold, this preparation is simple...and a great appetizer!

MEASURE	INGREDIENT
1 gal	water - boiling
2 Tbsps	salt
2 Tbsps	lemon juice
4 large	artichokes
1/4 cup	olive oil
1/2 cup	garlic cloves - diced
1/2 tsp	oregano
1 pinch	salt
1 & 1/2 cups	*Vegetable Stock*

Bring water - combined with salt and lemon juice - to a hard boil. Wash artichokes well, trim points and stems away, then immerse in boiling water. Boil artichokes for about 20 minutes; until leaves can be easily pulled away.

Heat the olive oil in a sauce pan (or skillet) and brown diced garlic lightly, with the oregano and a pinch of salt. Slowly add vegetable stock - to retard browning - and simmer 5 minutes.

Place artichokes in a greased baking dish. Pour garlic and oil mix over artichokes, making sure most of the garlic-bits are inside leaves. Bake artichokes - covered with foil - in a 450°F oven, for 20 more minutes. Serve hot or cold. [2-5 PORTIONS]

Baked Beans
**Good old fashioned baked beans...slow cooked all day.
Here's a 'Boston style' recipe.**

MEASURE	INGREDIENT
1/2 cup	water
1/2 cup	tomato paste
2 tsps	mustard powder
2 Tbsps	brown sugar
2 Tbsps	molasses
1 Tbsp	onion powder
1 tsp	garlic powder
1 tsp	cinnamon
2 Tbsps	soy oil
1 Tbsp	salt
2 Tbsps	apple cider vinegar
1 lb	great northern or navy beans - soaked & cooked
1 whole	onion - half cut
2 cups	**Vegetable Stock** (or drained cooking water from beans)

Mix the water, tomato paste, mustard powder, sugar, molasses, onion powder, garlic powder, oil, salt and vinegar in a bowl. Combine this mixture with the cooked beans.

Place onion, cut in half, at bottom of an earthen-ware cooking pot. Pour bean mixture into pot with onion. Bake 5 hours at 250°F. Periodically baste - with vegetable stock (or bean soaking water) - the surface of the baking beans, throughout the cooking process, to prevent drying out of surface beans.
[6-10 PORTIONS]

Baked Cauliflower
A good side dish to go with dinner and easy to make.

MEASURE	INGREDIENT
1 head	cauliflower - parboiled
1/2 cup	bread crumbs
1 cup	*White Sauce*

Parboil head of cauliflower for 5 minutes in a large pot of water. Grease a baking dish and place parboiled head of cauliflower in it. Cover the cauliflower with bread crumbs and bake in a 450°F oven for about 20 minutes.

Remove from oven. Transfer cauliflower to a serving plate and pour the heated white sauce over the top. Serve on a platter. [2-4 PORTIONS]

Baked Potato Fries
Here's a great way to use cold baked potatoes!

MEASURE	INGREDIENT
3	potatoes - prebaked & cross cut
1/4 cup	soy oil
(to taste)	salt & black pepper
(as needed)	*Ketchup*

Cross cut prebaked potatoes into large, one inch thick sections. Do not remove the skins. Heat a skillet and fry the potatoes in half the oil on one side until brown. Turn potatoes and fry other side in the rest of the oil. Serve with ketchup. Salt and pepper to taste. [2 PORTIONS - LARGE]

Baking Powder Dumplings

Soft little puff or clouds floating on soups or resting on stews and sautés. This easy recipe is a nice finishing touch.

MEASURE	INGREDIENT
1 cup	soy milk
1 cup	unbleached white flour (organic)
2 tsps	baking powder
1/4 tsp	salt
1 cup	**Mashed Potatoes** (optional ingredient)
1/2 cup	carrots - grated (optional ingredient)
1 cup	**Vegetable Stock** (for optional precooking)

Mix ingredients into a smooth batter. Let stand five minutes. Gently spoon into soups, turning once.

Method 2:
Follow above recipe and combine 1 cup **Mashed Potatoes** and/or 1/4 cup grated carrots with above ingredients. Sprinkle in additional flour if too wet.

Note: If adding to a sauté, first cook dumplings in a separate pan, with a small amount of vegetable stock; then immediately transfer to the sauté surface. Cover, then simmer in sauté for 3-5 more minutes, before serving.
[20-25 SMALL DUMPLINGS]

Barley

Barley is a healthy ancient grain with protein, B vitamins and carbohydrates. A high energy fuel for soups, salads or stuffed vegetables.

MEASURE	INGREDIENT
1 qt	water (or **Vegetable Stock**)
1 cup	unpearled barley
1/2 tsp	salt

Bring ingredients to a boil, then cover; and depending on age and quality of the grain, simmer 45 minutes to one hour. If using barley in salads - or as a loose grain - strain off liquid and save for stock.

Beans

To use dehydrated (dry) beans of any kind, they must first be soaked and cooked. Once the beans are cooked, they can be added to soaps, salads, sautés, wraps...etc. This process is recommended, when using dry beans in the preparation of - almost - all soups. Using good canned (organic) varieties is acceptable for other applications, but knowing how to prepare dry beans is a must...for every - good - chef.

Method 1:
Soak beans overnight in cold water not longer than 12 hours. If beans are tiny such as lentils or split peas, they can be cooked without soaking.
After soaking, the beans will have swelled to at least twice the original dry volume. Pour off the soaking water. This fluid contains the elements that make eating beans cause gas and flatulence. Rinse beans well and add enough water or stock to cover beans by three inches. Add seasonings, salt and cook until tender. Cooking time 20 minutes to one hour.

Method 2:
This is called the quick soak method. Put dry beans in a soup pot and add at least five parts water to one part beans. Boil water and beans two minutes, turn off heat, cover and let stand one hour. Pour off soak water. Rinse and add enough water or **Vegetable Stock** to cover beans by three inches. Bring to a boil, reduce heat and simmer until done. Cook 20 minutes to 1 hour depending on the size of the bean and its age.

Braised String Beans & Mushrooms

**A simple vegetable side, illustrating the braising method.
Works well with different combinations
of vegetables and herbs.**

MEASURE	INGREDIENT
1 Tbsp	olive oil
4 cups	string beans - trimmed & cut
2 cups	mushrooms - sliced
3 Tbsps	*Vegetable Stock*
1 Tbsp	fresh herb
1/4 tsp	salt

Heat oil in skillet, pan or wok. Toss in string beans and mushrooms. When string beans begin to wilt and change in color, add vegetable stock, herbs and salt, then steam until done. [4-8 PORTIONS]

Bread & Cornbread Stuffing

**Our standard holiday or everyday stuffing, easy
to make and a great American side dish.**

MEASURE	INGREDIENT
1/4 cup	soy oil
1 large	onion - chopped
1 & 1/2 cup	celery - chopped
1 Tbsp	thyme leaf
1 Tbsp	marjoram
1 tsp	black pepper
1 qt	*Vegetable Stock*
1 16-oz package	cornbread stuffing mix
1 16-oz package	wheat bread stuffing mix
	(or homemade croutons)

Heat the oil in a large soup pot, then add the chopped onions. Sauté onions on medium heat for 3 minutes, then add the chopped celery, herbs and pepper. Cover and simmer on low heat, for about 7 minutes.

Next, heat the vegetable stock to a boil. Add the two stuffing mixes (or croutons), and the previously sautéd mixture to the boiling stock, and stir vigorously until completely mixed. Remove from heat. Stuffing is now ready to serve, or can be baked in the oven to brown or reheat. [16-20 PORTIONS]

Brown Rice

Brown rice is a staple in the vegan diet. It is a perfectly balanced grain and goes well with almost everything.

MEASURE	INGREDIENT
2 cups	water
1 cup	brown rice (long or short grain)
2 pinches	salt

Boil water and rice together, then stir in salt and reduce heating of contents to a simmer - covered - for 40 to 60 minutes, until done.

Method 2:

MEASURE	INGREDIENT
(as needed)	brown rice (any amount)
(as needed)	water
several pinches	salt (use sparingly)

Put desired amount of rice in a pot, then add enough water to cover two and a half (2-1/2) inches above surface of rice. Cook rice as in Method 1.

Tofu Buffalo Wings

**No chicken here. Enjoy the goodness of soy
with these great little appetizers.**

MEASURE	INGREDIENT
1/2 lb package	firm tofu - strip cut
2 Tbsps	cajun spice blend
(as needed)	canola oil (for frying)
1/4 cup	**Buffalo Hot Sauce**

Cut tofu block into nine equal strips. Sprinkle with cajun spice and deep fry in oil, in a fryer or skillet.

Warm up the hot sauce and mix well. Use hot sauce for dipping.

Bulgar Wheat

**Traditional cracked wheat used in the Middle East in salads
such as tabouli, pilafs, casseroles and stuffed vegetables.**

MEASURE	INGREDIENT
2 cups	water
1 cup	bulgar wheat
2 pinches	salt

Boil water and bulgar wheat together, then stir in salt and reduce heating of contents to a simmer - covered - for 5 more minutes. Remove from heat and let stand covered ten more minutes, before using. [MAKES 2 CUPS]

Candied Yams

**Great holiday dinner side, this recipe is easy,
producing perfect results.**

MEASURE	INGREDIENT
4 large	yams (or 8 small sweet potatoes) - cross cut
1/2 cup	brown sugar
3 Tbsps	soy margarine
1/4 cup	molasses
2 tsps	salt

Peel and cross cut yams into half inch thick rounds. Boil yams until they begin to soften, yet are still firm. Drain yams and place them in a greased baking dish.

Crumble the brown sugar over the yams. Evenly distribute the margarine, molasses and salt over yams. Bake in a 450°F oven for about 20 minutes, turning once or twice. Remove and serve hot. [6-8 PORTIONS]

Collards Southern Style

**Our Yankee, vegan version of a classic side dish
served in the American south for generations.**

MEASURE	INGREDIENT
2 qts	collard greens - chopped
2 Tbsps	soy oil
1	onion - chopped
4 slices	vegan-style canadian bacon
1 tsp	powdered savory
1 cup	*Vegetable Stock*
(to taste)	salt & black pepper

Wash collard greens thoroughly, then chop up and set aside. Heat oil in a soup pot, then add chopped onions. Chop up the Canadian bacon and add this - with the seasonings - to the cooking onions. Maintain medium low heat and add chopped collard greens. Cover and slow cook, stirring occasionally for 15 minutes.

Pour in vegetable stock and increase heat to medium high. Stir while liquid cooks down, about five minutes. Serve when liquid is sufficiently reduced. This reduction process infuses flavor. Salt and pepper to taste.

Couscous
Couscous is a semolina pasta in granular form. Can be used in a variety of ways including cold salads and sautés.

MEASURE	INGREDIENT
1 pinch	salt
2 & 1/4 cups	boiling water
2 cups	couscous

Pour boiling salted-water over couscous, cover and let stand 5 minutes. Fluff up with a fork and serve, or let cool, then rinse with cold water, drain well and use in cold salads. [8-12 PORTIONS]

Corn or Vegetable Fritters
Goes well with American and Southern style meals. Corn can be combined with other diced veggies for a mixed vegetable fritter, as well.

MEASURE	INGREDIENT
1 16-oz can	corn - drained
3 Tbsps	soy milk
1/2 tsp	salt
1/2 tsp	baking powder
1/2 tsp	cajun spice blend

MEASURE	INGREDIENT
1 tsp	cornstarch
4 Tbsps	unbleached white flour (organic)
1 cup	soy oil

Beat ingredients together. Spoon into hot oil and fry, turning once, until golden brown. If batter is too wet, add another tablespoon of flour. [2-3 PORTIONS]

Escarole

This vegetable is a staple in Italy. It should be better integrated in the American cuisine.

MEASURE	INGREDIENT
2 heads	escarole
2 Tbsps	olive oil
4	garlic cloves - chopped
1/2 cup	***Vegetable Stock***
(to taste)	salt & black pepper

Cut bottom off escarole and wash leaves well. Heat oil in a soup pot (or sauce pan) and lightly brown the chopped garlic. Add vegetable stock and escarole leaves. Cook, covered, 10 minutes on low heat. Salt and pepper to taste. [4-6 PORTIONS]

Farfel or Matzoh Brie

An ancient tradition of the Jewish people, this recipe varies from family to family. Our basic recipe makes a fine cornerstone for more elaborate versions.

MEASURE	INGREDIENT
1 box	whole wheat matzoh meal crackers
2 cups	*Vegetable Stock*
2 Tbsps	soy oil
1 cup	onion - chopped
(to taste)	salt & black pepper

Break up the crackers into small pieces, approximately 1 or 2 inches in rough size. Place the cracker pieces into a deep bowl. Heat the vegetable stock to a boil, then pour this liquid over the crackers. Allow crackers to soak for 5 minutes, then drain off any unused liquid.

Heat a skillet or sauté pan and add the oil. Fry the onions on medium heat until translucent, then stir in the soaked crackers. Fry this mixture several minutes, flipping the mass occasionally, until evenly browned. Salt and pepper the mixture during this process. Serve as a breakfast entrée, or side to a dinner. [6-8 PORTIONS]

French Fried Potatoes

Make your own organic French fries and freeze them or serve them fried or baked with sandwiches.

MEASURE	INGREDIENT
6 large	potatoes - peeled & strip cut
2 qts	water - cold
1 Tbsp	salt
1/4 cup	soy oil

Peel and cut potatoes into thin strips. place them in the cold water with salt. Soak one hour. Remove from water, drain well and fry in the hot oil (350°F) or freeze for later use.

An alternate method is to toss drained fries in the oil then bake them in a 450°F oven, turning once, for 20 to 30 minutes. [4-8 PORTIONS]

Fried Noodles
Crispy garnish or topping for Asian foods, casserole topping, or simply as an appetizer.

MEASURE	INGREDIENT
1 pt	noodles - cooked
1 Tbsp	soy oil (or canola oil)

Deep fry noodles until crispy; or heat a skillet, add one tablespoon oil and lightly brown noodles, while stirring. The use of different cooking oils will impart a range of flavors. Roasted sesame oil adds a nutty flavor.

Grilled Corn on the Cob
An open grill or barbecue lends a distinctive, smoky flavor to fresh picked corn on the cob. Easy to prepare, goes great with summer barbecues.

MEASURE	INGREDIENT
4-12 ears	white corn fresh

Remove outer leaves, allowing inner leaves to remain on cob. Grill corn, turning four times, for five minutes. Remove and serve, allowing guests to remove husk and eat.

Hash Browns
Familiar breakfast potato side dish, it's easy to make and good to eat.

MEASURE	INGREDIENT
4 large	potatoes - grated
1 qt	water - cold
1 Tbsp	salt (for soaking water)
1/4 cup	soy oil (or canola oil)
(to taste)	salt & black pepper

Grate the potatoes and soak in the cold, salted water one hour. Remove, drain and pat dry potatoes. Spoon potatoes into the heated soy oil and flatten with a spatula. Fry, covered, on medium heat for 4 minutes, turn and fry 4 more minutes. Salt and pepper to taste. [4-6 PORTIONS]

Home Fries
Great American breakfast food and this recipe is foolproof.

MEASURE	INGREDIENT
6 medium	potatoes - peeled & sliced
1 qt	water - cold
1 Tbsp	salt (for soaking water)
1	onion - sliced
3 Tbsps	soy oil
(to taste)	salt & black pepper

Peel, wash and slice potatoes in half, lengthwise. Lay flat end of potato down and thinly slice. Soak potato slices in cold, salted water for twenty minutes.

Cut onion in half, then lay flat side down and thinly slice onion. Heat up a skillet and sauté onions with oil, on medium heat, for about three minutes.

Drain the potatoes well and pour them into the pan with onions. Stir contents well and cover to steam. Cook about 25 minutes, stirring five times to evenly brown potatoes. Salt and pepper to taste. [2-6 PORTIONS]

Indian Samosas
This delightful potato stuffed pastry is a staple of Indian cuisine. Our recipe is simple to make, with all the flavor and satisfaction of the original.

MEASURE	INGREDIENT
2 sheets	*Puff Pastry*
1 & 1/2 Tbsps	curry powder
1 cup	peas - frozen
3 cups	*Mashed Potatoes*
3 Tbsps	soy margarine

Roll out the sheets of puff pastry on a floured board to twice their original size. Score a matrix of 3 inch square pieces. Mix the curry powder and peas with the mashed potatoes, then spoon 2 tablespoons into the center of each pastry square. Fold the 4 corners around to the top. With wet fingers, crimp the peak of these corners together.

Brush margarine over pastry pockets, then bake on a greased cookie sheet at 400°F for 12 to 20 minutes or until golden brown. Serve with **Chutney**, or **Sweet & Sour Sauce**. [MAKES 24 SAMOSAS]

Jalapeno Poppers
Also known as Chili Rejenos, these tasty little gems require a little labor, but are well worth the effort.

MEASURE	INGREDIENT
1 qt	jalapeno peppers - whole
1 cup	unbleached white flour (organic)

Grains, Beans & Side Dishes

MEASURE	INGREDIENT
2 Tbsps	baking powder
1/2 cup	yellow corn meal
1 Tbsp	salt
1 cup	soy milk
1 Tbsp	canola oil (or soy oil)
1 lb	soy cheese

When handling this many hot peppers, latex gloves are a must! Cut stems off jalapeno ends and using a paring knife (or small spoon), remove the seeds.

Sift together the dry ingredients. Mix the oil and soy milk. Setting the peppers and cheese aside, combine the wet and dry ingredients, then beat into a batter.

Take the block of soy cheese and slice into 1/4 inch sheets. Cut the sheets into 1/4 inch strips and then cut these strips in half. Stuff each jalapeno pepper with a piece of cheese.

Roll or toss the stuffed peppers in a little flour, then dip them in the batter. Placed coated poppers on a stainless steel tray, or a metal tray that's covered with parchment paper. Freeze immediately! When ready to cook, plunge frozen poppers into 350°F oil and fry for five minutes, until well browned.
[4-6 PORTIONS]

Macaroni and Cheese
This recipe is included as a side dish, it is completely vegan, and is good for active children.

MEASURE	INGREDIENT
1 cup	elbow macaroni - dry
2 cups	water - boiling
1 tsp	salt
1 cup	**White Sauce**
1/2 cup	soy cheese - shredded

Cook the pasta in the boiling salted-water, until done. Rinse and set aside. Heat white sauce, then stir in cheese. Pour heated sauce over pasta and serve. For that casserole effect, bake an additional 10 minutes in a hot oven.
[2 PORTIONS]

Mashed Potatoes

An true American staple, this vegan recipe is easy and makes the best mashed potatoes in the world.

MEASURE	INGREDIENT
5 large	potatoes (organic) - peeled & chunked
2 qts	water - boiling
2 Tbsps	soy margarine
2 tsps	salt
1/4 cup	soy milk

Peel, wash and cut potatoes into fairly large chunks. Put potatoes in the boiling water and cook until soft. Drain potatoes well, then add margarine, salt and soy milk. Mash by hand or electric mixer. Smooth with rubber spatula.
[4-6 PORTIONS]

Millet

This ancient grain is seldom used in western cuisine, yet half the world eats it daily. It's easily digestible and can be eaten as a breakfast cereal or as a substitute for rice, in many dishes.

MEASURE	INGREDIENT
1 Tbsp	roasted sesame oil
1 cup	millet
3 cups	water (or **Vegetable Stock**)
1 tsp	salt

Heat the oil in a sauce pot. Stir in the millet and brown lightly. Combine water, salt, and millet, then bring to a hard boil. Reduce heat and cook for 20 more minutes. Fluff up with fork and serve. [8-12 PORTIONS]

'Mozzarella' Sticks

**This method is essentially the same as
the recipe for *Jalapeno Poppers*.**

MEASURE	INGREDIENT
1 6-oz block	soy mozzarella cheese
3/4 cup	soy milk
1 tsp	salt
2 Tbsps	baking powder
1 cup	unbleached white flour (organic)
2 cups	bread crumbs

Cut up the cheese into 1/4" x 1/4" x 3" strips. Mix soy milk, salt, baking powder and flour together to form a batter. Dip cheese strips into batter then roll in crumbs. Place on a tray and freeze. When ready to use, flash-fry frozen sticks in 350°F heated oil for 3 minutes. [MAKES 16-20 STICKS]

Nachos

**A popular appetizer found in Mexican restaurants,
this recipe is vegan and makes a great snack.**

MEASURE	INGREDIENT
1 medium	fresh tomato - diced
1/2	red onion - diced
1/2	green bell pepper - diced
1/4 cup	black olives - sliced (optional)
1 tsp	salt
1	jalapeno pepper - minced (optional)
1 qt	tortilla chips (plain)
1/2 cup	soy cheddar cheese - shredded

Dice up the tomato, onion, peppers and slice the olives (if used). Combine diced veggies and salt. For extra effect, you can also mix in a minced jalapeno pepper into veggie garnish. Shred the soy cheddar. Place a layer of tortilla chips on a greased baking pan. Sprinkle some cheese and veggies on this layer then repeat this process with a total of three layers. Oven bake at 450°F - 500°F for 15 to 20 minutes. [2-4 PORTIONS]

Pasta

This is just fundamentals. Pasta does vary however, requiring longer or shorter cooking periods, depending on pasta size or the type of grain the pasta is made with.

Some sensitive pastas such as oriental rice sticks or mung bean thread need only be soaked in hot water. Fresh made Durham wheat pasta need only be boiled as little as two minutes. Dry Durham wheat pasta should be boiled between eight and twenty minutes depending on pasta size.

Always cook pasta with plenty of salted water. Pasta should always be cooked aldente, or slightly undercooked. One should begin testing pasta by tasting, at the end of the prescribed cooking period. It is done when it is still a little chewy but not hard.

Cooked pasta can be rinsed with cold water after cooking but is not usually recommended. You can store cooked pasta for several days refrigerated. Just mix few drops of oil into pasta before storage.

Pilaf

Often wild rice, bulgar or kasha is combined into a 'pilaf' casserole. This is our basic recipe...so, feel free to improvise.

MEASURE	INGREDIENT
3 Tbsps	soy oil (other cooking oils can be used as well)
3 Tbsps	onion - diced
3	celery stalks - diced

Grains, Beans & Side Dishes

MEASURE	INGREDIENT
3	carrots - diced
1	green bell pepper - diced
1 tsp	salt
1 cup	*Brown Rice*
1 cup	wild rice
6 cups	*Vegetable Stock*

Heat a sauce or soup pot on the stove. Add oil (soy oil is an excellent neutral oil, olive, sesame or peanut oils will lend regional flavors to the pilaf) and sauté the vegetables with salt and herbs of your choice, until soft.

If combining, add the rice and other grain to the sauté. Stir this together and continue to sauté another five minutes. Next add the vegetable stock and bring mix to a boil. Reduce heat to very low and simmer about 1 hour.

To create a rice ring for a more elegant presentation, simply grease up a ring mold (spray with Pam) and pack mold with pilaf. Place mold (upside down) in a pan of boiling water and bake in a 400°F oven 30 minutes. Turn mold upright onto a platter and remove mold. Garnish. [8-12 PORTIONS]

Quinoa
**This ancient grain from South America offers high quality protein.
It has all the essential amino acids and can be substituted
for millet, bulgar, kasha or couscous, in dishes.**

MEASURE	INGREDIENT
1 cup	quinoa
2 cups	water
2 pinches	salt

Rinse grain well with cold water. This washes off a bitter tasting substance called saponin, the quinoa grain plant produces as a natural pesticide. Heat a sauce pot and pour cup of grain into hot pot. Reduce heat and lightly roast quinoa, stirring frequently. Pour in water and salt. Water should come to a boil quickly, reduce heat and simmer on low for 15 minutes.

Roasted Red Peppers
This delicacy is easy to prepare and is nice with antipasto or spiked hor'dourves.

MEASURE	INGREDIENT
3-4 large	red bell peppers
1	paper bag

Bake whole peppers at 450°F for 15 minutes. Remove and put into paper bag and close up bag. An alternate method is to grill peppers on low heat setting, turning several times, then removing to paper bag.

In about a half hour, peppers have cooled enough to remove from bag. Using a paring knife, score surrounding stem base area, and pull stem with seeds away - in one motion - then peel off skins. Chill. If desired, marinate in **Garlic and Oil** sauce.

Sautéed Cabbage & Potatoes
This peasant side dish from Eastern Europe, is both healthy and satisfying.

MEASURE	INGREDIENT
1/2	onion - chopped
2 Tbsps	soy oil (or canola oil)
1 small head	white cabbage - chunk chopped
4	potatoes - peeled
1 tsp	paprika
1/2 tsp	salt
1 cup	**Vegetable Stock**

Grains, Beans & Side Dishes

Sauté chopped onion in a pot with the oil. When onions have caramelized, toss in chunked cabbage, cover and simmer on low heat 10 minutes. This will sufficiently soften cabbage.

Meanwhile, boil chopped potatoes until they're soft, yet still firm. Next, drain parcooked potatoes, then add to sautéing cabbage. Mix paprika and salt into sautéing mixture, stirring often on medium high heat until cabbage is lightly browned. Add vegetable stock and cook down liquid. Serve hot.
[4-8 PORTIONS]

Sautéed Mushroom or Onions
Want fried onions or mushrooms on that burger? Or maybe that tofu or gluten steak. Here's the recipe.

MEASURE	INGREDIENT
1/2	onion - thinly sliced
1 cup	mushrooms - sliced
2 pinches	thyme leaf
1-2 tsps	soy oil
1 Tbsp	white wine (and/or **Vegetable Stock**)
(to taste)	salt & black pepper

Fry the onions, mushrooms and herbs in oil, on high heat setting. Toss and stir for a couple minutes, to sear. Lower heat and braise, covered, 3 minutes. Add wine (or vegetable stock) and continue cooking - covered - for 2 more minutes, or until liquid is reduced. Salt and pepper to taste. [2 PORTIONS]

Sautéed Spinach

Spinach is a deep green vegetable with plenty of minerals and lots of vitamin A. Makes a great side dish so here's a simple recipe.

MEASURE	INGREDIENT
1 Tbsp	olive oil
1/2 small	onion - diced
1 lb	spinach - fresh
1/4 cup	*Vegetable Stock*

Heat a soup pot, then add oil and fry diced onions. Add raw, whole, rinsed spinach to pot and lower heat. Add vegetable stock, then cover and continue simmering 5 more minutes, stirring once.

At this point spinach should have reduced its size. Mix well into the juices and simmer a few more minutes. Serve hot. [2-4 PORTIONS]

Sugar Glazed Beets or Carrots

Tasty little dish goes well with all world cuisine accompanying a variety of main courses. Kids love them!

MEASURE	INGREDIENT
2 Tbsps	soy margarine
2 Tbsps	raw sugar (or xylitol)
4	beets - sliced & cooked
	(or 1 cup baby carrots - organic)
1 tsp	cornstarch - dissolved in
	1/4 cup cold water

Heat the margarine with the sugar and add beets (or carrots). Cover and cook beets (or carrots) until soft, then slowly stir in cornstarch slurry, forming a glaze. Cook a couple of minutes reducing glaze, then serve. [4-6 PORTIONS]

Steamed Artichokes

Always a delight, this method is a simple way of preparing and eating artichokes. This recipe uses a dipping sauce for eating the leaves with.

MEASURE	INGREDIENT
4 large	artichokes
2 qts	water - boiling
2 tsps	salt
1	lemon - juiced
1/2 cup	soy margarine - melted

Trim the stems off artichokes (you may cut off the pointed tips on the leaves as well, for a more decorative look). Drop in boiling water and boil until leaves can be easily pull away from artichokes. Add salt and half of the lemon juice, into the boiling water.

Melt the margarine and add the other half of the lemon juice. Sprinkle a pinch or two of salt and this is your dipping sauce. To eat, pull leaves away one-by-one, then dip into sauce. Use this process until you reach the fuzzy heart. Remove all of the fuzz, then dip the heart into sauce and eat! [2-4 PORTIONS]

Stewed Tomatoes

Good canned organic tomatoes are expensive and hard to find, so consider growing your own for the best flavor.

MEASURE	INGREDIENT
(as needed)	water - boiling
10 - 100	plum tomatoes (organic)

Boil tomatoes whole for 3 minutes. Drain and let cool. Peel skins off and store tomatoes in refrigerator or freezer. Use in sauce, stews, soups sautés, etc...

Vegetable Medley

This is a nice little vegetable side dish that goes well with a variety of main courses.

MEASURE	INGREDIENT
2 cups	fresh corn - cut
1 large	carrot - diced
1/2 cup	peas
1	zucchini - diced
(to taste)	salt & black pepper
1 pinch	thyme
1/4 cup	**Vegetable Stock**

Combine all ingredients together, then simmer in a small amount of vegetable stock (or water), until carrots have softened. [4-6 PORTIONS]

Casseroles & Stuffed Things

Introduction

A casserole is a simple and efficient meal consisting of several ingredients, bound together by a heated protein - such as eggs or cheese. Casseroles can feed a group of people, as a main or side course and can be refrigerated or frozen for future 'ready made' meals.

This chapter will teach you how to create vegan casseroles that have perfect form, taste and nutritional value, without dangerous animal proteins.

The following section will explore the virtually infinite variety of baked stuffed foods. Everything from wraps and burritos, to stuffed vegetables, pizza pockets, squashes, pot pies, turnovers, and more will be covered here. Once familiar with the example recipes featured, you will have the confidence and knowledge to develop wonderful creations on your own.

The purpose of this chapter, as in every chapter, is to help establish the fundamental basis for every day vegan cooking. To lay the groundwork for a lifetime cuisine that provides perfect harmony with yourself, the environment and the world. Acquiring the skills and eating from the recipes illustrated in this book will help to center yourself physically, mentally and spiritually as a human being --- guaranteed.

'Beef' & Bean Burrito
Here's a very basic, but delicious burrito.
This one's for vegan 'carnivores'.

MEASURE	INGREDIENT
1 cup	black beans (or refried beans) - cooked

MEASURE	INGREDIENT
1 cup	*Taco-Style Ground 'Beef'*
1/2 cup	*Mexican Sauce*
1/2 cup	*Brown Rice* - cooked
1/2 cup	soy cheddar cheese - grated
2 large	tortillas

Apply the beans, ground 'beef', Mexican sauce, rice, and half the cheese, to the center of each heated tortilla. Fold sides and roll up burrito. Sprinkle the other half of the cheese over the top of the folded burrito and bake on a greased pan at 450°F for 20 minutes. Serve with *Guacamole*, *Mexican Sauce*, *Sour Cream* sides. [1-2 PORTIONS]

'Beef' Enchiladas

If you are an enchilada lover, this recipe's for you. If you have never tried one, you're in for a real treat!

MEASURE	INGREDIENT
4 large	tortillas
1 cup	*Sour Cream*
2 cups	*Taco-Style Ground 'Beef'*
1 cup	soy cheddar cheese - grated
2 cups	*Enchilada Sauce*

Heat the tortillas and evenly distribute the sour cream, ground 'beef' and soy cheese in the center of each tortilla. Take end nearest you and fold over center, then roll tortilla forward.

On a baking tray or casserole dish, smear some sauce on baking surface, to prevent enchiladas from sticking. Neatly lay enchiladas down on tray or dish and pour the remainder of the sauce over enchiladas. Sprinkle a little extra cheese over the tops and cover dish with foil. Leave the ends of enchiladas sauce-free for a more decorative look. Bake 20 minutes at 450°F. [2-4 PORTIONS]

Broccoli & Artichoke Casserole
This casserole makes a wonderful holiday side dish.
It's packed with balanced nutrition...

MEASURE	INGREDIENT
1 qt	artichoke hearts
2 qts	broccoli spears
3 cups	**White Sauce**
2 12-oz packages	silken tofu
(to taste)	salt & black pepper
2 cups	cracker meal / crumbs
(as needed)	**Vegetable Stock** (optional)

Obtain prepared (canned or jarred) artichoke hearts. Steam off broccoli aldente. Grease a baking pan or chafing dish evenly distribute the artichokes and broccoli. Use a dish of a size that will allow you to double stack vegetables.

Heat white sauce on stove top, then blend in tofu with infusion blender*. Adjust flavor with salt and pepper. Pour this mixture over vegetables in 8"x12" chafing dish. Cover with a rather thick layer of cracker crumbs, or meal, and bake in a moderate oven (400°) for 1 hour. [6-12 PORTIONS]

*If white sauce and tofu seem too thick, add a little **Vegetable Stock** to thin out and increase flavor.

Calzone

Calzones are basically pizza turnovers, and can be stuffed with a variety of vegetable combinations with cheese. The following two examples illustrate the possibilities.

MEASURE	INGREDIENT
fist-size ball	*Pizza Dough* - flattened
1 cup mixed:	vegetables - sautéed & diced
1/8 lb	tofu - diced
1/4 cup	*Marinara Sauce*
1/4 cup	soy mozzarella cheese

Roll the dough into a 1/8 inch thick - 12 inch round pizza. Place the vegetables, tofu, marinara sauce and cheese in the center, then fold over one side. Pinch the edge and roll edge over starting at one end and finishing at the other. Bake at 500°F for 15 to 20 minutes. [1 PORTION - LARGE]

Method 2:

MEASURE	INGREDIENT
fist-sized ball	*Pizza Dough* - flattened
1/2 cup	soy mozzarella cheese
1/4 cup	*Marinara Sauce*
1/2 cup	*Taco-Style Ground 'Beef'*

Roll the dough into a 1/8 inch thick - 12 inch round pizza. Put cheese, marinara sauce and ground 'beef' in center of rolled dough. Fold over, pinch and roll edges. Bake at 500°F for 15 to 20 minutes.

Chimichanga

Chimichangas are Mexican stuffed burritos that are deep fried or pan fried, with cheeses stuffed inside with the filling.

MEASURE	INGREDIENT
1/2 of 1 lb block	tofu - strip sliced
1 cup	*Mexican Sauce*
1 large	tortilla
3 Tbsps	refried beans
1/4 cup	soy cheese - grated
1/4 cup	*Brown Rice* - cooked
3 Tbsps	fresh corn - cut
3 Tbsps	*Salsa*

Slice the half block of tofu into long, thin strips. Immerse strips in the Mexican sauce, to marinate for several hours.

Heat the tortilla in an oven (or microwave), just long enough to soften and make it more pliable. Remove tofu strips from the marinade, then place these strips at the center of the tortilla. Combine remaining ingredients, piling into a stack at the center of the torilla. Dribble some of the marinating juices over the stack, then fold in ends and bring front edge over filling. Tuck this edge around filling and roll burro forward. All edges should be sealed as well as possible. You can dab a little water on problem areas then pinch together to seal.

Heat a skillet and add the oil. Lay the chimichanga, bottom side down, into the oil. Fry, covered, on medium heat until side is browned then turn to brown other sides. After browning all sides in a covered pan, chimichanga is ready to serve with sides of *Sour Cream*, *Guacamole*, more *Salsa*, shredded lettuce and fresh tomato slices. [1 PORTION - LARGE]

Chipped 'Beef' & Noodles

This hearty casserole is very inexpensive and will feed a family. A new twist on an age old tradition.

MEASURE	INGREDIENT
1 lb	durham wheat noodles
4 cups	***White Sauce***
(as needed)	soy oil (for frying)
3 cups	***Basic Seitan*** - sliced
2 cups	peas - frozen
3 cups	cracker meal
(to taste)	salt & black pepper

Boil noodles until aldente. Heat the white sauce slowly while stirring. Using the oil, either deep fry seitan slices for 30 seconds, or pan fry on medium heat, until lightly browned. Mix prepared seitan slices with peas, then set aside.

Grease a deep 8"x12" casserole dish and layer with noodles, then add seitan mixed with peas. Repeat layering process until these ingredients are layered into dish. Slowly pour and distribute white sauce over layered casserole ingredients, then top with cracker meal and bake in a moderate (350°F - 400°F) oven for 45 minutes. [4-8 PORTIONS]

Eggplant Parmigiani

This well known Italian-American casserole is quite easy to make. Our vegan version tastes the same...but is much healthier!

MEASURE	INGREDIENT
2 large	eggplants - thin sliced
(as needed)	salt
2 cups	whole wheat flour or unbleached white flour (organic)
1 cup	soy milk

Casseroles & Stuffed Things

MEASURE	INGREDIENT
3 cups	bread crumbs
1 cup	soy oil (for frying)
2 cups	*Marinara Sauce*
1 cup	soy mozzarella cheese
1/4 cup	soy parmesan cheese

Slice the eggplant into thin rounds and lightly salt each side. Place eggplant slices in a bowl to rest for 20 minutes. Drain off liquid then coat each slice, first with whole wheat flour then soy milk and finally the bread crumbs. Set aside.

Heat half the oil in a skillet and fry half the eggplant slices, on each side. Add the rest of the oil and fry up the rest of the eggplant. Drain all slices well, on paper towels.

Spread some sauce into a small casserole dish. Layer the eggplant into dish, sprinkle with the soy mozzarella and a little more marinara. Repeat this layering 3 stacks high. On top layer sprinkle the soy parmesan cheese to protect the browning of the mozzarella. Bake at 400°F 30 minutes. [4-6 PORTIONS]

Gluten Steak Parmigiani
This Italian entrée usually involves chicken or veal. Our gluten steak, will easily substitute for any animal dirived flesh.

MEASURE	INGREDIENT
4 medium	*Perfect Gluten Flank Steaks*
1 cup	whole wheat flour
1 cup	soy milk
1 cup	bread crumbs
1 cup	soy mozzarella cheese - grated
1 cup	*Marinara Sauce*
(as needed)	soy oil (for frying)

Cover steaks well in flour, then dip into soy milk, and finally dip into the bread crumbs. (Discard leftover flour, milk and bread crumbs.) Fry steaks on both sides, then coat with marinara and bake - covered with cheese - for 20 minutes at 450°F. [4 PORTIONS]

Grammy's Spaghetti

This delicious - homespun - casserole has evolved over generations, into a wonderful and satisfying vegan dish.

MEASURE	INGREDIENT
1 lb	TVP burger blend - dry mix
3 & 1/2 cups	ice cold water
1 lb	elbow macaroni
1 Tbsp	salt (for boiling water)
6 cups	water - boiling
1 large	onion - chopped
2	green bell peppers - chopped
1/4 cup	canola oil (or soy oil)
2 cups	mushrooms - sliced
3 cups	**Stewed Tomatoes** - hand crushed
1 Tbsp	salt
1 Tbsp	thyme leaf
1 Tbsp	oregano
2 cups	soy cheddar cheese - grated
2 cups	cornflakes

Mix the burger blend with the cold water, then refrigerate for at least 30 minutes, or more.

Cook the pasta in salted - boiling - water. When cooked, drain, rinse and set aside.

Chop up the onions and peppers and fry in preheated oil, in a large pot. Add in the burger, then cover and reduce heat for simmering. After five minutes, stir mixture and add sliced mushrooms. Contiue cooking - covered - for ten minutes, while stirring occasionally, then add tomatoes, salt and herbs. Simmer another 15 minutes on low heat setting.

Stir pasta into pot with cooked mixture. Grease an 8"x12" (or smaller size) baking dish and spread mixture into dish. Sprinkle grated cheese over casserole and top with crumbled corn flakes (or potato chips). Bake at 400°F for 45 minutes. [8-12 PORTIONS]

Incan Quinoa Casserole

This baked casserole brings together many of the staple foods commonly found in the markets of the ancient Inca empire.

MEASURE	INGREDIENT
1	onion - chopped
2 Tbsps	canola oil
4	garlic cloves - minced
2 large	chilies - dried & crumbled [see Hot Pepper Chart]
2 cups	lima beans (frozen)
3 cups	fresh corn - cut
2 cups	*Stewed Tomatoes*
1 Tbsp	salt
4 cups	*Vegetable Stock*
2 cups	*Quinoa* - precooked
4	potatoes - thin sliced
2	sweet potatoes (or yams) - thin sliced
2 tsps	cornstarch (for basting slurry)
4 cups	tortilla chips - crumbled

Sauté the chopped onions in preheated oil, in a pot, then add the minced garlic, crumbled dried chilies, lima beans, corn, tomatoes and salt. Pour in one cup vegetable stock and sauté on low heat - covered - for ten more minutes.

Evenly spread quinoa into a deep 8"x12" greased baking dish. Next, cover quinoa with a layer of one third the sauté mixture. Follow this layering with all of the thinly sliced white potatoes. Layer again with another third of the sauté mixture, then layer with all of the thinly sliced sweet potatoes. Apply remaining third of sauté mixture over the sweet potato slices.

Next stir cornstarch into remaining stock and evenly distribute slurry over casserole. Top dish with crumbled tortilla chips. Bake at 400°F for 1 hour.
[6-12 PORTIONS]

Ispanakli Borek
This traditional Turkish spinach - filo pastry pie is rendered vegan in this recipe. A wonderful casserole that can serve as a portion in a Mediterranean theme dinner.

MEASURE	INGREDIENT
1	onion - chopped
1 Tbsp	soy oil
1 pinch	salt
2 cups	spinach - steamed
2 lb block	tofu - course crumbled
1 Tbsp	salt
1 Tbsp	garlic powder
1 Tbsp	onion powder
1 Tbsp	nutritional yeast
1 box	filo pastry - thawed
1/2 cup	soy margarine - melted

Chop up onion and sauté in preheated oil, with a pinch of salt. When onions are finished, combine them - in a bowl - with lightly steamed spinach. In another bowl, mix coursely crumbled tofu with one tablespoon of salt, garlic powder, onion powder and nutritional yeast.

Using a pastry brush, grease a 12"x18" (large) casserole dish. Using two sheets of thawed out filo pastry, paint a thin coat of melted margarine on top of each double-layered sheet. Repeat this process with 4 more (2 layer) sheets, placing each basted sheet on top of the other. Note: As it's very difficult to separate

Casseroles & Stuffed Things

individual layers from a flattened filo pastry roll, you can prevent undue tearing, by carefully drawing away two layers at a time.

Take half of the spinach and onion mixture and apply it evenly to the surface of the four layers of pastry. Next, take half of the tofu mixture and crumble it over the spinach and onion layer.

Repeat above process with 4 more sheets of filo pastry then another layer of fillings. Top with 3-4 more double layered sheets of filo pastry. Preheat oven to 400°F and bake casserole 30 - 35 minutes or until golden brown. Slice into equal portions and serve. [8-12 PORTIONS]

Lasagna

Lasagna is an Italian casserole baked with layers of cheese and wide noodles. Different 'meats' and vegetables are frequently added as layers.

MEASURE	INGREDIENT
1 lb	lasagna noodles - boiled aldente
1 lb package	firm tofu
1 12-oz package	silken tofu
1 Tbsp	nutritional yeast
1 Tbsp	onion powder
1 tsp	garlic powder
2 Tbsps	soy parmesan cheese
2 cups	soy mozzarella cheese - grated
2 tsps	salt
1 tsp	black pepper
2 lbs	*Taco-Style Ground 'Beef'*
1/2	onion - chopped
4	garlic cloves - crushed
1/4 cup	olive oil
2 cups	mushrooms - sliced
3 cups	*Marinara Sauce*

Boil noodles aldente and let rest in cold water. Mix the two types of tofu together, then combine with yeast, onion powder, garlic powder, soy parmesan, a third the soy mozzarella, one teaspoon of salt and pepper, to produce mock ricotta cheese.

Sauté sliced mushrooms, then set these aside.

In a medium sized glass baking dish apply a thin layer of marinara sauce. Take one noodle and use it to measure the breadth of the baking dish. Cut this noodle to the appropriate size and use as a template to cut all the noodles this size. Place one noodle in dish and overlap half the noodle with the next noodle until bottom layer is complete.

Sprinkle a third of the remaining mozzarella cheese over noodle layer. Next, evenly apply the 'ricotta cheese' mix, then dribble marinara over this layer. Now evenly layer all of the sautéed mushrooms over this first layer.

Repeat another layer of noodles and mozzarella cheese, evenly distribute all of the sautéed burger mix, then dribble marinara over this second layer. Repeat a third (top) layer of noodles, also covered with mozzarella cheese. Finally, spread a small amount of marinara over top of noodles and top with a sprinkling of parmesan cheese. Bake 300°F - 400°F for 45 minutes. [6-8 PORTIONS]

The Maximilian
Named after a former emperor of Mexico for it's multifarious splendor and opulence, this stuffed tortilla has it all.

MEASURE	INGREDIENT
2 cups mixed:	carrots, cauliflower, broccoli, mushrooms, celery, colored bell peppers, onions, squashes, string beans, peas, asparagus and yams - chopped and steamed
1 cup	*Taco-Style Ground 'Beef'*
1/2 cup	tofu - cubed

Casseroles & Stuffed Things

MEASURE	INGREDIENT
1/2 cup	refried beans
1/2 cup	black beans - cooked
1 cup	*Salsa*
1/2 cup	*Guacamole*
1/3 cup	*Sour Cream*
1 cup	soy cheddar cheese - grated
2 extra-large	tortillas (or 4 large tortillas)
1/4 cup	*Enchilada Sauce*
1/4 cup	*Mexican Sauce* (optional)

Chop and steam all vegetables first, then combine all ingredients to form a filling for the tortillas. Divide filling into equal quantities, then place individual filling in center of each heated tortilla. Tuck in sides and fold near end over filling then roll tightly forward. Place stuffed tortillas on a greased baking tray. Pour **Enchilada Sauce** (or **Mexican Sauce**) over tortillas and bake - covered - for 20 minutes at 450°F. [2-4 PORTIONS]

The Neapolitan
A sauce-free pizza...topped with a plethora of Mediterranean delights!

MEASURE	INGREDIENT
(as needed)	zucchini, portabella mushrooms,
(")	leeks, eggplant - all sliced
1/2	red onion - sliced
1	red bell pepper - sliced
(as needed)	*Grill Goddess Sauce* (for grilling)
fist-sized ball	*Pizza Dough* - flattened
1/4 cup	olive oil
2 Tbsps	garlic clove - diced
1/4 cup	black olives - sliced
1/4 cup	soy parmesan cheese - grated

Casseroles & Stuffed Things

Using a grill, baste sliced zucchini, portabella mushrooms, (well washed) leeks, eggplant, onion, and bell pepper - with prepared sauce - then grill at a medium temperature setting. Don't overcook, as these ingredients will be further cooked.

Roll out dough and bake crust for 7 minutes at 500°F. Remove crust from oven, then paint on olive oil, add diced garlic, grilled vegetables, sliced black olives and grated parmesan cheese. Re-bake 10 min. [MAKES 1 MEDIUM SIZE PIZZA]

New World Stuffed Peppers
**A delicious combination of corn, vegetables and soy burger.
This filling represents the bounty of the Americas.**

MEASURE	INGREDIENT
1/2 lb	TVP burger blend - dry mix
2 cups	ice cold water
4-6	colored bell peppers
1	onion - diced
1/4 cup	soy oil
1 Tbsp	salt
1 tsp	thyme leaf
1 tsp	marjoram
1/2 tsp	rubbed sage
3	celery stalks - chopped
4	garlic cloves - diced
1 cup	fresh corn - cut
1 cup	baby lima beans
1	eggplant - cubed
1	zucchini - cubed
1 cup	**Stewed Tomatoes** - hand crushed
1/2 cup	**Brown Rice** - cooked
1 cup	tofu - cubed
2 cups	**Vegetable Stock**

Casseroles & Stuffed Things

Mix the burger blend with the cold water, then refrigerate for at least 30 minutes, or more.

Using a small paring knife, carefully cut around pepper stems, and lift out seed core, then remove all loose seeds with a spoon. Blanch peppers in boiling water for 5 minutes or until color begins to change. Remove peppers and plunge into cold water, for later use.

Sauté diced onions in preheated soy oil, with salt and herbs. After a minute, add chopped celery, diced garlic and burger, then continue cooking - covered - on a low-medium heat setting, for 5 to 10 more minutes. Next, stir in corn, lima beans, cubed eggplant and zucchini, then continue cooking - covered - for an additional ten minutes. When vegetables are fully sautéd, stir in tomatoes, rice, cubed tofu and only half of the vegetable stock into mix. After an additonal 5 minutes of simmering, remove from heat.

Grease a baking dish, place peppers in dish open side up. Stuff the peppers with a mixture of the sauté filling, then pour remaining stock into baking dish. Bake at 400°F - covered - for 30 minutes. Remove cover and top peppers with bread crumbs or soy cheese then bake ten more minutes. Serve as a dinner entrée, or main course! The recipe's filling can also be used to stuff squashes, eggplant or portabella mushroom caps, too. [2-6 PORTIONS]

Polenta

Polenta is a form of cornmeal mush, that is prepared on the stove top. Fashion into crusts, pies, layers and bases for casseroles, pizzas, hor d'ourves and sautés.

MEASURE	INGREDIENT
1 cup	polenta corn meal
1 tsp	salt
1 cup	water - cold
4 cups	water - boiling

Mix the polenta corn meal with the salt and cold water to form a mash. Bring four cups of water to a boil. Slowly stir in the polenta mash into the boiling water - gradually - so as not to alter this water's temperature to greatly.

Reduce heat and continue to stir mixture for three minutes until it stiffens. Remove and cool. When cooled it can be spread into a crust like pizza, covered with toppings and baked. [4-8 PORTIONS]

Potato Pocket
All the wholesomeness of mashed potatoes, with diced - steamed - veggies, encased in a wheat pocket, then baked golden brown.

MEASURE	INGREDIENT
1 cup mixed:	carrots, yams (or sweet potatoes), string beans - diced & steamed
1/2 cup	peas
2 cups	**Mashed Potatoes**
(to taste)	salt
1 tsp	curry powder (or cajun spice blend, or other spice blend)
2 small balls	**Pizza Dough** - flattened

Dice up the vegetables, then steam. Combine steamed vegetables, peas, mashed potatoes, salt and seasoning to produce a filling. Divide dough in half, then roll out into two 1/8" thick - 10 inch rounds. Divide filling mix, and place each half into the center of the two flattened dough rounds.

Using a knife, slice off rounded edges of dough to form a square. Fold each corner up over center filling. Wet each edge and overlap to seal up pocket. Repeat with second pocket. Bake the two pockets at 450°F for 20 minutes.
[2 PORTIONS]

Pot Pie

An alternative version to the classic meat and vegetable pies everyone is familiar with. Everything you've ever desired in a pot pie, is in this recipe.

MEASURE	INGREDIENT
3 Tbsps	soy oil
1	onion - chopped
1/2 cup	*Perfect Gluten Flank Steak* - diced
4	celery stalks - diced
2	carrots - diced
2	broccoli stalks - skinned & diced
1/3 cup	string beans - diced
1-2 tsps	salt
1/2 tsp	thyme leaf
1/4 tsp	rubbed sage
3	potatoes - diced
1 small	zucchini - diced
1/4 cup	baby lima beans (optional)
1 cup	tofu - diced
1 cup	fresh corn - cut
1 Tbsp	cornstarch - dissolved in
	2 cups cold *Vegetable Stock*
4 fist-sized balls	*Pot Pie Dough* (quantity of dough may vary with size of pie pans...)
(as needed)	soy margarine (for pie crust basting)

Note: This recipe makes two small pot pies, so small pie pans must be on hand. If this is not an option, and you wish to use a regulation sized pie pan to make one large pie, use one ball of dough for the bottom and the other ball of dough for the top crust. For two pies divide each doughball in half.

In a soup pot, sauce pot, or large skillet, preheat oil and begin sautéing chopped onions. Reduce heat to medium and add diced up gluten steak bits. Stir around a couple of minutes then add diced celery and carrots. Cut the tough skin off broccoli stalks and discard. Dice up the remaining marrow and add this and the string beans to the sauté.

Combine the salt, herbs, diced potatoes, diced zucchini, baby lima beans, diced tofu, and cut corn with the sautéing mixture. Reduce heat to low, cover and simmer for ten more minutes, stirring occasionally.

Mix the cornstarch with the cold vegetable stock and slowly stir in this mixture into the simmering sauté. When done, gradually bring the sauté mix to a boil, then remove from heat. Allow resulting filling to cool at least 30 minutes.

Roll out each doughball 1/8 inch thick - 8 inches in diameter.   Grease the inside of 2 small pie pans and center one dough round into each pan. Brush margarine (or oil) on inside of pie shell as well and prick shell with a fork.

Divide filling, putting half inside each pan. Wet edge and cover with second dough round to top pie, sealing edges with a fork. Prick holes in top and bake at 400° for 30 minutes.

Quesadilla
These delicious Mexican tortilla-turnovers are quick, easy and impressive. They can be stuffed with a variety of combinations. Here's one basic version.

MEASURE	INGREDIENT
2 tsps	*Mexican Sauce*
2 Tbsps	*Guacamole*
1 large	tortilla
1/4 cup	soy cheddar cheese - grated
1/4 cup	refried beans
1/4 cup	vegetables - diced

Casseroles & Stuffed Things

Mix the Mexican sauce with the guacamole and spread this over tortilla. Layer other ingredients over half of tortilla. Fold empty half of tortilla over, forming a turnover. Place on a pizza screen (or cookie sheet) and bake for 7 minutes at 500°F. Slice and serve with **Salsa** and **Sour Cream**.

The quesadilla can also be baked first, then grilled, for a more dramatic effect than simple baking. [1-4 PORTIONS]

Shepherd's Pie

This ancient dish has its roots all over the western world. An oven-baked stew with large cut vegetables, tofu and seitan, topped with mashed potatoes.

MEASURE	INGREDIENT
2 cups	**Basic Seitan** - diced
3	carrots - chopped
6	celery stalks - chopped
2-3	yams (or sweet potatoes) - chopped
2	onions - chopped
2 tsps	salt
1 tsp	powdered thyme
1 cup	string beans - cut
2 cups	peas
1 qt	**Vegetable Stock**
1 lb package	firm tofu - cubed
4 Tbsps	cornstarch - mixed with
	1/2 cup cold water
3 cups	**Mashed Potatoes**

Fry diced seitan in a deep fryer (if need be, pan fry on range in preheated oil until browned) for 30 - 45 seconds, then drain and set aside.

Chop up carrots, celery, yams and onions - into large pieces - and sauté them in a soup or sauce pot on low heat, - stirring occasionally - for 15 minutes. When fully heated, add in the salt, thyme, string beans and peas, then pour in vegetable stock and bring (what is now a stew) to an easy boil. Combine cubed tofu and prefried seitan bits into this stew, then lower heat and continue cooking - about 20 more minutes - until carrots have softened. Next, stir in cornstarch slurry, reduce heat and simmer for another 10 minutes.

Scoop out stew to individual baking crocks, topping each with mashed potatoes; or pour stew into a baking dish and cover with three cups of mashed potatoes. Which ever method you choose make sure you peak the mashed potatoes with a fork, so that they brown evenly. A fancy method is to force potatoes through a pastry decorators bag. Bake individual crocks or casserole for 25 minutes at 450°. [4-8 PORTIONS]

Spanish Rice Casserole

This variation on an ethnic recipe features tofu as a meat substitute. The body and flavor of this casserole is authentic.

MEASURE	INGREDIENT
1/4 cup	olive oil
1 large	onion - chopped
6	garlic cloves - diced
4	celery stalks - chopped
2	green bell peppers - chopped
1 lb package	firm tofu - cubed
1 Tbsp	salt
2 tsps	paprika
1/2 tsp	cumin
1 cup	black olives - sliced
1/4 cup	capers
2 cups	*Vegetable Stock* - cold
4 cups	*Brown Rice* - steamed
2 cups	tomato puree - cold

Casseroles & Stuffed Things

MEASURE	INGREDIENT
2 Tbsps	cornstarch
1 cup	bread crumbs

In a large skillet, heat oil, then sauté chopped onions, diced garlic, chopped celery, chopped peppers, cubed tofu, salt and spices. Cook five minutes at medium heat then add olives and capers. Pour about one-half cup of vegetable stock into skillet, cover and steam this mixture for another five minutes.

Grease a medium casserole dish and evenly layer one third of the brown rice contents into the dish. Take half the sauté mixture and layer it over the rice. Repeat another layer of rice, then layer the remainder of the sauté mix. Cover this sauté layer with the remainder of the rice.

Completely mix the cold tomato puree, cold vegetable stock and cornstarch in a separate mixing bowl, then pour this flavored slurry over the casserole contents. Bake in a 400°F oven for 45 minutes, topped with bread crumbs.
[6-10 PORTIONS]

Stromboli
This baked, stuffed wheat pocket is similar to a Calzone, yet distinguishes itself by the way it is stuffed and rolled. Use different fillings for unique Strombolis.

MEASURE	INGREDIENT
2 slices	eggplant - grilled
4 slices	zucchini - grilled
2-3 slices	fresh tomato - grilled
1/2 cup	*Grill Goddess Sauce*
fist-sized ball	*Pizza Dough* - flattened
1	onion - diced
1	colored bell pepper - diced
1	portabella mushroom - diced
1/4 cup	soy mozzarella cheese - shredded

Grill sliced vegetables with prepared sauce, then set aside. Roll out dough to 1/4 inch thickness. Layer center of flattened dough with both grilled and diced vegetables, shredded cheese, then fold over two sides and roll forward.

Bake on a greased sheet for 15 minutes, at 450°F. Serve, covered with heated **Marinara Sauce**. [1 PORTION - LARGE]

Stuffed Acorn Squash

Acorn squash is featured in this recipe, however, butternut squash may be substituted. The flavor will vary with type of squash used.

MEASURE	INGREDIENT
3 large	acorn squash
3 Tbsps	soy margarine
1	onion - chopped
4	garlic cloves - diced
1	eggplant - cubed
2 cups	kale leaves - chopped
1 tsp	salt
1/2 tsp	powdered thyme
2 pinches	black pepper
1 cup	*Vegetable Stock*
1 lb package	firm tofu - cubed
1 cup	*Brown Rice* - precooked
1/2 cup	bread crumbs

Cut unpeeled squashes in half and scoop out seeds. Bake - covered - squashes in a 400°F oven for 30 to 45 minutes, until soft. Remove the cooked meat from one whole squash (2 halves), chop it up and set aside in separate bowl. Grease a baking dish and place - upright -the 4 remaining squash halves, in dish.

Heat a pot on the stove top, then add 3 tablespoons of the margarine, chopped onion and diced garlic. Sauté on low until onions becomes translucent, then add

Casseroles & Stuffed Things

cubed eggplant, chopped kale, salt, thyme, pepper and chopped squash. Continue sautéing - covered - on low, for 10 more minutes, then add one-half cup of vegetable stock, cubed tofu, precooked brown rice, then continue cooking - covered - for another five minutes.

Divide filling into four equal parts and spoon into waiting squash. Bake in a preheated oven, at 400°F - covered - for 20 minutes. Remove baking dish cover and sprinkle bread crumbs over the squashes. Bake another 10 minutes until bread crumbs are slightly browned. Serve immediately. [4 PORTIONS]

Stuffed Baked Tomatoes

If you want to use up those tomatoes or if you just want to make something special with them, the following recipe will do the trick.

MEASURE	INGREDIENT
4-8 large	fresh tomatoes - cored
2 tsps	salt
1/4 cup	brown sugar
1/2 tsp	black pepper
2 cups	**White Sauce**
1 cup	soy mozzarella cheese - grated
1/2 cup	bread crumbs

Core out a cylindrical hole through the stem side of the tomato. Mix the salt, sugar and black pepper, then spoon equivalent quantities into each tomato. Heat the white sauce and melt the cheese into it. Fill the individual tomatoes with the cheese sauce, then top with bread crumbs and bake at 450°F for 15 minutes. [4-8 PORTIONS]

Stuffed Cabbage Leaves

This Eastern European casserole makes a great dinner in the home cooked tradition. This recipe is easy to make, tastes authentic and is vegan.

MEASURE	INGREDIENT
1 lb	TVP burger blend - dry mix
3 & 1/2 cups	ice cold water
1 large head	green cabbage - cored
2 Tbsps	soy oil
1	onion - diced
5	garlic cloves - crushed
1 tsp	thyme leaf
1 Tbsp	paprika
1 tsp	salt
2 pinches	cayenne pepper
2 Tbsps	soy margarine
1 tsp	apple cider vinegar
1/2 cup	tomato puree
1 cup	*Vegetable Stock*

Mix the burger blend with the cold water, then refrigerate for at least 30 minutes, or more.

Cut core out of cabbage and leave head intact. Blanch head in boiling water for at least six minutes. Remove head and allow to cool. Remove ten or twelve best outer leaves. You can trim ribs to make them easier to bend.

Mix burger with oil, diced onions, crushed garlic, thyme, paprika, salt and cayenne pepper. Divide this mixture into 4-5 ounce oblong shapes. Place shaped filling onto center of cabbage leaf, curled side up. Fold over left and right sides and roll leaf forward. Pierce with a toothpick to hold together. Use the margarine to grease a baking dish then pack the stuffed cabbage leaves into the dish.

Casseroles & Stuffed Things

Mix the vinegar and tomato puree with vegetable stock, then pour half this mixture over stuffed cabbage leaves. Preheat an oven to 400°F and bake casserole 45 minutes. After thirty minutes pour other half of the tomato sauce mixture into baking dish. Remove from heat, and cover until ready to serve. [6-12 PORTIONS]

Stuffed Mushrooms Italienne

This stuffed mushroom recipe utilizes silver dollar mushrooms, for hor d'ourves. The caps are easily fill, yet still bite sized.

MEASURE	INGREDIENT
1 lb	silver dollar mushrooms
1/4 cup	olive oil
1/2	onion - diced
6	garlic cloves - diced
1 tsp	salt
1/2 tsp	oregano
1/2 tsp	basil
1/3 cup	soy parmesan cheese - shredded
1/3 cup	bread crumbs
1/2 cup	***Vegetable Stock***

Remove the stems from the mushrooms by twisting away from caps. Chop these stems up and set aside.

Heat oil in a skillet and sauté diced onions, diced garlic, diced mushroom stems, salt and herbs. Remove sauté mix from heat, and allow to cool ten minutes.

Grease a medium sized baking dish and place mushroom caps neatly in dish, underside up (stemside). Thoroughly combine shredded parmesan cheese with bread crumbs and sauté mix, then spoon this combined mixture into each cap. Sprinkle a little more bread crumbs over the top, add one-half cup vegetable stock to baking dish and bake at 450°F for 20 to 30 minutes. Serve as hors d'oeuvres.

Stuffed Peppers with Rice

This simple, yet delicious, recipe provides a fundamental starting point from which to create stuffed peppers.

MEASURE	INGREDIENT
4 large	colored bell peppers
1 cup	*Brown Rice* (uncooked)
3 cups	*Vegetable Stock*
1 Tbsp	soy margarine

Using a small paring knife, carefully cut around pepper stems, and lift out seed core, then remove all loose seeds with a spoon. Blanch peppers in boiling water for 5 minutes or until color begins to change. Remove peppers and plunge into cold water, for later use.

Cook the brown rice in vegetable stock, with one tablespoon of margarine.

Stuff the cooled peppers with the cooked rice, then bake - covered - in a greased baking dish at 400°F for 30 minutes.

Stuffed Portabella Mushroom

Portabella mushrooms have very large caps that are great for stuffing. This recipe uses Whoopie Wrap stew as filling.

MEASURE	INGREDIENT
4 large	portabella mushroom caps
1/4 cup	olive oil
2 cups	*Whoopie Wrap* stew filling
1 cup	soy mozzarella cheese - grated

Carefully remove stems from mushroom caps.

Heat the oil in a large skillet and add the mushroom caps. Cover, reduce heat and sauté 5 minutes. Turn caps and sauté another five minutes.

Casseroles & Stuffed Things

Grease a baking dish and place sautéed mushroom caps underside up. Divide stew filling into four equal parts and spoon filling onto caps. Bake ten minutes in a 450°F oven. Sprinkle grated cheese over stuffed mushrooms and bake another five minutes. [4 PORTIONS]

Tantric Dumplings
A delicious wheat dumpling stuffed with shredded greens, seitan and spices that is served with a sauce featured in this book.

MEASURE	INGREDIENT
3 Tbsps	roasted sesame oil
6	*Basic Seitan* medallions
2 cups	nappa greens - shredded
1 cup	daikon radish - grated
1 Tbsp	ginger root - minced
2 cups	bok choy leaves - shredded
1 bunch	green onions (scallions)
3 Tbsps	soy sauce
1 tsp	apple cider vinegar (or rice vinegar)
1 cup	*Barley* - cooked
1 lb	*Pierogies* dough
2 cups	*Sweet & Sour Sauce*

Heat a skillet (or wok) and add sesame oil. Chop up the seitan into small chunks and sear in the oil; then add shredded nappa, grated daikon radish, minced ginger root, shredded bok choy and chopped scallions. Stir fry this mixture with soy sauce and vinegar, for 2 more minutes. Mix in the cooked barley, then remove from flame. Mixture should be lightly cooked, but not well done. Allow to cool to room temperature.

Roll out chilled pierogi dough to 1/4 inch thickness and cut out 3 inch rounds. Stuff the pierogi rounds by spooning one tablespoon of mixture onto one side of the round. Wet the edge of the dough and fold it over the filling. Crimp the edges with a fork to seal (what is now a) dumpling.

When all dumplings are completed, place them in a large skillet and cover with cold water. Heat skillet slowly and bring it to a boil. Simmer dumplings 5 minutes. Remove and cover with heated Sweet and Sour Sauce.
[MAKES 6-8 DUMPLINGS]

Tofu Tamales
These adorable, stuffed corn husks are like little wrapped presents, hiding a delicious vegan filling.

MEASURE	INGREDIENT
8 -10	corn husks
2 cups	white corn (unsalted hominy)
2 cups	tofu - crumbled
1/2 cup	soy cheese - shredded
2 tsps	salt
1/2 cup	xylitol
tiny pinch	habenero pepper - crushed
1 roll	cooking string (for binding)

Buy some fresh corn on the cob and carefully remove the husks. [Note: cut the corn away from the cobs, and save for another recipe.] We will be using the husks for making tamale wraps, in this recipe! To prepare the husks for wrapping, plunge them in boiling water for 5 minutes.

Drain hominy and put them in a mixing bowl. Add crumbled tofu, shredded soy cheese, salt, xylitol (birch) sugar, and a tiny pinch of habenero pepper. Combine this hominy-tofu together, by mixing thoroughly.

Place the corn husk down on a flat surface. Put another husk directly on top of the first husk. Next, drop 3 tablespoons of the hominy-tofu mixture into the center of the husks. Now fold the two sides over the center, then pull the bottom up and the top down. This forms a cute package! Finally, tie the tamale together by wrapping a single cooking string, around the center and tying a bow.

Casseroles & Stuffed Things

There are 2 methods that you can use to cook these food packets off. The first method is by placing them in a large steamer over boiling water, covered for 20 minutes.

Method two, is by placing all the tamales in a large skillet and adding enough water to almost cover them. Cover the skillet and simmer 15 minutes, or until water is reduced.
[4-6 PORTIONS]

Tofu / Tempeh Parmigiani
This recipe substitutes thinly sliced tofu and/or tempeh for eggplant.

MEASURE	INGREDIENT
3-4 slices	tofu - thinly sliced
1 cup	flour
1 cup	soy milk
2 cups	bread crumbs
1/4 cup	soy oil (for frying)
1/2 cup	*Marinara Sauce*
1/4 cup	soy mozzarella cheese - grated

Dredge tofu through flour, soy milk and bread crumbs. Fry tofu in oil, on both sides and drain.

Layer a small baking dish with marinara, then tofu and grated cheese, then marinara again. Reheat process until complete. Bake at 400°F for 20 minutes.
[1-2 PORTIONS]

Tofu 'Tuna' Casserole

**Many of our childhood memories include a tuna noodle casserole.
This vegan recipe has all the flavor of the original.**

MEASURE	INGREDIENT
1/2	onion - diced
2 cups	mushrooms - sliced
2 Tbsps	soy oil
1 tsp	salt
1/3 tsp	black pepper
1/2 tsp	powdered thyme
2 cups	lasagna noodles (cooked)
1 cup	**_Vegetable Stock_**
2 cups	tofu - cubed
1 & 1/2 cups	peas - frozen
1 Tbsp	cornstarch - dissolved in
	1 cup of cold Vegetable Stock
2 cups	cornflakes

Sauté the onions and mushrooms in preheated oil, with salt, pepper and thyme.
When onion's are translucent, pour in one cup of vegetable stock and add the
cubed tofu. Lower heat and simmer for 10 minutes.

Grease a small casserole dish and layer down 1 cup of cooked noodles. Next
add a layer of the finished sauté mix, then evenly distribute half of the frozen
peas over layer. Add another layer of noodles, then the remainder of sauté and
peas. Top with the remaining noodles.

Evenly distribute the cornstarch / vegetable stock slurry over the entire casserole.
Crumble up the cornflakes and layer this over the top of the casserole. Bake in a
400° oven for 30 minutes. [4-6 PORTIONS]

Tuscan Wrap

This recipe is a combination of old world and new world traditions. Combining Mediterranean, Oriental, and Meso American characteristics, this one is for the fusion enthusiast.

MEASURE	INGREDIENT
1 large head	broccoli - quarter cut
2 large	leeks - long strip cut
1	onion - thin sliced
1 large	portabella mushroom - thinly sliced
1	red bell pepper - sliced
1 small bunch	asparagus spears - slant cut
1/2 lb package	firm tofu - long strip cut
4 large	tortillas
1 cup	*Grill Goddess Sauce*
1 cup	*Pepper Steak Sauce*

Cut broccoli into four quarters. Thoroughly wash, then slice leeks lengthwise, into long strips. Cut onion into thick rounds. Cut portabella mushroom in thin strips. Slice up bell pepper. Cut asparagus spears diagonally. Slice tofu into long strips

Grease a broiling pan and preheat broiler setting to medium, then place all prepared veggies and tofu strips into pan and cover with grill goddess sauce. Broil until done, turning occasionally. Heat tortillas and fill with broiled veggies. Roll up tortillas and cover with pepper steak sauce. Bake - foil covered - tortillas at 400° in broiler, for 10 more minutes. [4 PORTIONS]

Vegetable Bean Loaf

An alternative to the soy 'meat' loaf, this hearty loaf is packed with nutrition, and will feed up to ten people. Makes a great centerpiece for holiday dinners.

MEASURE	INGREDIENT
4 cups	beans (or lentils) - cooked
3 cups	potatoes (precooked) - diced
2 cups	carrots - grated
1 cup	onion - diced
1/2 cup	parsley - chopped
1 cup	peas - frozen
1/2 cup	whole wheat flour
2 Tbsps	vital wheat gluten
1 & 1/2 cups	bread crumbs
1 Tbsp	salt
1/2 tsp	black pepper
2 Tbsps	soy margarine

Use any bean, remembering that some cooked beans have strong flavors. The type or combination of beans you choose will tailor the flavor of this recipe.

Mix all ingredients, pack into a greased loaf pan and bake for an hour at 400°F. Serve hot from the oven, with **Walnut Gravy** or **Brown Gravy**.
[8-12 PORTIONS]

Vegetable Bean Burritos

This Mexican staple has become very familiar in America in recent decades. This recipe is a basic version.

MEASURE	INGREDIENT
2 extra-large	tortillas
1 & 1/2 cups	black beans (or refried beans) - cooked
1/2 cup	mixed vegetables - diced
1/2 cup	fresh corn - cut
1/2 cup	soy cheese - shredded
1 cup	**Brown Rice** - cooked
1/4 cup	**Salsa**
(as needed)	**Sour Cream**, **Guacamole**,
(")	**Salsa** (for sides)
(as needed)	fresh tomatoes and
(")	shredded lettuce (for garnish)

This recipe makes two large burritos. Heat the tortillas briefly in a hot oven to make them pliable. Lay tortilla down flat and fill each center with beans, diced veggies, corn, cheese, rice and salsa. Fold up sides of tortillas and roll closest end around center to meet other end. Pack tightly.

Grease a baking pan and bake burritos, covered with the rest of the cheese and salsa for 20 minutes at 400°F. When finished, serve with sour cream, guacamole and salsa sides, topped with diced tomatoes and shredded lettuce.

Whoopie Wrap

This wild and wacky wrap is one of our restaurant's most popular dinners. A real crowd pleaser.

MEASURE	INGREDIENT
1/2 lb	TVP burger blend - dry mix
2 cups	ice cold water
1/4 cup	olive oil
2	onions - chopped
1 each:	green, red, yellow bell peppers - chopped
4	garlic cloves - diced
1 Tbsp	salt
1/2 tsp	black pepper
2 tsps	thyme leaf
2 tsps	marjoram
2	portabella mushrooms - sliced
2 cups	*Stewed Tomatoes* - hand crumbled
1/2 of 1 lb block	tofu - cubed
1 & 1/2 cups	*Brown Rice* - cooked
4-6 large	tortillas
1/2 cup	soy cheese - shredded

Mix the burger blend with the cold water, then refrigerate for at least 30 minutes, or more. In a soup pot, preheat the oil and begin sautéing chopped onions, peppers, diced garlic, with only half the herbs and spices. Break up raw burger into pot and cover immediately. Cook on medium low for five minutes. This will firm up the burger blend.

Slice up the portabella mushrooms and add them to the sauté mix, return cover and simmer for five more minutes. Next, pour in hand crumbled tomatoes, with remaining herbs and spices, and slowly bring (what is now a) stew to a boil. Combine cubed tofu and precooked rice with the stew, then simmer on low heat for another 10 minutes.

Heat the tortilla wraps and grease a baking tray. Divide the stew into equal parts and fill the center of each tortilla. Sprinkle the grated soy cheese over each filling. Roll the edge nearest your body forward until wrap is tightly rolled. This action pushes the filling towards the ends. Bake at 400°F for 25 minutes. [4-6 PORTIONS]

From the Grill

Introduction

The grill or barbecue has always been associated with the primitive carnivorous diet of Americans. What could be easier than grilling a piece of meat? Together with the broiler, the grill seems to be the most popular method of preparing animal flesh for consumption.

The grill can also be a wonderful and versatile tool for vegetarians. Vegetables and meat analogs grill beautifully, imparting distinctive flavors to the meals you can prepare. In this chapter you'll learn the principals of marinating, using glazes, reverse marinating, preparing foods for the grill and perfect grilling technique.

Learn how to become the master of the summer barbecue, impressing friends and family with great tasting and satisfying vegan meals. Mesmerize them with your knowledge and skill while demonstrating the power of the grill for great vegan cooking.

Grilling Tips

There are some general guidelines concerning the use of the open grill or barbecue. Having a properly heated grill surface, grilling accessories, food preparation skills and good technique are all necessary in achieving good results. The following will help you get started:

Gas Grill Setup

Use ceramic briskets or volcanic rock for coals. Start on high with grill cover down. Reduce heat after ten minutes to medium and leave cover on until ready to grill. If indoor, make sure there is adequate exhaust ventilation.

Kettle, Hibachi or backyard fireplace: This type of grill requires the use of charcoal which must first be ignited with a small fire strong enough to start burning the coals. The most common method is to use a starting fluid which, when ignited, provides a short lived, but strong enough flame to ignite the coals. Other starting methods include using a blowtorch on the charcoal for a few seconds or burning a small pyramid of kindling material surrounded by charcoal.

In any case, the charcoal, once ignited, should be piled together to build up heat. When the charcoal is substantially burning, it can be spread over the grill bottom. The cover can then be lowered and the grill surface allowed to heat up.

Grill Accessories

A surface cover, metal spatulas, tongs, grill brush, heat mitten, pot holder, temperature guage and timer.

Grill Temperature

Here's an easy way of determining surface temperature: hold the palm of your hand over the surface grate. If you can count to 4 before you have to pull your hand away, the temperature is high. If you can count up to 8 --- surface temperature is medium. If you can hold your hand over surface for longer than a 12 count, surface is too cold to cook anything.

Heat Control

Gas grills usually have two or more controls for heat. Many grills have adjustable grate heights for temperature control. For non-gas powered grills, piling or thinning out the charcoal to one side of the grill will supply two operating temperatures on the surface. Moving the food around provides the control. In any event, having multiple control over the surface temperature is essential.

Food Preparation

Any food about to be grilled should be brought up to room temperature or pre-heated before grilling. Attempting to grill anything cold usually results in the food sticking to the grill.

Many vegetables should be parboiled before grilling or marinating. This creates a more evenly cooked result. Hard vegetables such as potato, yam, peppers, onion and carrots should always be parboiled. Semi-hard veggies such as broccoli, cauliflower or asparagus also require parboiling or steaming before grilling.

Softer foods such as zucchini, summer squash, eggplant tomato, tofu, gluten, seitan, tempeh, pineapple, orange slices or banana do not require parboiling. These foods should be at least 70°F or more before grilling, or they will stick to grill surface.

From the Grill

Marinating

Marinating is a method of preparing foods to be grilled with a specific flavor. Soaking foods in an diluted liquid - from thirty minutes to overnight - will impart the flavor of the liquid to the soaking food.

The numerous variety of marinades include the use of vegetable stock, salts, sugars, fruit juices, spices, herbs, vinegars, prepared sauces and oils.

Reverse Marinade

If you want to grill something without first marinating it but want all the flavor of a marinade, first grill the food with a glaze. Once grilled, the food can be baked in a hot oven with a mixture of the marinade and the glaze for 15 minutes. This will create a perfect result.

Glazing

A glaze is a thickened sauce or marinade applied to food when grilling. A basting brush is the best tool for glazing. As food grills, glaze is painted on. Thicken marinades with cornstarch to create glazes with the same flavor.

Smoked Flavoring

Mesquite, hickory or other flavored wood chips can be thrown into the grill before cooking food to impart special flavors. Soak chips before using.

Burgers & Hotdogs
Vegan burgers and hotdogs are as satisfying as their animal-based counterparts.

MEASURE	INGREDIENT
(as needed)	vegan-style burgers and hotdogs
small amount	soy oil

Start with a preheated grill and a surface temperature of medium hot. Burgers and franks should be at room temperature to prevent sticking to grill surface. Brush or spray oil on grill and underside of burger or frank.

Grill burgers for at least three minutes before turning, cook evenly on both sides. Franks should be turned enough to impart even grill marks on all sides.

Grilled Leek Portabella Soup

Surprised to see a soup in this section? That's because this soup's almost entirely made from grilled contents.

MEASURE	INGREDIENT
2	red bell peppers - grilled, skinned & chopped
6	portabella mushrooms - thin sliced
4 bunches	leeks - washed & strip cut
2 large	onions - thick cut
1 & 1/2 cups	*Grill Goddess Sauce*
2 qts	*Vegetable Stock*
4	fresh corn cobs (in husk)
2 Tbsps	cornstarch - dissolved in
	2 cups cold water
(to taste)	salt & black pepper

Grill peppers whole on all sides and remove to cool in a closed paper bag.

Thinly slice mushrooms; clean leeks thoroughly, then slice them lengthwise into long strips; peel onion, then slice into 1/4 inch thick rounds.

Combine one-half cup of prepared sauce with one cup of the vegetable stock into a bowl, then immerse mushroom slices, leeks and mushrooms in this marinade.

While veggies are marinating, peel the outer leaves off corn cobs - leaving several inner leaves intact. Place cobs on the medium-hot grill and grill all sides for several minutes. Set aside when cooked, and allow corn to cool.

Place marinated onions on grill surface, then baste with the marinade until well grilled. Set onions aside on a large bowl. Now grill the portabella slices, basting with the marinade, until soft and evenly lined. Dump grilled mushrooms into the

From the Grill

bowl, with the grilled onions. Next, grill the leek strips while basting with the remaining marinade, until sufficiently done and put them in the bowl.

Mix remaining marinade with stock, then heat to a slow boil, in a soup pot. When marinade-stock is heated to a boil, combine grilled vegetables with soup, then reduce heat to a simmer. Cut the kernels off the cooled corn cobs, and these to the simmering soup.

Next remove the peppers from the paper bag and pull out the stems and seeds. Using your paring knife and thumb, remove skins. Chop up skinned peppers and add them to the soup.

Bring the soup to a slow boil, then reduce heat and simmer 15 minutes. When ready, slowly stir in cornstarch slurry into simmering soup. Simmer another five minutes. Adjust flavor with salt and pepper, then serve. [MAKES 2-1/2 QTS]

Grilled Mexican Fajitas
As a complete dinner or to accompany a multi-course feast, this dish presents distinct and unique flavors.

MEASURE	INGREDIENT
1	onion - thick sliced
1	fresh tomato - thick sliced
1	zucchini - thin sliced
1	yellow squash - thin sliced
1/2 cup	*Mexican Sauce*
3	*Mexican Gluten Strips*
1 package	tortillas (taco size)
1 cup	lettuce - shredded

Have the grill hot and ready. Slice the onion and tomato into thick rounds, then slice zucchini and yellow squash into thin rounds. Grill these vegetable slices evenly on both sides using the prepared sauce as an unthickened glaze. When vegetables are done, remove to a bowl with tongs.

Prepare Mexican-style gluten strips, and add these to the bowl with the grilled veggies. Veggies may be sliced up once grilled. Serve with preheated tortillas, **Salsa**, shredded lettuce, with sides of **Brown Rice** and **Mexican Pinto Bean Soup**, for a complete meal. [1-2 PORTIONS]

Happy Family Kebabs
This skewered kebab features chunks of veggie meats, alternated with onions, peppers, mushrooms and tomatoes.

MEASURE	INGREDIENT
1	**Perfect Gluten Flank Steak** (4 pieces) - chunked
1/2 of 1 lb block	tofu (4 pieces) - chunk cut
1/2 of 1 lb block	tempeh (4 pieces) - chunk cut
1	onion (4 pieces) - cut
1	green bell pepper (4 pieces) - cut
1	red bell pepper (4 pieces) - cut
2	skewers (stainless or bamboo)
4 pieces	**Basic Seitan** - chunk cut
4 small	mushrooms - whole (quarter cut if large)
1 cup	**Vegetable Stock**
4	cherry tomatoes
(as needed)	**Jamaican Jungle Sauce** (for glazing)

Cut gluten steak, tofu and tempeh into 4 individual pieces. Cut up the onion and peppers into 4 pieces each. Skewer chunked seitan, onion, gluten, green bell pepper, tofu, single mushroom, tempeh and red bell pepper, then repeat the alternating sequence.

Using a large skillet, steam the kebabs in vegetable stock, until the green peppers change color. [Note: stock will impart additional flavor to the kebabs.] If using a tall pot, substitute the stock with about 1 quart of water, as the kebabs can't benefit from the stock. In either case, after kebabs are parboil-steamed, top-off each skewer tips with two cherry tomatoes.

From the Grill

Paint the kebabs with a chosen glaze - such as **Jamaican Jungle Sauce** - then grill on low heat, turning several times until done. Serve over **Brown Rice**.

Steaks

Gluten, tempeh, tofu and seitan make excellent steaks, when grilled. Marinades, ingredient flavoring, glazes and meat cuts, all play important roles when grilling these meats. To learn how to prepare these meats in a variety of ways, refer to the chapter on Vegan Meats. These high protein, low fat meats are easily grilled. Just follow the section on Grill Tips, for rules in grilling. The following are examples:

Barbecued Gluten Steak
Try this recipe next time you fire up the grill.
You won't be disappointed.

MEASURE	INGREDIENT
1	*Perfect Gluten Flank Steak*
(as needed)	*Vegetable Stock*
1/4 cup	*Basic Barbecue Sauce*

Note: Gluten steak is created and cooked in vegetable stock to flavor, as described in the Vegan Meats chapter. Have steak at - or above - room temperature, before grilling.

With a medium hot grill surface, paint prepared sauce on side to be grilled, then place steak on grill. Paint top side and grill for about three minutes. To avoid tears, turn steak over by loosening the underside first, with a spatula, then flipping it over. Grill this side and baste top side again. Steak is now done. If you'd like, you can turn steak perpendicular, flip, then grill again, to create cross lines.

Grilled Tofu Steak

This recipe demonstrates the effectiveness of marinating with a flavored liquid, then converting this liquid into a grill glaze.

MEASURE	INGREDIENT
1 lb package	extra-firm tofu - slab cut
1/2 cup	*Grill Goddess Sauce*
(as needed)	*Vegetable Stock* (for simmering)
1 Tbsp	cornstarch

Cut the tofu into four steaks and soak these steaks in the grill goddess sauce for 30 minutes, or overnight. Be sure the steaks are at room temperature or above. Prior to grilling, preheat steaks in an oven (or skillet) by simmering in a little vegetable stock (or water) that's been mixed with the prepared sauce.

Mix the cornstarch with the prepared sauce and heat this in a pan on the stove until it boils and thickens. Preheat grill to medium hot and place warmed steaks on the grill. Baste steaks with thickened sauce and flip when grill lines appear. Turn steak perpendicular and flip again to create cross lines. Steak is done when grilled surfaces are well marked.

Teriyaki Tempeh

Here's a great way to enjoy grilled tempeh.

MEASURE	INGREDIENT
10 oz block	tempeh - sliced
1/4 cup	*Teriyaki Sauce*

Thinly slice tempeh into two or three wide sheets depending on the original thickness of the tempeh block. Paint one side, of each sheet, with teriyaki sauce.

Place glazed side down on a medium hot grill. Baste top side and turn sheet perpendicular after one or two minutes of grilling. Flip tempeh and repeat process,

From the Grill

basting often. Serve grilled tempeh sheets over **Brown Rice**, with steamed veggies, or build a club sandwich.

Polynesian Seitan Medallions
High protein seitan morsels prepared and grilled Polynesian style.

MEASURE	INGREDIENT
4-6	*Seitan Supreme* medallions
1/4 cup	*Polynesian Sauce*
1/2 cup	*Vegetable Stock* (for preheating)

Note: As seitan has a delicate surface, it must be brought up to a higher temperature before grilling.

Place the seitan one-half cup of vegetable stock, then bring stock to a hard boil.

When seitan is sufficiently preheated, remove and paint the medallions with the prepared sauce, then grill on a medium hot grill. Baste and turn the seitan until well marked. Serve seitan as the meat portion in a dinner.

Mexican Gluten Strips
This is an excellent substitute for chicken or beef in Mexican recipes.

MEASURE	INGREDIENT
1	*Perfect Gluten Flank Steak*
1/2 cup	*Mexican Sauce*

Have steak at - or above - room temperature, before grilling.

Paint the steak with the prepared sauce on one side and lay this side down on the surface of a medium hot grill. Baste top side and flip after a few minutes. Turn and flip once more after basting.

193

Remove steak from grill and place it on a cutting board. Cut steaks into strips and use these strips to stuff a taco, enchilada, burrito or quesadilla.

Quesadilla

The quesadilla is a traditional tortilla turnover from Mexico. Stuffed with a variety of fillings, it is easy to prepare and can serve as an appetizer, sandwich or a complete dinner! Grilled or baked, they can be unique and delicious. Here are two quesadilla recipes that explore the possibilities of this traditional Mexican wrap.

Mucho Mexican Quesadilla
The Quesadilla is the Mexican answer to the sandwich. They can be stuffed with a variety of fillings. This recipe demonstrates the possibilities.

MEASURE	INGREDIENT
1 large	tortilla
1/4 cup	**Mexican Sauce** (for basting)
1/4 cup	refried beans
4-6 ozs	**Taco-Style Ground 'Beef'**
2 Tbsps each:	vegetables - diced
1/4 cup	soy cheddar cheese - shredded

Lay the tortilla out flat. Work on top side only. Paint the tortilla with a table-spoon of Mexican sauce. Spread the refried beans over one half the tortilla. Apply the ground 'beef' on top of the beans. Sprinkle the diced veggies (onions, peppers, tomatoes, cucumbers, corn) and shredded soy cheese over the refried beans. Fold the empty half of the tortilla, over the layer half.

Note: If the tortilla and/or its contents are cold, quesadilla can be prebaked before grilling. This - preheating - enables a quick 'grill-off', which results in evenly heated contents, without the burning of tortilla wrap!

From the Grill

Use a preheated grill - at medium temperature - and grill tortilla-turnover on one side. Turn quesadilla on a perpendicular angle and grill a couple of minutes more. Flip quesadilla and repeat process until quesadilla is well marked and well heated. Serve with sides of **Salsa**, **Guacamole** and **Sour Cream**.

Spinach & Gluten Quesadilla
Another kind of quesadilla. This one features a filling of sautéed spinach, tasty grilled gluten steak and soy cheese.

MEASURE	INGREDIENT
4 ozs	**Mexican Gluten Strips** - chopped
1/3 cup	spinach - chopped
1 large	tortilla
2 Tbsps	**Mexican Sauce**
1/4 cup	soy monterey jack cheese - grated

Prepare Mexican-style gluten strips, chop up and steam the spinach, then set these ingredients aside. Next, lay the tortilla out flat and paint the entire upper side with Mexican sauce. Sprinkle some grated cheese over one-half of the tortilla, then evenly distribute the prepared spinach over this same half. Chop up the gluten, then layer over spinach and follow-up with the rest of the grated cheese.

Note: If the tortilla and/or its contents are cold, quesadilla can be prebaked before grilling. This - preheating - enables a quick 'grill-off', which results in evenly heated contents, without the burning of tortilla wrap!

Use a preheated grill - at medium temperature - and grill tortilla-turnover on one side. Turn quesadilla on a perpendicular angle and grill a couple of minutes more. Flip quesadilla and repeat process until quesadilla is well marked and well heated. Serve with sides of **Salsa**, **Guacamole** and **Sour Cream**.

Vegetable Kebabs

Great meal from the summer barbecue or the oven broiler. Whether marinated or simply glazed on the grill, these skewered vegetables pack a lot of flavor and nutrition.

MEASURE	INGREDIENT
1 large	carrot (parboiled) - thick slant cut
1 medium	yam (or sweet potato) (parboiled) - sliced
(as needed)	*Grill Goddess Sauce*
1	onion - thick sliced
1	green bell pepper - chunk sliced
1	red bell pepper - chunk sliced
8-12 large	mushrooms - chunk sliced
1 small head	cauliflower - chunked
1 head	broccoli - chunked
1	zucchini - sliced
1	summer squash - sliced
12-20	cherry tomatoes
4-6 large	skewers (stainless or bamboo)
(as needed)	flavored wood chips
	(optional - for barbecue)
(to taste)	salt (for sprinkling on finished kebabs)

Note: Hard vegetables should be parboiled for 5 minutes before marinating, grilling or broiling. Parboiling hard vegetables, insures that they're evenly cooked, and avoids excessive burning of surfaces when grilling.   In addition, the resulting parboiled vegetables' are moist and easily accept the flavor of the glazing sauce (or marinade). Softer veggies or fruits - such as squash, tomatoes, eggplant, pineapple or orange slices - need not be parboiled.

When marinating, always parboil hard vegetables first, before soaking in marinade.

From the Grill

The assortment of vegetables listed in recipe should be cut into appropriate sizes, and proportioned, so each skewer can receive an equal combination when assembled.

Divide the parboiled and raw vegetables into equal amounts, and assemble on each skewer. Make sure kebabs are at - or above - room temperature. You can let them stand for one hour before grilling or they can be preheated - in an moderately heated oven - for ten to fifteen minutes.

Have your grill or broiler preheated to medium hot. Place kebabs on the grill and paint glaze* on kebabs with a pastry brush. Use tongs and metal spatula to grab and turn kebabs. Baste often. Toss optional wood chips over heated coals to impart a smokier flavor. Once grilled on all sides, kebabs are ready to eat. Serve as the main entrée, with **Brown Rice**, or as a side to a sautéd dinner!

Kebabs should be served immediately, after grilling; or reheated in an oven. To reheat in an oven, pour a small amount of liquid (diluted marinade, vegetable stock, water), into an appropriately sized baking dish, then place grilled kebabs in, and cover dish.   The oven temperature should be at a moderate setting, wherein the kebabs should be adequately heated within 15-20 minutes.

*If you want to turn your marinade liquid into a glaze, add one or two tablespoons of cornstarch to the cold marinade. Bring this to a boil to thicken the glaze. This can be stored refrigerated for later use.

Sautés

Introduction

Sautés are the main conduit for creativity in any restaurant environment. A sauté can be simple or relatively complex. In this chapter, you'll use the proper combination of materials to create great tasting meals that are unique, yet ethnically accented.

Sauté techniques, as well as steaming, braising and stir frying methods, are also explored here. Individually portioned dinners are usually prepared on the stove top in a skillet, wok, or sauté pan. When combined in various ways, you will see how prepared meats [see chapter on Vegan Meats], fresh produce, herbs, spices, condiments, vegetable stock and spirits, enable the chef to discover a world of global-cuisines.

By working through recipes in this chapter, you'll learn about preparing vegetables and veggie meats; how different shapes, create different effects and cooking times. And of course, sauces - the key to many sautés - will be explored here as well.

Note: Whenever a cooking process calls for sautéing, this will require the preheating of both sauté pan (or other prerequisite cooking vessel) and cooking oil. The pan - and oil - must first be brought up to an acceptable temperature, whereupon, the ingredients are only then considered ready for cooking.

American Stew
This hearty stew can be cooked in about twenty minutes.

MEASURE	INGREDIENT
1	potato
1/4 cup	baby lima beans - (frozen)
2 Tbsps	soy oil
1/2 large	onion - chopped
2	celery stalks - chopped
1	carrot - chopped
3 pieces	**Seitan Supreme** medallions - cut
2 pinches	salt
2 pinches	thyme leaf
8	string beans - slant cut
2 Tbsps	whole wheat flour
1/2 cup	**Vegetable Stock**
1/4 cup	peas

Slice a skinned potato into large chunks, then parboil with the frozen lima beans, for about 10 minutes. Pour off water and set parboiled vegetables aside.

Remove tips and stems, then slant cut string beans and set aside.

Heat a sauté pan (or skillet) and add the oil, then add chopped onion, celery and carrot. Turn heat to medium low and cover pan. Shake covered pan - or stir - until onions soften-up a little. Slice seitan into six or eight pieces, then add seitan to sautéing mix. Work the seitan to the bottom the pan to sear meat surfaces.

Continue cooking this mixture for several minutes, then thoroughly mix in salt and thyme. Next, mix in the parboiled potatoes and lima beans with string beans and flour, then continue sautéing for 3 minutes.

Slowly pour vegetable stock into sauté mix, then stir in the peas. Turn up heat until contents - begin - to bubble, then immediately lower heat and cover. Sim-

Sautés

mer - what is now a - thickening stew for several minutes more, until carrots are soft. If stew becomes too thick, gradually add a little water and continue cooking until stew is the right consistency. [1-2 PORTIONS]

Balti Stir Fry
A quick and easy sauté with authentic flavors of northern India.

MEASURE	INGREDIENT
2 Tbsps	soy oil
1/4 cup	onions - chopped
1	carrot - thinly sliced
1/4 cup mixed:	green, yellow and red bell peppers - diced
1/2 cup	cauliflower - sliced
10 each	string beans - trimmed & half cut
2-3 Tbsps	chickpeas - cooked
1/4 cup	yam (or sweet potato) - slivered
2 pinches	salt
1-2 tsps	curry powder
1/4 cup	**Vegetable Stock**
1/4 cup	peas
1/4 cup	**Stewed Tomatoes** - hand crushed peeled & mashed
1 tsp	cornstarch - dissolved in 3 Tbsps cold water

Heat a skillet or sauté pan and add the oil. Begin to stir fry the chopped onions, thinly sliced carrots and diced peppers at medium-high heat. After two minutes, add sliced cauliflower, trimmed and half cut string beans, cooked chickpeas, slivered yams and salt. Shake pan to flip contents frequently or stir to prevent burning.

Next add the curry powder and flip contents for several seconds to lightly brown spices. Now pour in the vegetable stock, add the peas and hand crushed stewed tomatoes, then lower heat to medium. Cover and simmer for five more minutes. Stir in cornstarch slurry and cook another minute to thicken juices. Serve over cooked **Brown Rice** or basmati rice. [2 PORTIONS]

Couscous Succotash

A sauté of sliced and diced Mediterranean vegetables, ethnic spices and couscous. A bright and flavorful dinner.

MEASURE	INGREDIENT
1/4 cup	sundried tomatoes - soaked & chopped
2 Tbsps	olive oil
3 slices	red onion - chopped
1/4 cup	colored bell peppers - diced
2	garlic cloves - crushed
2 pinches each:	cumin, allspice, salt & black pepper
1/4 cup	carrot - thin rounds
1/4 cup	yam (or sweet potato) - slivered
1/4 cup	tiny cauliflowerettes
1/4 cup	string beans - trimmed & slant cut
1/4 cup	chickpeas - cooked
1/2	lemon - juiced
1/3 cup	couscous (uncooked)
1/2 cup	**Vegetable Stock**
1/4 cup	peas

Put the sundried tomatoes in a small sauce pan with enough water to just cover the tomatoes, then bring contents to a boil. Reduce heat and simmer for 3 minutes, covered. Remove from heat and let steep for another 5 minutes before draining and use.

Sautés

Heat a skillet or sauté pan and add the oil. Chop the onions and begin to fry them with diced peppers. After two minutes add crushed garlic and spices. Adjust heat to medium low and mix in the thin cut carrots, slivered yam, cauliflowerettes, trimmed and slant cut string beans, chopped sundried tomatoes, precooked chickpeas and lemon juice. Cover and sauté 5 more minutes.

Pour couscous over sauté mix, add vegetable stock and peas, then cover and simmer for 3 more minutes. To set couscous, turn off heat and allow to stand 5 minutes covered. Shake pan or use a fork to fluff up mixture. [2 PORTIONS]

Creole Madness

This dish explores some Cajun and Creole styles. The thinly sliced vegetables, diced veggie meats and hot peppers make this a highly charged meal.

MEASURE	INGREDIENT
2 Tbsps	soy oil
1/2	onion - thin sliced
1/2 each:	green, yellow and red bell peppers - thin sliced
1	jalapeno pepper - diced
1/4 cup each:	tofu, tempeh, **Perfect Gluten Flank Steak** and **Basic Seitan** - diced
1-2 tsps	cajun spice blend
1/2	habenero pepper (optional) - diced
2 pinches	salt
1/4 cup	summer squash - shredded
1/4 cup	zucchini - shredded
1 small	carrot - shredded
1/4 cup	**Vegetable Stock**
1/4 cup	**Brown Rice** - cooked

Heat a sauté pan (or skillet), then add oil, thinly sliced onions and peppers, then stir fry for several minutes. Next, add veggie meats, cajun spice blend, dice habenero pepper (optional ingredient, for extra hot effect), and salt. After a few more minutes of frying, stir in shredded summer squash, zucchini, carrot with vegetable stock. Reduce to medium heat, cover, and continue cooking for three more minutes. Stir in precooked brown rice, then cook for two more minutes. Serve immediately. [1-2 PORTIONS]

Curried Enlightenment
This creamed curry sauté is reminiscent of traditional southeast Asian meat curries.

MEASURE	INGREDIENT
1/2 cup	potato - chopped & parboiled
1 Tbsp	soy oil
3-4 whole	onion hearts
1	carrot - shard cut
3 large	cauliflowerettes
1/4 cup	spinach - shredded
1/4 cup	string beans - chopped
2 Tbsps	chickpeas - cooked
2 Tbsps	peas
6-8 chunks	*Basic Seitan*
2 tsps	curry powder
2 pinches	salt
1/3 cup	*Vegetable Stock*
3 Tbsps	*Sour Cream*

Chop up and parboil potatoes, then set aside.

Heat a sauté pan (or skillet), then add oil, whole onion hearts. Meanwhile, cut carrot into shards, then add to skillet. Reduce heat to low, then add cauliflowerettes. Cover and simmer 5 minutes. Next, add shredded spinach, chopped string beans, cooked chickpeas, peas, prepared potatoes, chunked seitan, curry powder, salt., vegetable stock, then mix in sour cream. Increase heat, cover, then continue cooking for about 3 more minutes, to thicken. Serve over a bed of cooked *Brown Rice*. [1-2 PORTIONS]

Darwin's Natural Selection

Dedicated to the famous vegetarian and founder of the theory of evolution, this sauté contains many of the native ingredients from Darwin's historic trip to South America and the Galapagos Islands.

MEASURE	INGREDIENT
2 Tbsps	soy oil
5 small slices	yam (or sweet potato) - thin sliced
4-5 pieces	carrot - shard cut
1/4 cup	pineapple - chunked
5-6 small pieces	colored bell pepper - sliced
2	**Seitan Supreme** medallions - chopped
1/4	**Perfect Gluten Flank Steak** - chopped
1	plantain - sliced
1/4 cup	cashews - raw
1 pinch	salt
1 pinch	allspice
1 pinch	cinnamon
2 Tbsps	fresh corn - cut
2-5	tofu cutlets (prefried)
1 whole	orange - juiced
1/4 cup	pineapple juice
1 tsp	cornstarch (or arrowroot powder)
1/4 cup	**Vegetable Stock**
2 Tbsps	brewed coffee (strong)
2 Tbsps	coconut milk

Heat a sauté pan (or skillet), then add oil, thinly sliced yams, carrot shards, pineapple chunks, sliced bell peppers, chopped seitan medallions and gluten steak, sliced plantain, cashews, salt and spices. After 3 minutes add corn and prefried tofu cutlets. Next, cover and braise everything with fresh squeezed orange juice

and pineapple juice. Mix the cornstarch with the cold vegetable stock, brewed coffee, and coconut milk. Add this mixture to the sauté and simmer, covered, for 3 minutes. Serve over a bed of cooked **Brown Rice** or toss with pasta.
[1-2 PORTIONS]

The Joe Hercules
This super charged, high protein sauté is centered around a 12 ounce burger patty that's stuffed with veggies, and simmered in an herb sauce with shredded vegetables.

MEASURE	INGREDIENT
6 ozs	TVP burger blend - dry mix
1 & 1/2 cups	ice cold water
1/4 cup mixed:	onions, bell peppers, mushrooms - minced
1/2 tsp	garlic clove - minced
1 tsp	cajun spice blend
3 Tbsps	olive oil
3 pinches mixed:	thyme, oregano, marjoram and basil leaf
2 cups mixed:	carrots (julienned), onions, leeks, portabella mushrooms, zucchini, string beans, & bell peppers - chopped
1/2 cup	raw spinach - chopped
1/2 cup	raw kale - chopped
3-4	broccoli buds
1/2 tsp	garlic clove - minced
2 pinches mixed:	salt & black pepper
1/2 cup	**Vegetable Stock**
3 Tbsps	tomato puree
1 tsp	cornstarch - dissolved in 3 Tbsps cold water

Mix the burger blend with the cold water, then refrigerate for at least 30 minutes, or more.

Sautés

Combine minced veggies and half teaspoon minced garlic with cajun spice blend, then thoroughly mix into the raw burger. Form burger into a patty and flatten into an oval shape.

Heat a sauté pan (or skillet), add oil, then place the burger patty into the pan, reduce heat and cover pan.

When one side of patty has browned, flip burger, add herbs, mixed veggies, chopped spinach and kale, broccoli buds, the other half teaspoon of minced garlic, salt and pepper. Cover pan then continue cooking on low heat for 5 more minutes.

Add the vegetable stock and tomato puree, cover and simmer 5-7 more minutes. Finally, add the cornstarch slurry and cook one more minute to thicken sauce. [1-2 PORTIONS]

The Etruscan
This lively sauté combines fresh Mediterranean vegetables with the sundried tomato 'Etruscan Sauce'.

MEASURE	INGREDIENT
1 Tbsp	olive oil
5 slices	zucchini
5 pieces	carrot - shard cut
1 small	portabella mushroom - thick sliced
1 small head	broccoli - quartered
5	asparagus spears - 1/3 cut
5 leaves	escarole - course chopped
5-10	string beans - trimmed & halved
5 small pieces	tofu (prefried)
5 small pieces	**Perfect Gluten Flank Steak** (prefried)
1 handful	spinach - fresh
1/4 cup	**Vegetable Stock**
3 Tbsps	**Etruscan Sauce**

Heat a sauté pan (or skillet), add oil, then fry sliced zucchini pieces on one side and turn over.   Lower heat, then add shard cut carrots and thick sliced portabella mushrooms. Cover and slow cook 3 minutes.

Toss in a quarter cut broccoli head, asparagus (that's been cut into 3 sections), coursely chopped escarole leaves, then string beans which have been trimmed and cut into two pieces. Shake covered pan vigorously (or stir occasionally) to prevent sticking and burning, and continue cooking another 3 minutes.

Next add the prefried tofu and gluten steak pieces with handfull of spinach, then cover and cook 3 more minutes. Pour in vegetable stock and steam down contents, covered, for a few more minutes. Now mix in the Etruscan sauce. Replace cover and cook 3 more minutes. Toss or stir sauté a little more and serve over a bed of cooked **Brown Rice** or toss with pasta. [1 PORTION - LARGE]

Gado Gado
This our restaurant's rendition of a classic Thai dish. A healthful sauté of vegetables, tempeh and tofu in a spicy peanut sauce.

MEASURE	INGREDIENT
2	bok choy stalks - strip cut
1 Tbsp	roasted sesame oil
1	carrot - shard cut
1/4 cup	colored bell peppers - thinly slivered
1/4 cup	yams (or sweet potatoes) - slivered
1/4 lb package	firm tofu - (prefried) - small strip cut
6-8 pieces	tempeh (prefried) - 1/2" x 2" strip cut
1/3 cup	**Vegetable Stock** (or water)
5-6	snow peas
3 Tbsps	peanuts - shelled
1/3 cup	**Thai Peanut Sauce**
1 cup	raw spinach

Sautés

Cut the bok choy into small wide strips.   Heat a sauté pan (or skillet), add oil, stir in bok choy strips, shard cut carrots, thinly slivered peppers and slivered yam, then reduce heat to medium low and slow fry, covered, for five minutes.

Pre-fry tofu and tempeh for best results, and then into the sauté. Stir fry the sauté for 3 more minutes, add vegetable stock (or water), snow peas then shelled peanuts. Cover and steam for 2 minutes, then add prepared sauce. Allow sauce to heat up for a couple of minutes then stir or shake pan to blend sauté ingredients. If you think sauce is too thick, add a little more stock (or water) to pan.

Place the raw spinach on top of the sauté and cover. Simmer three minutes until the spinach has wilted considerably, then flip sauté so spinach is now on the bottom. Simmer one minute, then slide entire contents over a plate of cooked **Brown Rice**. [1-2 PORTIONS]

Garlic Sesame Tofu
This is a popular sauté on our menu with braised vegetables and tofu in a Southeast Asian sauce with roasted sesame seeds and garlic.

MEASURE	INGREDIENT
1-2 Tbsps	roasted sesame oil
3-4 whole	onion hearts
1 small	carrot - share cut
4 large slices	yam (or sweet potato)
2 slices	extra-firm tofu - slab cut & triangled
2 medium	mushrooms - sliced
4-5 pieces	colored bell pepper - sliced
1 large	bok choy stalk - quartered
5-6	snow peas
2 Tbsps	mung bean sprouts (optional)
1/4 cup	**Vegetable Stock** (or water)
3 Tbsps	**Garlic Sesame Sauce**

Heat a sauté pan (or skillet), add oil, then fry the onion hearts, carrot shards and yams on medium heat for 3 minutes. Cut two 1/4 inch thick lengthwise slabs from tofu block, then slice diagonally across each slab to form triangles. Add the four resulting tofu triangles to the sauté; carefully working pieces down to pan surface to enable browning. When tofu's adequately browned, add sliced mushrooms, peppers, and a stalk of bok choy that's been cut in four 'squares' (quartered). Cover sauté pan and continue cooking on medium heat for 3-5 more minutes. Toss or stir pan occasionally.

Add vegetable stock (or water), increase heat and steam (to soften contents), then add the prepared sauce. Toss pan a little to blend and heat the sauce. Serve over a bed of cooked **Brown Rice** or toss with pasta. [1-2 PORTIONS]

Gluten Diablo

This spicy sauté with large fillets of gluten steak, tomatoes and Italian herbs is great with rice or pasta. Adjust the heat range to your taste.

MEASURE	INGREDIENT
3-5 small	colored bell pepper - sliced rounds
1 Tbsp	olive oil
3-5	onion hearts
1	**Perfect Gluten Flank Steak** - chunk sliced
1	carrot - shard cut
1 Tbsp	garlic clove - crushed
1 medium	portabella mushroom - sliced
2 pinches	salt
(as needed)	hot peppers (see Hot Pepper Chart) - minced
3 pinches	cajun spice blend
1 pinch each:	oregano, marjoram, basil
1/4 cup	**Vegetable Stock**
1 handful	spinach
1/4 cup	**Stewed Tomatoes** - hand crushed
4	asparagus spears - slant cut

Sautés

MEASURE	INGREDIENT
1 tsp	cornstarch (mixed with 3 Tbsps cold water)

Carefully slice off small round pieces from bell pepper, then set these pieces aside.

Heat a sauté pan (or skillet), add oil, and sauté the onion hearts, then gradually add sliced pepper rounds, chunk sliced gluten steak, shard cut carrot, crushed garlic, sliced mushrooms, salt, pinch of minced hot peppers, and other spices. Continue cooking, covered, for 5 more minutes, then add vegetable stock, spinach leaves, hand crushed stewed tomatoes, and slant cut asparagus spears. Mix in cornstarch slurry, then continue cooking for 5 more minutes. Serve over a bed of cooked **Brown Rice** or toss with pasta. [1 PORTION - LARGE]

Gypsy's Fortune
Rugged, folk dish with deep flavor and energy packed ingredients. Satisfying and easy to make with pierogies, seitan and brown gravy.

MEASURE	INGREDIENT
1 Tbsp	soy oil
2 Tbsps	onions - chopped
6	potato stuffed **Pierogies** (or mixed vegetable)
2	**Seitan Supreme** medallions - thin sliced
1 pinch	thyme
1 pinch	salt
1/4 cup	**Vegetable Stock**
2 Tbsps	**Brown Gravy**

Heat a sauté pan (or skillet), add oil, and sauté onions until translucent, then throw in pierogies and lower the heat. With tongs or cooking fork, turn pierogies, to brown on both sides. Thin slice seitan, then fry these pieces with the sautéd onions and pierogies. Sprinkle in the thyme and salt.

When everything is well browned, pour in vegetable stock and cover pan. Keep heat on low and simmer, covered, for 3-5 minutes then add prepared gravy. Cook this for a few more minutes until sauce thickens, then serve.
[1-2 PORTIONS]

The Hispania
Named for its Spanish flavors and ingredients. With tofu and gluten cutlets, brown rice and ethnic vegetables, the 'Hispania' is easy to make.

MEASURE	INGREDIENT
2 Tbsps	olive oil
1/4 cup	onion - chopped
2	celery stalks - chopped
1 small	carrot - sliced rounds
1 tsp	garlic clove - crushed
1/2 tsp	salt
2 pinches	cumin
1-2 tsps	spanish paprika
1/2 tsp	thyme leaf
2	Italian frying peppers (mildly hot) - diced
2 Tbsps	chickpeas - cooked
1/4 cup	black olives - pitted & sliced
2 tsps	capers
1/2 lb package	extra-firm tofu - thin sliced cutlets
1/2	*Perfect Gluten Flank Steak* - thin sliced cutlets
1/4 cup	*Brown Rice* - cooked
1/4 cup	*Stewed Tomatoes* - hand crushed
1/4 cup	*Vegetable Stock*

Heat a sauté pan (or cast-iron skillet), add oil, and sauté chopped onion and celery. Adjust heat to medium then gradually add sliced carrots, crushed garlic, salt, spices, diced frying peppers, precooked chickpeas, pitted and sliced olives,

Sautés

capers, thin sliced tofu and gluten steak cutlets. Cover and slow fry on medium low 5 minutes, stirring occasionally.

Next stir in precooked brown rice and hand crushed stewed tomatoes. Turn up heat and cook 2 minutes. Pour in the vegetable stock, cover and simmer on low heat 5 more minutes.   [1-2 PORTIONS]

Hunter's Bounty

A hearty sauté with the flavor of woodland things, cooked on a campfire.

MEASURE	INGREDIENT
2 Tbsps	soy oil
3 Tbsps	onions - chopped
1/4 lb package	firm tofu - chunk sliced
8 slivers	**Seitan Supreme** steak - chunk sliced
5-10 small cubes	tempeh - cubed
5-8 small pieces	**Perfect Gluten Flank Steak**
1	carrot - thin cut shards
3	button mushrooms
1/2	portabella mushroom - sliced
1-2 pinches mixed:	salt & black pepper
1/2 tsp	thyme leaves
1/4 cup	**Vegetable Stock**
3 Tbsps	**Brown Gravy**

Heat a sauté pan (or skillet), add oil, and sauté onions and veggie meats on medium low until browned. When ready, mix in shard cut carrots, mushrooms, salt, black pepper and thyme, then cover, and continue cooking on low heat setting for 5 more minutes. Next, add vegetable stock and prepared gravy, then cover and simmer sauté 3 more minutes. Serve over bed of cooked **Brown Rice** or toss with pasta. [1 PORTION - LARGE]

Hungarian Goulash

This sauté, with cabbage and potatoes, is typical of eastern European cuisine. The addition of protein rich gluten and tofu cutlets substitute for commonly used meats.

MEASURE	INGREDIENT
2 Tbsps	olive oil
1/4 head	white cabbage - chopped
1 large	potato - cubed
1	carrot - sliced
1/4 cup	onion - chopped
several leaves	kale, chard (or spinach) - chopped
5-6 small	tofu cutlets - sliced
5	*Perfect Gluten Flank Steak* cutlets - sliced
3-4 pinches	salt
1-2 tsps	paprika
2 pinches	thyme leaf
2 pinches	cayenne pepper
1/3 cup	*Vegetable Stock*

Heat a sauté pan (or skillet), add oil, and slowly sauté vegetable-based ingredients. When cabbage and potatoes are adequately cooked, slowly stir in veggie meats, salt and spices. Cover pan and continue cooking on low heat, stirring occasionally, for about 10 more minutes. Eventually, add vegetable stock and simmer for 5 more minutes. [1-2 PORTIONS]

Hungarian Style Pierogies
**A traditional Hungarian sauté with pierogies, spinach
and onions. Served with vegan sour cream.**

MEASURE	INGREDIENT
2 Tbsps	soy oil
1 medium	onion - thin sliced
6	potato stuffed **Pierogies** (or mixed vegetable)
2 cups	spinach - fresh
(to taste)	salt & black pepper

Heat a sauté pan (or skillet), add oil, and slowly sauté onions on medium heat until they begin to caramelize. Add in pierogies and slow fry them with the onions until they brown on both sides.

Now place spinach on top of the sauté and cover pan. Keep heat low and steam down spinach. After a few more minutes spinach has wilted enough to be tossed with the onions and pierogies. Toss until spinach is well cooked, then slide sauté onto a plate. Salt and pepper to taste, and serve with side of **Sour Cream**.

Imam's Delight
**A favorite of ancient Persian royalty. With ground soy-based 'beef',
vegetables and Persian spices, resting on a bed of
brown rice and grilled eggplant.**

MEASURE	INGREDIENT
6 ozs	TVP burger blend - dry mix
1 & 1/2 cups	ice cold water
1	eggplant
1/2 cup	**Grill Goddess Sauce**
1/4 cup	olive oil
1 medium	onion - thin sliced

MEASURE	INGREDIENT
1/2 each:	green, yellow, red bell peppers - thin sliced
4	garlic cloves - crushed
1/4 cup	leeks - rinsed & chopped
1 tsp	salt
1/4 tsp	black pepper
1 tsp	allspice
1/3 tsp	cumin
1/4 tsp	cardamom
2 pinches	cayenne pepper
1	portabella mushroom - sliced
1/3 cup	*Stewed Tomatoes* - hand crushed
1/2 tsp	dill
1/4 cup	*Vegetable Stock*
1 cup	*Brown Rice*
1 tsp	cornstarch (mixed with 3 Tbsps cold water)

Mix the burger blend with the cold water, then refrigerate for at least 30 minutes, or more.

Slice the eggplant into rounds and marinate them in Grilled Goddess sauce. After 10 minutes of marinating, the eggplant should be grilled and set aside. If a grill is not convenient, a grill surfaced sauté pan will work.

Heat a large sauté pan (or cast-iron skillet), add oil, and sauté thinly sliced onions and peppers for several minutes on medium heat. When onions become translucent, thoroughly mix in crushed garlic, well cleaned and chopped leeks, salt, black pepper and spices. Next, form 5 small barrels with the burger, using wet hands, then place barrels on top of the sauté. Cover and simmer for 5 minutes.

Slice up portabella and gently mix into pan. Cover and simmer 5 more minutes. Add hand crushed stewed tomatoes, dill and vegetable stock, then continue simmering for 5 more minutes, stirring occasionally. Mix in the cornstarch slurry to thicken juices, then layer the grilled eggplant pieces over cooking sauté, and put cover back on. Simmer 2 more minutes.

Sautés

To serve, make a bed of cooked **Brown Rice** on a plate. Use tongs to pick up steamed eggplant and place pieces on the rice. Now slide the rest of the sauté contents over the eggplant. [1-2 PORTIONS]

Indian Vegetable Curry

This flavorful sauté incorporates the culinary principals of Heaven and Earth. Combining deep-earth root vegetables, such as potatoes, yams and turnips, with surface vegetables, like peas and peppers, and the highest growing food...coconuts.

MEASURE	INGREDIENT
1/2 cup mixed:	green, yellow, red bell peppers - round cut
1 Tbsp	soy oil
1/4 cup	onion - chopped
1/2 large	turnip - sliced
4 large slices	yam (or sweet potato) - sliced
1	parsnip - large round slices
4 large slices	potato
4 thin slices	rutabaga
1	carrot - thin sliced
3 Tbsps	water (for steaming)
4-5	string beans - trimmed & slant cut
3-4	cauliflowerettes
2 Tbsps	chickpeas - cooked
2 pinches	salt
1-2 tsps	curry powder
1/3 cup	**Vegetable Stock**
3-4	broccoli buds
1/4 cup	peas
1/4 cup	coconut milk
1 tsp	raw sugar

Carefully slice off small round pieces from each bell pepper, then set these pieces aside.

Heat a large sauté pan (or cast-iron skillet), add oil, and sauté chopped onions with other root vegetables. Stir fry three minutes, on medium heat, tossing occasionally. Add the water and cover to steam sauté contents for 5 minutes.

Next toss in the round sliced bell peppers, trimmed and slant cut string beans, cauliflowerettes and precooked chickpeas. Stir fry another three minutes, then add salt and curry powder, toss a little more, then pour in vegetable stock, mix in broccoli buds, peas, coconut milk and raw sugar. Reduce heat, cover and simmer until all root veggies are soft. Serve over a bed of cooked **Brown Rice**, or basmati rice. [1-2 PORTIONS]

Jamaican Jungle

This meal transports you to Jamaica, with braised, large cut vegetables, tofu and seitan, simmered in a spicy sauce.

MEASURE	INGREDIENT
1 Tbsp	soy oil
1	carrot - large cut shards
2 large	onion hearts
1/2	yam (or sweet potato) - large slices
1/2 each:	yellow, green, red bell peppers - sliced
1/4 lb package	firm tofu (prefried or raw) - chunk sliced
5 large pieces	*Basic Seitan*
3 Tbsps	water (for steaming)
1/4 cup	*Jamaican Jungle Sauce*

Heat a sauté pan (or skillet), add oil, and sauté large shard cut carrot, onion hearts and yam slices on medium heat, covered for 3-5 minutes, shaking pan to prevent burning. Add sliced peppers, chunk sliced tofu (prefried or raw) and seitan pieces, then cover and fry another three minutes.

Sautés

Turn up heat and add a small amount of water. Steam contents soft by continuing to add small amounts of water while using medium-high heat. When yams are soft enough, stir in Jamaican Jungle sauce. Shake pan to mix thoroughly and heat up. Cover and simmer 3 minutes on low heat. Serve over a bed of cooked **Brown Rice**. [1-2 PORTIONS]

Jambalaya
This authentic Cajun stew is loaded with flavor and nutrition.
Reflects the highlights of a night on the Bayou.

MEASURE	INGREDIENT
1/2	potato - parboiled & chopped
2 Tbsps	soy oil
1/2 small	onion - chopped
1/2 cup	colored bell peppers - chopped
1/2 tsp	garlic clove - crushed
1/2	carrot - thin sliced rounds
1/2-2	jalapeno peppers
(to taste)	salt
1/2 tsp	thyme leaf
1-2 tsps	cajun spice blend
1/2 cup mixed:	tofu, tempeh, gluten, seitan - chunked
3 slices	zucchini
2 Tbsps	whole wheat flour
1/4 cup	**Vegetable Stock**
2 Tbsps	white wine
3 Tbsps	tomato puree

Chop up and parboil potatoes, then set aside.

Heat a large sauté pan (or cast-iron skillet), add oil, then sauté onion slices, chopped bell peppers, salt and spices. Stir fry on medium heat for 3 minutes, then add chopped up parboiled potatoes, crushed garlic, thinly sliced carrot, jalapeno pepper(s), chunks of prepared veggie meats, sliced zucchini and flour. Cover and cook on medium heat for 5 more minutes, stirring occasionally. When ready, stir in vegetable stock, wine and tomato puree, then simmer 5 more minutes. Serve over a bed of cooked **Brown Rice**. [1-2 PORTIONS]

Leonardo's Vision
Pierogies, tofu cutlets, asparagus spears and broccoli tips in a vegan white sauce, with melted vegan mozzarella cheese. In honor of Leonardo da Vinci, a vegetarian genius!

MEASURE	INGREDIENT
1 Tbsp	olive oil
1 tsp	garlic clove - diced
1/4 cup	**Vegetable Stock**
4	potato stuffed **Pierogies** (or mixed vegetable)
5-6	tofu cutlets (prefried)
1 cup	broccoli buds
6	asparagus spears - slant cut
1/4 cup	basic **White Sauce**
2 ozs	soy mozzarella cheese - grated

Heat a sauté pan (or skillet), add oil, and fry the diced garlic until it starts to brown, then add the vegetable stock. Remove the garlic by straining off liquid. Steam the pierogies and tofu cutlets in the strained stock for 3 minutes, covered, on medium low heat. Next add the broccoli buds, slant cut asparagus spears, then mix in prepared sauce and grated cheese. Continue heating for a few more minutes, then shake pan to blend and serve. [1 PORTION]

Mediterranean Pasta Toss
**This delightful sauté makes a great meal,
with plenty of flavor and nutrition.**

MEASURE	INGREDIENT
4-5	sundried tomatoes - mixed with
	1/4 cup soaking water
2 Tbsps	olive oil
1/2 small	onion - chopped
1/4 cup	carrot - thin sliced rounds
1/2 cup	colored bell pepper - sliced
1 cup	cauliflower - sliced
1 cup	string beans - trimmed & slant cut
1/4 cup	yam (or sweet potato) - thin slivers
1/4 cup	chickpeas - cooked
1/2 cup	tofu - cubed
1/2	lemon - juiced
1/4 cup	***Vegetable Stock***
2 pinches	salt
2 pinches	cumin
1 pinch	powdered thyme
1/2 cup	peas - frozen
1 Tbsp	fresh dill - chopped
2 cups	penne pasta - cooked

Put the sundried tomatoes in a small sauce pan with enough water to just cover the tomatoes, then bring contents to a boil. Reduce heat and simmer for 3 minutes, covered. Remove from heat and let steep for another 5 minutes, then drain away most of the the soaking water, retaining a 1/4 cup of soaking water with tomatoes.

Heat a sauté pan (or skillet), add oil, then sauté the chopped onions and sliced carrots for 3 minutes, then gradually add sliced bell peppers, sliced cauliflower, trimmed and slant cut string beans, slivered yam slices, precooked chickpeas, cubed tofu, prepared sundried tomatoes with a 1/4 cup of their soaking water, one-half juiced lemon and vegetable stock, then cover and simmer on low heat for 4-5 minutes.

Add salt and spices, peas and dill. Increase heat and stir fry for 3 minutes. Add precooked pasta, toss another 2 minutes and serve. [1-2 PORTIONS]

Neptune's Gift
For seafood lovers, this tofu preparation is reminiscent of a white fish sauté with lemon and herbs.

MEASURE	INGREDIENT
5-6 whole	baby red potatoes - unpeeled & parboiled
2 Tbsps	soy margarine
2	onion hearts
1 lb package	extra-firm tofu - fillet cut
1/3 cup	*Vegetable Stock*
1 Tbsp	lemon juice
1 tsp	salt
2 pinches	black pepper
1 pinch each:	thyme, marjoram, rosemary, tarragon
6 inch sheet	wakame seaweed (or dulse seaweed)
1 cup mixed:	carrots, cucumber, kale, zucchini - slivered
4-5	fresh snap peas
1 tsp	cornstarch (mixed with 3 Tbsps cold water)

Select smallest (baby) size potatoes. Parboil unpeeled and whole, then set aside.

Heat a sauté pan (or skillet), add margarine and onion hearts.

Sautés

Slice the tofu into thin, long fillet shaped pieces, then fry with onion hearts, on low heat. Using a cooking fork, tongs or other utensil, carefully turn and brown each fillet.

When tofu is adequately seared, pour in vegetable stock and lemon juice, then stir in salt, black pepper, herbs, and prepared potatoes. Place seaweed (in one piece) over sauté mixture, then cover pan and simmer for 3 minutes. Remove seaweed, add slivered veggies, snap peas and continue cooking, covered, for 3-5 more minutes. Finally add cornstarch slurry and shake pan to blend. Serve over a bed of cooked **Brown Rice**, or with a side of **Pilaf**.

Newton's Law
Named in honor of Isaac Newton, father of modern physics and calculus...who was also a vegetarian!

MEASURE	INGREDIENT
1	**Perfect Gluten Flank Steak** - thick sliced
1/4 cup	whole wheat flour
1/4 cup	soy milk
1/2 cup	bread crumbs
2 Tbsps	soy oil
1/4 cup each:	portabella mushroom, zucchini, onion, carrot, and asparagus - slivered
1 pinch	salt
1 pinch	thyme leaf
2 pinches	cajun spice blend
1/2 cup	**Vegetable Stock**
1 tsp	cornstarch (mixed with 3 Tbsps cold water)

Thick slice steak into 3-4 pieces and bread by dredging in flour, soy milk and then bread crumbs. Heat a sauté pan (or skillet), add oil, then brown gluten steak pieces. Pour off excess oil, then add slivered veggies, salt, herbs and spices. Cover and steam contents on low heat for 5 minutes, then add vegetable stock, cover again and continue cooking for 3 more minutes. Stir in cornstarch slurry and thicken. Serve as main course with side dishes.

The Olympian

A favorite dish of the Gods. With bright mediterranean vegetables, festive herbs and spices, tender morsels of gluten and tofu, and a delicious citrus sauce.

MEASURE	INGREDIENT
2 Tbsps	sundried tomatoes - soaked & chopped
1 Tbsp	olive oil
2 Tbsps	red onion - chopped
5-10 slices	yam (or sweet potato) - sliver cut
5	carrot - shard cut
1/4 cup mixed:	red, yellow, green bell peppers - diced
1/4 cup	tofu - cubed
1/4 cup	*Perfect Gluten Flank Steak* - chopped
1 tsp	garlic cloves - crushed
5 thin slices	zucchini
1/4 cup	eggplant - diced
1/4 cup	string beans - chopped
1/4 cup	cauliflower tips
1/4 cup	broccoli buds
1/4 cup	asparagus tips
3 Tbsps	black olives - pitted & sliced
2 pinches	salt
2 pinches	cumin
1/4 tsp	allspice
2 pinches	coriander
2 pinches	thyme leaf
1/2	orange (for squeezing over sauté mix)

MEASURE	INGREDIENT
1 Tbsp	lemon juice
1 Tbsp	cornstarch - dissolved in
	1/ 4 cup cold Vegetable Stock

Put the sundried tomatoes in a small sauce pan with enough water to just cover the tomatoes, then bring contents to a boil. Reduce heat and simmer for 3 minutes, covered. Remove from heat and let steep for another 5 minutes before draining and use.

Heat a sauté pan (or skillet), add oil, then begin frying the chopped onions. In two minutes add the thinly sliced yam, shard cut carrots, diced peppers, cubed tofu and chopped gluten steak. Simmer, covered, on medium heat for five minutes then toss in the crushed garlic, sliced zucchini, diced eggplant, prepared sundried tomatoes, chopped string beans, cauliflower tips, broccoli buds, asparagus tips, pitted and sliced olives, salt, herbs and spices. Simmer on low heat, covered, for 5 more minutes.

Squeeze the orange over the sauté, then add the lemon juice. Increase heat and stir or shake pan. After a minute or two, stir in cornstarch-vegetable stock slurry, while bringing sauté to a boil, then immediately lower heat and simmer for 2 more minutes. Serve over a bed of cooked **Brown Rice** or toss with pasta. [1-2 PORTIONS]

Oriental Stir Fry

A potpourri of thinly sliced vegetables, stir fried with delicious Oriental flavors. Expand this recipe-for-one and create dinner for the whole family.

MEASURE	INGREDIENT
1 tsp	roasted sesame oil
1 small	carrot - thin slice strips
1/2 cup	colored bell peppers - thin slice strips
1/2 small	leeks -washed & thin slice strips
3	asparagus spears - thin slice strips
2	bok choy stalks - thin slice strips

MEASURE	INGREDIENT
1/2 small	zucchini - thin slice strips
3	nappa stalks - thin slice strips
2	mushrooms - thin slice strips
1" thin sliver	ginger root
2 pinches	garlic clove - crushed
1/4 cup	water
3 Tbsps	*Tamari* sauce
6	broccoli buds
1/2 cup mixed:	kale & spinach leaves
5-10	snow peas
1/4 cup	fresh bean sprouts
1 tsp	cornstarch (mixed with 3 Tbsps cold water)

Thinly slice carrots, bell peppers, well washed leeks, asparagus spears, bok choy, zucchini, nappa, mushrooms, into long strips and set aside.

Heat a sauté pan (frying pan or wok), add oil, then sauté crushed garlic and minced ginger root. Toss pan (or stir) a moment then add the thinly sliced strips of carrot, bell peppers and well washed leeks. Add a third of the tamari and a third of the water, cover pan and steam rapidly on high heat for one minute.

Now add the broccoli, asparagus spears, bok choy, zucchini, nappa, kale, spinach and mushrooms. Add another third of the remaining tamari and water, then toss (or stir) in cover pan. Reduce heat a little and combine the snow peas, sprouts, the rest of the tamari and water. Steam a few minutes then slowly stir in cornstarch slurry. Toss pan as juices rapidly thicken. Remove from heat and immediately serve over a bed of cooked **Brown Rice**, or toss with pasta.
[1-2 PORTIONS]

Pasta Primavera
This stir fried sauté features a variety of small cut vegetables, garlic, herbs and tomato, tossed with pasta.

MEASURE	INGREDIENT
1 Tbsp	olive oil
1/4	onion - thin sliced
2 Tbsps	carrots - julienned
1/4 each:	red, yellow, green bell peppers - thin sliced
1 Tbsp	garlic clove - crushed
2 pinches	salt
1 pinch	black pepper
2 pinches each:	oregano, marjoram, basil
4	string beans - trimmed & chopped
3	asparagus spears - chopped
5-6 small	broccoli buds
1/2 small	zucchini - thin sliced
1/4	portabella mushroom - thin sliced
1-2	mushrooms - sliced
2 Tbsps	chickpeas - cooked
5-6	black olives - pitted & sliced
2 Tbsps	pignoli nuts
2 Tbsps	white wine
3 Tbsps	**Vegetable Stock**
1/4 cup	**Stewed Tomatoes** - hand crushed
1 cup	penne pasta - cooked

Heat a sauté pan (frying pan or wok), add oil, then sauté chopped onions, julienned carrots and thinly sliced peppers. Stir fry 2-3 minutes, then add crushed garlic, salt, black pepper and herbs. After a minute - with the exception of the tomatoes - combine all other vegetables, sliced mushrooms, precooked chick peas, pitted and sliced black olives, and pignolis nuts. Return cover to pan and continue stir frying, with a tossing motion, on medium heat for 3-5 more minutes.

Next, pour in the wine, shake pan to distribute, then add vegetable stock and cover. Simmer on low heat for 2 minutes and then add hand crushed stewed tomatoes. Cover and simmer for another 3 minutes, then add pasta over top of stir fried mix, cover again and simmer for 2 more minutes. Uncover, toss saute with precooked pasta and serve immediately. [1-2 PORTIONS]

The Paul Bunyon
This pan fried steak-burger, with mushroom gravy is supercharged with protein, and rich in flavor.

MEASURE	INGREDIENT
6 ozs	TVP burger blend - dry mix
1 & 1/2 cups	ice cold water
2 Tbsps	onions - minced
3 Tbsps	colored bell peppers - minced
1 tsp	garlic clove - minced
3 Tbsps	mushrooms - minced
1-2 tsps	cajun spice blend
1/4 cup	soy oil
1/2 cup	mushrooms - sliced
1/4 cup	**Vegetable Stock**
3 Tbsps	**Brown Gravy**

Mix the burger blend with the cold water, then refrigerate for at least 30 minutes, or more.

Mash the minced onions, bell peppers, garlic and mushrooms, then - using your hands - thoroughly mix this mash with the cajun spice and ground burger, then flatten to form a steak-burger. Heat a cast-iron skillet (or frying pan) and add the oil. Place the patty into the heated pan then lower the heat, replace cover, and cook 3 minutes to brown.

Sautés

Flip the steak-burger, and cook 2 more minutes. Add the sliced mushrooms, cover and fry 3 more minutes until mushrooms cook down.

Pour in vegetable stock, increase heat a little and cover again. In a minute or two, add prepared gravy and cook another minute to heat all contents thoroughly. Slide off pan onto a plate and voila! The Paul Bunyon.
[1 PORTION - LARGE]

Penne Alfredo Toss

**Here is an easy pasta dish you can whip up in almost no time.
Use the Alfredo Sauce recipe to complete this simple dish.**

MEASURE	INGREDIENT
6-10	broccoli buds
1/4 cup	*Vegetable Stock*
1/4 cup	*Alfredo Sauce*
6-10 small pieces	*Perfect Gluten Flank Steak* (prefried)
1 cup	penne pasta (cold) - cooked

Steam the broccoli and prefried gluten steak with the vegetable stock on low heat, covered. Mix in prepared sauce and cover to heat up sauce. Throw in cold precooked noodles, cover again and continue cooking over low heat. Uncover after two minutes, toss and serve. [1 PORTION - LARGE]

Pierogie Italia

**A delicious sauté, with potato stuffed pierogies,
broccoli and other vegetables, in a light sauce,
flavored with garlic and Italian herbs.**

MEASURE	INGREDIENT
2 Tbsps	olive oil
1 small	portabella mushroom - quartered
4	potato stuffed *Pierogies* (or mixed vegetables)
1 pinch	salt

MEASURE	INGREDIENT
1 large pinch each:	oregano, marjoram, basil
1 tsp	garlic clove - crushed
1 small head	broccoli - quartered
5-6	string beans - trimmed & half cut
5	asparagus spears - slant cut
1 handful	spinach - fresh
1 Tbsp	cornstarch - dissolved in
	1/3 cup cold **Vegetable Stock**

Heat a sauté pan (or frying pan), add half the olive oil, then fry mushroom pieces, covered, for about two minutes. Next, add the other tablespoon of olive oil, pierogies, salt, herbs and crushed garlic. Using low heat, cover pan, and lightly brown pierogies, occasionally turning pierogies to brown all sides.

After pierogies are well browned, toss in sliced up broccoli head, trimmed and half cut string beans, slant cut asparagus and spinach. Cover pan and slow cook this for 4-5 minutes on low heat. Next, add the cornstarch-vegetable stock slurry. Simmer another 5 minutes on medium low heat, to thicken the sauce, then slide contents onto a plate and serve. [1 PORTION - LARGE]

Polynesian Tofu & Vegetables

This sauté delivers the warmth and color of the South Pacific, with vegetables, tofu and pineapple, in a sweet and sour sauce.

MEASURE	INGREDIENT
1 Tbsp	roasted sesame oil
3	bok choy stalks - large sliced
1/4 cup	carrots - julienned
1/4 cup	yam (or sweet potato) - julienned
1/2	green banana (or plantain) - sliced
6	string beans - trimmed & length split
5	tofu cutlets (prefried) - cubed
1/4 cup	pineapple - chunked

Sautés

MEASURE	INGREDIENT
3 Tbsps	water (for steaming)
1/4 cup	*Polynesian Sauce*
5-10	snow peas
1/4 cup	mung bean sprouts

Heat a sauté pan (or skillet), add oil, then stir fry large slices of bok choy, julienned carrots and yams, first. After a minute or two, add the sliced plantain, trimmed and length split string beans, cubed tofu (prefried), chunks of pineapple, and a couple of tablespoons water, then cover and steam for a few more minutes. Now add prepared sauce, snow peas and sprouts. Shake or stir in sauce, reduce heat and cover pan. Cook contents for 2 minutes, then serve over a bed of cooked *Brown Rice*. [1-2 PORTIONS]

Ratatoulli

**With origins in southern France, this is a well known vegetable stew.
Large cut garden vegetables highlight this dish.**

MEASURE	INGREDIENT
3 Tbsps	olive oil
1 medium	onion - chunk chopped
1 tsp	salt
1 tsp	oregano
1 tsp	garlic clove - crushed
1/2	eggplant - cubed
1 small	zucchini - chunk chopped
1 small	summer squash - chunk chopped
1	green bell pepper - chopped
1	red bell pepper - chopped
5	button mushrooms
1/3 cup	*Stewed Tomatoes* - hand crushed

Heat a sauté pan (or skillet), add oil, large pieces of a chopped onions, then stir in salt and oregano. After a few minutes gradually stir in crushed garlic, cubed eggplant, chopped vegetables and mushrooms. Cover and cook on low heat for five minutes. Combine hand crushed stewed tomatoes and simmer contents for 10 minutes. Serve as a stew with fresh bread on the side. [1-2 PORTIONS]

Seitan Stroganoff

Modeled after the traditional Russian classic, with seitan slices and mushrooms in a creamy brown gravy. Hearty and delicious.

MEASURE	INGREDIENT
1 Tbsp	soy oil
2 Tbsps	onions - chopped
1-2 pinches	salt
1 pinch	black pepper
2 pinches	thyme leaf
4-5 slices	*Seitan Supreme* or
	Basic Seitan medallions - thin sliced
6	mushrooms - sliced
1/4 cup	*Vegetable Stock*
2 Tbsps	*Sour Cream*
2 Tbsps	*Brown Gravy*

Heat a sauté pan (or skillet), add oil, then fry the chopped onions with salt, black pepper and thyme. As onions begin to caramelize, toss in thin sliced pieces of seitan and brown with the onions.

When seitan is sufficiently seared, add in sliced mushrooms, replace cover and cook on low heat. Toss pan and fry for several minutes, then add vegetable stock and bring to a boil. Mix in sour cream and simmer 2 more minutes. Finally, thoroughly mix in prepared gravy, and serve over a bed of cooked *Brown Rice* or toss with pasta. [1 PORTION - LARGE]

Singapore Sunset

With the color of the Pacific sunset, and flavor of the South Seas, this tasty sauté combines large cut vegetables, meaty seitan and tofu, in a Southeast Asian citrus sauce.

MEASURE	INGREDIENT
1/2 each:	green, red, yellow bell peppers - sliced rounds
1 Tbsp	roasted sesame oil
2 large	onion hearts
1/2 large	carrot - shard cut
3 Tbsps	water (for steaming)
1/4 lb package	firm tofu (prefried) - large wedge cut
2	**Seitan Supreme**, or **Basic Seitan** medallions (prefried)- cut into 4-5 wedges
3-4	broccoli buds
1/2	portabella mushroom - large sliced
1/4 cup	**Singapore Sunset Sauce**

Carefully slice off small round pieces from each bell pepper, then set these pieces aside.

Heat a sauté pan (or skillet), add oil, then fry onions hearts. When onion hearts are lightly seared, throw in sliced bell pepper rounds, shard cut carrot pieces and large slices of portabella mushroom. Continue searing sauté contents on medium-high heat. Add a small amount of water, then replace cover. Periodically toss pan contents, while steaming for 5 more minutes.

Next add large slices of wedge cut tofu and seitan (both prefried), broccoli buds, a tablespoon of water, then replace cover, and continue steaming for another 3-5 minutes. Add prepared sauce, then heat blend for 2 more minutes while tossing pan contents to blend. Serve over a bed of cooked **Brown Rice** or toss with pasta. [1 PORTION - LARGE]

Southern Comfort

With tofu, carrots, broccoli and peas, this mellow sauté delivers old fashioned Southern flavor.

MEASURE	INGREDIENT
2 Tbsps	olive oil
1	carrot - shard cut
1/2 lb package	extra-firm tofu
1 pinch	salt
2 pinches	powdered thyme
3-5	broccoli buds
1/4 cup	peas - frozen
1/2	orange - juiced
1/4 cup	*Vegetable Stock*
1 tsp	cornstarch - dissolved in
	3 Tbsps water

Heat a sauté pan (or skillet) and add the oil and carrot shards. Stir fry carrots for two minutes on medium-high heat, then add small wedge cut pieces of tofu. Brown tofu for several minutes, while tossing pan occasionally to prevent burning. When tofu pieces are partially browned, season sauté mix with salt and thyme.

Next, squeeze juice from the orange over sauté contents, add broccoli buds and peas, then pour in the vegetable stock and replace cover. Cook on low heat for 3 more minutes, then thicken with the cornstarch slurry and serve over a bed of cooked **Brown Rice** or toss with pasta. [1-2 PORTIONS]

Teriyaki Tofu

An easy stir fry, using tofu and thinly sliced vegetables. Use the delicious teriyaki sauce to complete this recipe.

MEASURE	INGREDIENT
2	bok choy stalks - thin strip cut
1/4	red bell pepper - thin strip cut
1	carrot - thin strip cut
1/2	portabella mushroom cap - thin strip cut
1/2 lb package	extra-firm tofu - cubed
1 Tbsp	roasted sesame oil
4-5	broccoli buds
4-5	snow peas
2 Tbsps	water (for steaming)
1/4 cup	**Teriyaki Sauce**

Slice bok choy, red pepper, carrot and portabella mushroom into thin strips. Cut tofu into small cubes or small cutlets

Heat up a sauté pan (or skillet) and add the oil, then gradually stir in the thinly sliced vegetables and portabella mushrooms, cubed (or small sliced) tofu, broccoli buds, and snow peas. Stir fry on medium heat for several minutes until tofu browns a little, then add two tablespoons of water and steam, covered, for 3 minutes. Add prepared teriyaki sauce, then stir fry 2 more minutes to heat up mixture. Mix contents well, and if necessary, add only a tablespoon or two more of water. Serve over a bed of cooked **Brown Rice** or toss with pasta.
[1-2 PORTIONS]

The Thomas Edison

Named for the famous vegetarian inventor. Featuring hearty seitan in a deep brown sauce, with slivered carrots, portabella mushrooms, onion hearts, and broccoli buds.

MEASURE	INGREDIENT
2 Tbsps	soy oil
3-4	*Seitan Supreme* medallions - half cut
1	carrot - sliver cut
1/2	portabella mushroom cap - thin sliced
3	onion hearts
5-8	broccoli buds
1 pinch	salt
1 pinch	thyme leaf
2 pinches	cajun spice blend
2 Tbsps	*Tamari* sauce
2 Tbsps	cornstarch - dissolved in
	1/4 cup cold *Vegetable Stock*

Heat up a sauté pan (or skillet) and add the oil, throw in onion hearts and half cut seitan chunks, reduce heat to a medium setting and sauté until seitan is well seared. Next, add sliver cut carrot, replace cover and periodically toss sauté mix while cooking for 2 more minutes, then add thin sliced portabella mushroom. Replace pan cover and simmer for 2 more minutes, add broccoli buds and cover. Cook two more minutes then slowly stir in salt, herbs, spices, tamari and corn-starch-vegetable stock slurry. Simmer another 3-5 minutes to thicken the sauce and serve over a bed of cooked *Brown Rice* or toss with pasta.
[1 PORTION - LARGE]

Tofu Cacciatore

**This sauté demonstrates pre-flouring and prefrying of tofu,
which can produce a classic styled veal, chicken or fish.**

MEASURE	INGREDIENT
1/2 lb package	extra-firm tofu - thin sliced
(as needed)	whole wheat flour - for dredging
1/4 cup	olive oil
3 Tbsps	onions - chopped
2 large	mushrooms - sliced
1 Tbsp each:	red, yellow and green bell peppers - chopped
2 pinches	salt
1 pinch each:	oregano, marjoram, basil and black pepper
2 Tbsps	white wine
1/4 cup	**Vegetable Stock**
1/4 cup	**Stewed Tomatoes** - hand crushed

Slice the half block of tofu into 8-10 thin pieces, carefully dredge pieces in the flour.   Heat a sauté pan (or skillet) and add the oil. Brown both sides of thin sliced tofu in the preheated oil. Remove browned tofu pieces, then drain on paper towels.

Pour off most of the oil, then, with the exception of the tomatoes, sauté all vege-tables with salt and seasoning for a few minutes. Return the browned tofu pieces back to the pan, then lightly toss mixture for two more minutes. Add the wine, toss again, then pour in the vegetable stock. Cover pan and continue cooking on medium heat for 3 more minutes.   Finally add the hand crushed stewed tomatoes, replace cover and cook 3 more minutes. Serve over a bed of cooked **Brown Rice** or toss with pasta. [1 PORTION - LARGE]

Tofu Dijon

A delightful sauté, made with vegetables, tofu, in a white wine and mustard sauce...reminiscent of the French countryside.

MEASURE	INGREDIENT
1 Tbsp	soy oil
2-3	onion hearts
1/2 lb package	extra-firm tofu - chunk sliced
1 Tbsp	soy margarine
1/2 large	portabella mushroom - sliced
1 small head	broccoli - quartered
5-8	string beans - trimmed & half cut
5-6	asparagus spears - slant cut
2 Tbsps	dijon mustard
2 pinches	salt
1 pinch	black pepper
1 pinch	thyme leaf
1 pinch	tarragon
1/4 cup	white wine
1 Tbsp	cornstarch - dissolved in
	1/4 cup cold **Vegetable Stock**

Heat a sauté pan (or skillet) and add the oil, add onion hearts and fry on medium setting for 2-3 minutes, then add chunk sliced tofu pieces and margarine. Continue frying until tofu pieces begin to brown, then add sliced portabella mushroom. Return cover, then simmer on low heat for 5 minutes. Next add a quarter cut head of broccoli, trimmed and half cut string beans, and slant cut asparagus spears. Return cover and fry a few minutes more.

Add the dijon mustard, salt, black pepper, seasonings and wine to sautéing mix, then toss contents to spread the mustard. Stir in cornstarch-vegetable stock slurry, then return cover, reduce heat and continue slow cooking for 3-5 more minutes. Serve over a bed of cooked **Brown Rice** or toss with pasta.
[1 PORTION - LARGE]

Tofu Marsala

Though very similar to our Italian Cacciatore sauté, this recipe features a delicious Marsala wine sauce.

MEASURE	INGREDIENT
1/2 lb package	extra-firm tofu - thin sliced
(as needed)	whole wheat flour - for dredging
1/4 cup	olive oil
3 Tbsps	onions - chopped
2 large	mushrooms - sliced
1 Tbsp each:	red, yellow and green bell peppers - chopped
2 pinches	salt
1 pinch each:	oregano, marjoram, basil and black pepper
1/4 cup	marsala wine
1/4 cup	**Vegetable Stock**

Slice the half block of tofu into 8-10 thin pieces, then carefully dredge pieces in the flour. Heat a sauté pan (or skillet) and add the oil. Brown both sides of sliced tofu in the preheated oil. Remove browned tofu pieces, then drain on paper towels.

Pour off most of the oil, then sauté all vegetables with salt and seasoning for a few minutes. Return the browned tofu pieces back to the pan, then lightly toss mixture for two more minutes. Add marsala wine, toss again, then pour in the vegetable stock. Cover pan and continue cooking on medium heat for 3 more minutes. Finally, sprinkle in a teaspoon of flour, replace cover and cook 3 more minutes. Serve over a bed of cooked **Brown Rice** or toss with pasta.
[1-2 PORTIONS]

Tofu Scalloppine

Another in the series of Italian tofu sautés. This one uses of white wine and lemon, to create a wonderful lemon-herb sauce.

MEASURE	INGREDIENT
1/2 lb package	extra-firm tofu - thin sliced
(as needed)	whole wheat flour - for dredging
1/4 cup	olive oil
3 Tbsps	onions - chopped
2 large	mushrooms - sliced
1 Tbsp each:	red, yellow and green bell peppers - chopped
2 pinches	salt
1 pinch each:	oregano, marjoram and black pepper
1/2	lemon - juiced & sliced rind
1/4 cup	white wine
1/4 cup	**Vegetable Stock**

Slice the half block of tofu into 8-10 thin pieces, then carefully dredge pieces in the flour.   Heat a sauté pan (or skillet) and add the oil. Brown both sides of sliced tofu in the preheated oil. Remove browned tofu pieces, then drain on paper towels.

Pour off most of the oil, then sauté all vegetables with salt, black pepper and seasoning for a few minutes. Return the browned tofu pieces back to the pan, squeeze lemon juice over sauté contents, slice up rind and add to mix, then lightly toss mixture for two more minutes. Add white wine, toss again, then pour in the vegetable stock. Cover pan and continue cooking on medium heat for 3 more minutes.   Finally, sprinkle in a teaspoon of flour, replace cover and cook 3 more minutes. Serve over a bed of cooked **Brown Rice** or toss with pasta.
[1 PORTION - LARGE]

Tuscan Toss

**This recipe truly brings out the flavor of Northern Italy, with
its combination of vegetables, pasta, and herbs.**

MEASURE	INGREDIENT
2 Tbsps	olive oil
1/2 medium	onion - thin sliced
1/2 each:	green, red and yellow bell peppers - thin sliced
1 pinch each:	salt, black pepper,
	thyme leaf, oregano & marjoram
2-3	garlic cloves - sliced
1 large	portabella mushroom cap - thin sliced
1 small head	broccoli - quarter cut
1/4 cup	*Vegetable Stock*
1/2 cup	cooked pasta

Heat a sauté pan (or skillet) and add oil, then begin frying thinly sliced onions and peppers. Cover pan, reduce heat and cook for 3 minutes.

At this point, gradually combine salt, pepper, herbs, sliced garlic and thinly sliced portabella mushroom into sauté mix, then return cover and simmer for 3 more minutes. Next, cut the broccoli head into quarters and add these to the sauté, cover and continue to simmer for another 3 minutes.

Next, pour in half of the vegetable stock, cover, increase heat and braise sauté in stock for 3 more minutes. This process quickly steams down the mixture, while adding flavor.

Now, pour in remaining vegetable stock and repeat the braising process. At the end of this period, add the pasta, cover and steam for 30 more seconds. Finally, uncover pan and toss the sauté with the pasta. Serve at once.
[1-2 PORTIONS]

The Westerner
With all the majesty and promise of the great outdoors...

MEASURE	INGREDIENT
1	*Perfect Gluten Flank Steak*
1/3 cup	*Grill Goddess Sauce*
1/3 cup	*Basic Barbecue Sauce*
1/3 cup	A-1 sauce
1/2 cup	*Vegetable Stock*
1 cup mixed:	onions, carrots, asparagus spears, zucchini & portabella mushroom - all sliver sliced
1 Tbsp	soy oil
1 tsp	cornstarch - dissolved in
	3 Tbsps water
(to taste)	salt & black pepper

Begin by grilling off gluten steak on medium-high temperature, basting several times with a combined glaze, made from equal parts of Grill Goddess, Barbecue and A-1 sauces. Baste several times, until steak is done. When finished, place steak in a bowl (or other container) with 1/4 cup of vegetable stock and a small amount of the remaining glaze combination. Allow steak to marinate for several minutes.

Sliver slice all vegetables and portabella mushroom. Heat a sauté pan (or skillet) and add oil, then toss in slivered vegetables and mushroom slices and sauté on medium-high heat for about 5 minutes.

Pour remaining 1/4 cup of stock in sauté and simmer, covered, for 3 minutes. Remove cover and stir in cornstarch slurry to thicken sauté juices. Next, place grilled steak on top of sauté mix. Return cover, then simmer 2 more minutes. Finally, slide entire contents of sauté over a bed of cooked *Brown Rice*. Salt and pepper to taste. [1 PORTION - LARGE]

Breads & Doughs

Introduction

What is more 'real' than the appearance and odor of fresh baked bread? If you are lucky enough to have been born in the 1950's or earlier in America, you might share some fond childhood memories of Mom's fresh baked bread. Unfortunately, today, breadmaking is fast becoming a lost art form that has been relegated to the professional bakery. This gradual erosion of this basic family practice - which had been passed down through the generations - may be linked to some core fundamental social problems that plague our country today. Acquiring the skills of bread making instills a sort of confidence and joy that only a baker can truly appreciate.

What we will discover in this chapter is that working with dough is easy, economical and extremely versatile. You will learn how to create breads of almost infinite variety through working out a few simple recipes. Dinner rolls, biscuits and buns are concisely described, providing you with an arsenal of tasty accompaniments. Several basic dough recipes used for pizzas, pierogies, dumplings and veggie pockets are covered in this chapter. Breakfast pastries such as pancakes, crepes and coffee cake are included here as well.

The recipes in this chapter are simple and concise. Like all the recipes in this book, those included in this chapter are intended to provide the reader with reliable instructions and advice. The recipes are basic and fundamental, supplying the reader with a springboard for more elaborate designs. There are many secrets and revelations about bread making that can only be discovered through immersing oneself in the process. Working with the recipes in this chapter will enable you to become adept at several categories of bread making.

There are many mixed opinions circulating, in today's media, about the benefits - or hazards - of consuming wheat products. It must be made clear that wheat and bread have been the 'Staff of Life' of western civilization, for thousands of years. The modern American diet, rich in dairy and animal flesh, is about as unhealthy a diet for an entire culture as has ever existed on this planet. Adulterated and heavily processed breads have replaced the hearty whole grain breads our ancestors consumed. Couple this with the consumption of processed sugars and chemicals and you have the stage set for sickness and death.

Learn to bake with vegan ingredients. The results are excellent as long as one follows the simple rules outlined in this chapter and this book. The benefits to your life from making and consuming this food will rapidly become apparent. The positive ripples that you create in this universe from your act of vegan baking are immeasurable.

Baking Powder Biscuits
**Those Flaky, moist biscuits made fresh from a
hot oven have been a favorite in this
country since colonial times.**

MEASURE	INGREDIENT
2 cups	unbleached pastry flour (or whole wheat pastry flour)
1 tsp	salt
2 & 1/2 tsps	baking powder
1/4 cup	soy margarine (at room temperature)
3/4-1 cup	soy milk

Sift and combine the flour, salt and baking powder together in a bowl. Cut the margarine into the dry ingredients until mixture is granulated. Stir in the soy milk quickly - but gently - to prevent excessive development of gluten.

Turn the dough onto a floured board and roll out to a thickness of about a quarter of an inch. Cut with a floured, round cookie cutter, 2 to 3 inch discs. Bake biscuits on a greased baking pan in a preheated 450°F oven for 12-15 minutes. Serve immediately with gravy or room temperature margarine.
[MAKES 12-16 BISCUITS]

Corn Bread
Completely vegan, with all the flavor of traditional corn bread recipes.

MEASURE	INGREDIENT
2 & 1/2 cups	yellow corn meal
1 & 1/2 cups	unbleached white flour
2 & 1/2 tsps	baking powder
1 tsp	salt
1 cup	soy milk
1/2 cup	soy margarine
2 Tbsps	molasses
2 Tbsps	raw sugar (or xylitol)

Mix together corn meal, flour, baking powder and salt in a bowl, and set aside. In another bowl, beat together soy milk, melted margarine, molasses and raw sugar. Gradually pour the bowl of wet ingredients into the bowl with the dry ingredients and fold mixture while turning the bowl. When well mixed, pour batter into a greased medium-sized baking pan and bake 20-25 minutes at 425°F. [4-8 PORTIONS]

Croissants
Croissants are French puff pastry delicacies. Here is a recipe for completely vegan croissants with all the flavor of the traditional version.

MEASURE	INGREDIENT
1 tsp	salt
2 & 1/2 cups	unbleached white flour
1 cup	soy milk - preheated to 110°F
1 Tbsp	active dry yeast
1 Tbsp	raw sugar

MEASURE	INGREDIENT
1 Tbsp	soy oil
1 cup	soy margarine - melted

Stir the salt into the flour and set aside.

Heat the soy milk to about 110°F and mix in the yeast and sugar. When the yeast has risen and the liquid has a foam on top, add the oil to the liquid, then mix the liquid and salted-flour mix. Knead resulting dough, and set aside, covered for about 45 minutes.

Punch down the expanded dough and knead until it becomes smooth and elastic, then cover the dough and refrigerate for half an hour. When set, remove dough and turn onto a floured board. Roll dough out into an oblong a quarter of an inch thick. Using a pastry brush, paint on melted (not warmer than 70°F) margarine.

Fold one third of the dough into the center. Take the other end and fold that over the doubled side. You now have three layers. Roll this out again to the same dimensions as the first time. Repeat entire process a total of four times. The last time do not roll out but refrigerate folded.

Preheat oven to 400°F. Roll refrigerated dough into large rectangle a quarter of an inch thick. Mark and cut into 6 equal squares. Next cut each square in half diagonally. Roll the triangle starting from base to apex and place on a greased baking dish. Refrigerate again for twenty minutes. Finally, bake in oven for 20-25 minutes. [MAKES 12 CROISSANTS]

French Bread
Why bother making your own French bread? After creating this completely vegan version, you'll know why!

MEASURE	INGREDIENT
2 cups	whole wheat flour
2 cups	unbleached white flour
2 Tbsps	vital wheat gluten
2 tsps	salt
1 cup	soy milk - preheated to 110°F
1 cup	water - preheated to 110°F
2 Tbsps	active dry yeast
3 tsps	raw sugar (or xylitol)
3 Tbsps	soy margarine - melted

Sift and thoroughly combine flours with the vital wheat gluten and salt together, in a large mixing bowl.

Combine soy milk and water, then heat to around 110°F. Next, mix in the yeast and sugar and set aside until froth forms on the surface. When ready, mix the melted margarine into the yeast liquid, then form a well in the center of salted-flour mix, and pour liquid into well. Stir thoroughly, but do not knead at this time. Cover dough with a wet towel and let rise about one hour until in has doubled in size.

Punch down and knead dough for about one minute, then break into two halves and form each half into a long cigar shape. Next, roll this flat into a 1/4 inch thick rectangle, then take one edge of the flattened dough and roll this into a tight cylindrical form. Taper in the ends and make small incisions along the top of the loaf. Set loaves aside to rise for 15-20 minutes.

Preheat oven to 400°F. Place a pan of hot water in the oven to provide some moisture. Put loaves on a well greased flat baking tray and bake 40 minutes. Brush tops with margarine after 35 minutes. Remove from oven and allow to stand 10 minutes before slicing.

French Toast

Great French toast without eggs! You won't find This recipe lacking in flavor or satisfaction. In fact, the nutritional value is superior to the egg version.

MEASURE	INGREDIENT
1 Tbsp	soy margarine
1	*Eggless Egg*
1/2 cup	soy milk
2 pieces	whole grain bread
(as needed)	maple syrup

Heat a skillet and add 1 tablespoon of margarine. Beat up the eggless egg with the soy milk, then dredge the bread through the liquid. Fry on both sides and serve with maple syrup.

German Coffee Cake

Made with German "kuchen" dough, or sweet yeast bread. Very tasty and great for breakfast.

MEASURE	INGREDIENT
4 cups	unbleached white flour
2 Tbsps	vital wheat gluten
1 tsp	salt
1 cup	water - preheated to 110°F
2 Tbsps	active dry yeast
1/2 cup	raw sugar (or xylitol)
1/2 cup	soy margarine (at room temperature)
1	*Eggless Egg*
1 Tbsp	lemon rind - grated

MEASURE	INGREDIENT
1 cup	soy milk
(as needed)	*Morning Coffee Cake Glaze*

Thoroughly combine flour with the vital wheat gluten and salt, in a large mixing bowl. Heat water to 110°F then stir in yeast and one tablespoon of the raw sugar. Allow this to rest for about ten minutes or until it becomes frothy on the surface.

Cream the margarine, remaining raw sugar, eggless egg and lemon rind together with a whisk, then mix in the soy milk and add this liquid to the yeast water. Form a well in the flour, then thoroughly stir in the liquid slurry into the flour, then knead lightly. Place a wet towel over the dough and allow to rise until dough is doubled in size.

Knead dough at this time until smooth and elastic. Wrap up tightly with plastic and refrigerate at least 2 hours before using.

Preheat oven to 375°F. To create a coffee cake ring grease a ring pan and cut the dough in half. Refrigerate one half. Take the other half and shape it into a fat snake the size of the pan's inner circumference, by hand rolling on a lightly floured board.

Place the dough snake in the ring bold and bake at 350°F for 20 minutes. Remove from oven, dribble on the *Morning Coffee Cake Glaze* and bake for another ten minutes. Remove, let stand at least five minutes before serving. [6-8 PORTIONS]

Hot Cross Buns
**Hot Cross buns...everybody's heard about them.
Here's how to make fine vegan buns with
German Kuchen dough.**

MEASURE	INGREDIENT
(as needed)	*German Coffee Cake* dough
(as needed)	*Morning Coffee Cake Glaze*
few pinches	cinnamon

Grease a cookie sheet or baking pan and preheat oven to 400°F. Form little balls of kuchen, or German Coffee Cake dough and place tightly together on the baking pan. Bake for ten minutes then open oven and make crisscross indentations on each one. Bake another ten minutes or until buns have more than doubled in size. Remove and fill the gashes with **Morning Coffee Cake Glaze** and sprinkle on the cinnamon. Great breakfast treats. [MAKES 16 BUNS]

Garlic Bread
Simple to make, using the *French Bread* recipe.
Makes a great accompaniment to Italian dishes.

MEASURE	INGREDIENT
1/4 cup	olive oil
1/4 cup	garlic cloves - diced
1 tsp	salt
1 loaf	**French Bread**
1/2 tsp	oregano (optional)

Heat the oil in a small pan and fry the diced garlic and salt on low heat until it garlic begins to brown, then remove from heat. Cut the loaf in half, lengthwise and apply the oil and garlic mixture to the opened surfaces of the loaf with spoon or pastry brush. If desired, sprinkle a little oregano as well.

Preheat oven 400°F and bake the bread for 15 minutes, loosely covered with foil. Remove foil and bake 5 minutes more. Serve hot.

Home Style Quick Bread
**This bread is made from a cornbread like batter,
fortified with whole grains and nutritious soy.
Easy to make in about an hour.**

MEASURE	INGREDIENT
1 & 1/2 cups	whole wheat flour
1 cup	unbleached white flour
1 Tbsp	vital wheat gluten
1 tsp	salt
2 tsps	baking powder
1 12-oz package	silken tofu
1 cup	soy milk
1/4 cup	molasses
2 tsps	raw sugar
2 tsps	**Egg Substitute**

Sift and thoroughly combine flours with the vital wheat gluten, salt and baking powder. Blend the tofu and soy milk with the molasses, sugar and egg replacement substitute. Stir wet mix into dry mix and pour this into a greased small baking dish. Bake in a preheated oven at 400°F for about 45 minutes. Use a toothpick to test that loaf is thoroughly baked.

Muffins

The following are some recipes for dinner muffins. The important thing to remember when making muffins is to not beat batter too much. This causes gluten to form, making muffins dense and hard. Mixing must be limited to an absolute minimum.

Basic Muffins

This recipe illustrates vegan muffin making fundamentals. Enjoy light and tasty whole grain muffins any time with this easy recipe.

MEASURE	INGREDIENT
1 cup	whole wheat pastry flour
1 cup	unbleached white flour
2 Tbsps	vital wheat gluten
1/2 tsp	salt
2 tsps	baking powder
2	*Eggless Egg*s
1 cup	soy milk
1/3 cup	raw sugar
4 Tbsps	soy margarine - melted

Thoroughly combine flour with the vital wheat* gluten and salt, in a large mixing bowl. Beat the eggless eggs with the soy milk, raw sugar and melted margarine.

Make a well inside the flour in the mixing bowl. Pour liquid ingredients into the center of this well. Using a rubber spatula, begin folding the flour into the well while spinning the bowl with the other hand. Do this gently and quickly.

Grease a muffin pan and have oven preheated to 400°F. Use a table spoon to drop balls of dough into the muffin forms. Leave a few forms empty and fill these with water to create moisture in the oven while cooking. Bake muffins for 20 to 25 minutes. Once removed, allow muffins to stand for a minute or two before removing from forms. This will insure that they pop out cleanly and easily. [MAKES 8-10 MUFFINS]

Breads & Doughs

*Note: Although over-development of gluten in muffin dough is detrimental to muffin making, the addition of a small amount of vital wheat gluten does produce a better textured muffin.

Corn Muffins
Another variation on Basic Muffins, this recipe produces a delicious corn muffin.

MEASURE	INGREDIENT
2 cups	yellow corn meal
1 cup	unbleached white flour
1/2 tsp	salt
2 tsps	baking powder
2	**Eggless Egg**s
1 cup	soy milk
3 Tbsps	raw sugar
3 Tbsps	molasses
3 Tbsps	soy margarine - melted

Mix the cornmeal with the flour, salt and baking powder. Beat the eggless eggs with the soy milk, sugar, molasses and margarine.

Make a well inside the flour in the mixing bowl. Pour liquid ingredients into the center of this well. Using a rubber spatula, begin folding the flour into the well while spinning the bowl with the other hand. Do this gently and quickly.

Grease a muffin pan and have oven preheated to 400°F. Use a table spoon to drop balls of dough into the muffin forms. Leave a few forms empty and fill these with water to create moisture in the oven while cooking. Bake muffins for 20 to 25 minutes. Once removed, allow muffins to stand for a minute or two before removing from forms. This will insure that they pop out cleanly and easily.
[MAKES 6-8 LARGE MUFFINS]

Morning Coffee Cake
**Here's a healthy, guilt-free coffee cake,
that's completely vegan.**

MEASURE	INGREDIENT
1 & 1/2 cups	unbleached white flour
1/2 cup	whole wheat flour
2 Tbsps	vital wheat gluten
1/2 tsp	salt
2 tsps	baking powder
2/3 cup	soy margarine
3/4 cup	brown sugar
3/4 cup	*Sour Cream*
1 tsp	vanilla extract
1/4 cup	soy milk
(as needed)	*Morning Coffee Cake Glaze*

Sift flours together with the vital wheat gluten, salt and baking powder, then cut margarine into this flour mix. In a separate bowl, beat sugar, sour cream and vanilla together with the soy milk, then thoroughly combine this mixture with the prepared flour mix, to form batter.

Preheat oven to 350°F and grease a ring mold. Pour in batter. Bake for 25 to 30 minutes. Dribble warm *Morning Coffee Cake Glaze* over cake top 5 minutes before cake is done. [6-8 PORTIONS]

Morning Coffee Cake Glaze

**Use this sweet white glaze on *Morning Coffee Cakes*,
Hot Cross Buns or *Cinnamon Rolls*.**

MEASURE	INGREDIENT
1/4 cup	soy margarine
1/4 cup	soy milk
1/4 cup	maple syrup
1/2 cup	raw sugar (or xylitol)
1/4 cup	walnuts - broken

Combine all ingredients into a sauce pan and slowly bring to a boil while stirring. Pour over **Morning Coffee Cake** or pastry while hot.

Pizza Dough

Perfect pizza dough is easier to make than you might have guessed. This recipe can be used for making pizza, stromboli, calzone and more.

MEASURE	INGREDIENT
2 & 1/2 cups	whole wheat flour
1 & 1/2 cups	unbleached white flour
3 Tbsps	vital wheat gluten
3 tsps	salt
2 Tbsps	active dry yeast
3 cups	water - preheated to 110°F
1 tsp	xylitol (or raw sugar)
1/3 cup	soy oil

Sift and thoroughly combine flours with the vital wheat gluten and salt, into a large mixing bowl, then set aside. Stir the yeast into the hot water with the xylitol (or raw sugar) and set aside. When surface of yeast water becomes frothy, mix in the oil. Next stir this into the dry ingredients until you have a soggy dough. Set this aside, covered, until dough has risen and doubled in size. Punch this down and knead one minute. Add a little flour if needed, to firm up dough. Cover well and refrigerate at least one hour before using. [MAKES 6-8 PIZZAS]

Lefsa

A flatbread of eastern European descent. Made with a dough of mashed potatoes, sour cream and flour.   Can be stuffed with a various fillings, then baked with sauces to create unique meals.

MEASURE	INGREDIENT
1 cup	*Mashed Potatoes*
1/2 cup	*Sour Cream*
1 tsp	raw sugar (or xylitol, or Sucanat)
1 tsp	salt
1 cup	unbleached white flour

Mix all ingredients into a dough ball and refrigerate overnight. Roll out thin on a floured board. Have a griddle, large skillet or grill surface hot and place one side of the lefsa down. Turn once after surface begins to bubble. Remove from heat source and lefsa is ready to stuff.

Nordic Rye Bread

There's Norwegian rye, Swedish rye and Jewish rye bread, so we'll call this one Nordic rye. Easy to make and nutritious, too.

MEASURE	INGREDIENT
2 & 1/2 cups	rye flour
1 cup	unbleached white flour
1 cup	whole wheat flour
2 Tbsps	vital wheat gluten
2 Tbsps	salt
1/4 cup	raw sugar

Breads & Doughs

MEASURE	INGREDIENT
1 Tbsp	fennel seeds
2 tsps	caraway seeds
3 Tbsps	active dry yeast
1 & 1/2 cups	water - preheated to 110°F
1/4 cup	molasses
1/4 cup	soy oil
1 cup	soy milk

Sift and thoroughly combine flours with the vital wheat gluten, salt, raw sugar, caraway and fennel seeds into a large mixing bowl, then set aside.

Mix yeast into the hot water with the molasses and set aside for at least ten minutes or until surface becomes frothy. When the yeast water is frothy, add the oil and soy milk. Pour this into the center of the mixing bowl with the flours and mix well into a moist dough. Cover and allow to rise about 1 hour.

When ready, punch dough down and knead well until it is smooth and elastic. Cover again and let rise another 20-30 minutes.

Flour a board and punch down dough. Knead lightly and then cut dough in half. Take each piece and form a loaf by lightly rolling in the dough and then, while holding in both hands, pull dough underneath with your fingers while stretching the top until a nice loaf shape is achieved.

Grease a baking sheet. Place each loaf on the sheet. Bake 45 minutes in a 375°F oven. Remove from pans and let rest several minutes before slicing.

Pita Bread

This great Middle Eastern leavened flatbread has a multitude of uses. Falafel or salad stuffers are a common usage. You can be as creative as you want to be with pitas.

MEASURE	INGREDIENT
1 cup	whole wheat flour
1 Tbsp	vital wheat gluten
1 tsp	salt
1/2 tsp	baking soda
1 Tbsp	soy oil
1/2 tsp	apple cider vinegar
3/4 cup	water

Sift and thoroughly combine flour with the vital wheat gluten, salt and baking soda. Mix the oil with the water and vinegar and add this to the prepared flour mixture. Combine well and let rest for 20 minutes.

Knead dough one minute then break off balls of dough 3 inches in diameter. Roll these flat on a floured board. Preheat oven to 450°F with a flat baking stone on the oven rack. Make sure flat breads are well floured, then place them on the stone. Bake 10 minutes on one side, five minutes on the other. Remove and cool down 10 minutes. [MAKES 4-5 PITAS]

Pierogies

Pierogies are wonderful stuffed dumplings with strong elastic casings. They hold fillings well and yet, are still delicate. They can be stuffed with a variety of fillings and are used in a variety of dishes.

MEASURE	INGREDIENT
1 cup	unbleached white flour
1 Tbsp	vital wheat gluten
1 tsp	salt
3/4 cup	water

Sift and thoroughly combine flour with the vital wheat gluten and salt, then add the water. Knead lightly and let rest 20 minutes. Knead dough about 1 minute and roll out dough to an eighth inch thickness.

Use a round cookie cutter or jar lid about 3 inches in diameter and cut out discs of dough. Apply desired filling (such as **Mashed Potatoes**) in the middle and slightly off center of the dough. Use a small paint brush and brush a little cold water around the rim. Fold long side over filling and crimp down edges with a fork. Boil or fry before using. [MAKES 6 PIEROGIES]

Pot Pie Dough

Great for whole grain pot pie shells, vegetable turnovers or other dinner pastry ideas, this recipe is reliable with great flavor.

MEASURE	INGREDIENT
1 cup	whole wheat flour
1 & 1/2 cups	unbleached white flour
1 tsp	salt
1 tsp	baking powder
1 cup	soy margarine
5 Tbsps	water

Take one quarter cup of the white flour and set aside. Sift the remaining flours, salt and baking powder in a mixing bowl. Have the margarine about 70°F and cut this into the flour mix until well granulated.

Mix the five tablespoons of water with the quarter cup of flour and make a slurry. Mix this slurry into the flour mix and knead dough into a ball. Cut into four equal pieces and refrigerate at least 30 minutes before using.
[MAKES 2 PIE CRUSTS WITH TOPS]

Pancakes

Here are some easy basic pancakes recipe that are entirely vegan. Nothing makes breakfast so special like flapjacks. Use these recipes and feel free to experiment once you've learned the fundamentals.

Basic Wheat Pancakes
How about adding the goodness of whole wheat to your pancakes

MEASURE	INGREDIENT
1 cup	unbleached white flour
1/4 cup	whole wheat pastry flour
1/2 tsp	salt
4-5 tsps	raw sugar
1 tsp	baking powder
1/2 tsp	baking soda
1 tsp	*Egg Substitute*
3 Tbsps	soy margarine - melted
1 cup	soy milk
2 Tbsps	soy oil

Sift the dry ingredients into a mixing bowl. Mix the melted margarine into the soy milk and stir this into the flour mix making a loose batter.

Breads & Doughs

Heat up a skillet and add 2 tablespoons of oil. Use a ladle to drop batter into hot pan. Turn heat to medium and lightly brown both sides. Serve with maple syrup. [MAKES 6-8 PANCAKES]

Potato Pancakes
A vegan version of an old world classic.

MEASURE	INGREDIENT
2 cups	raw potatoes - grated
2 Tbsps	unbleached white flour
1/2 tsp	baking powder
2 tsps	salt
2 Tbsps	soy oil
1 Tbsp	*Egg Substitute*
2 Tbsps	onion - minced (optional)

Soak the grated potatoes in cold water for at least an hour. When ready, thoroughly mix the soaked potatoes with the other ingredients. Spoon into a hot skillet with the soy oil and fry until browned on both sides. Serve with *Sour Cream* or apple sauce. [MAKES 6-12 PANCAKES]

Matzoh Cracker Pancakes
This delicious pancake is a great way to use matzoh crackers.

MEASURE	INGREDIENT
4	whole wheat matzoh meal crackers - hand crumbled
2 Tbsps	soy oil
2	*Eggless Egg*s
3 Tbsps	unbleached white flour
1/2 cup	soy milk

MEASURE	INGREDIENT
1-2 tsps	salt
2 tsps	soy margarine - melted

Crumble matzohs with your hand, into a small bowl, then pour just enough boiling water over them to cover. Let stand 15 minutes.

Heat a skillet and add the soy oil. Mix the soaked matzohs with the eggless eggs, flour, soy milk, salt and melted margarine. Drop batter into skillet with a spoon and brown on both sides. Serve with maple syrup or fruit preserves.
[MAKES 6-8 PANCAKES]

Waffles
You need a waffle iron for this one...but its worth it.

MEASURE	INGREDIENT
2	*Eggless Egg*s
1 & 1/2 cups	soy milk
1/4 cup	soy margarine - melted
4 Tbsps	raw sugar (or xylitol)
1/2 cup	*Sour Cream*
1 cup	whole wheat pastry flour
1 cup	unbleached white flour
1/2 tsp	salt
2 tsps	baking powder
1/2 tsp	baking soda

Preheat waffle iron until it is hot and ready. Beat eggless eggs with the soy milk, melted margarine, sugar and sour cream.

Sift the flours with the salt, baking powder and baking soda. Mix the liquid ingredients with the dry ingredients forming a batter. Pour this batter in the center of each waffle section.

Breads & Doughs

Close lid and cook until waffle iron stops steaming or, if automatic, a light, bell or whistle will warn you that it is done. If iron doesn't open readily, cook one more minute. Iron should open and waffle eject easily. Serve with melted margarine and maple syrup. [MAKES 12-15 SMALL WAFFLES]

Corn Meal Pancakes
This light flapjack is a real favorite family classic.

MEASURE	INGREDIENT
2 Tbsps	raw sugar (or xylitol, or Sucanat)
1 cup	yellow corn meal
1 cup	boiling water
1/2 cup	unbleached white flour
1 tsp	salt
2 tsps	**Egg Substitute**
2 tsps	baking powder
3/4 cup	soy milk
2 Tbsps	soy margarine - melted
2 Tbsps	soy oil

Mix the raw sugar with the corn meal and then pour the boiling water in and stir well. Cover and set aside five minutes.

Sift the white flour with the salt, egg substitute and baking powder into a mixing bowl.

Mix the soy milk, melted margarine with prepared corn meal mash. Pour this thinned slurry into the bowl with the prepared flour mix. Stir this into a batter.

Heat a skillet and add the 2 tablespoons soy oil. Pour the batter in with a ladle allowing to flow in the desired sized pancake. Cook an medium, lightly browning both sides. [MAKES 4-8 PANCAKES]

Oatmeal Pancakes

Mix the best of both breakfast worlds -- oatmeal and pancakes -- in one delicious flapjack.

MEASURE	INGREDIENT
1 cup	boiling water
1/2 cup	rolled oats
1/2 cup	unbleached white flour
1 tsp	salt
1 tsp	baking powder
1 cup	soy milk
2 Tbsps	raw sugar (or xylitol)
2 Tbsps	soy margarine - melted
2 Tbsps	soy oil

Bring the cup of water to a boil in a small sauce pan. Add the oatmeal, reduce heat to low. Cook, covered for 3-5 minutes.

Mix the white flour with the salt and baking powder. Add the soy milk, sugar, and melted margarine, to the hot oatmeal. Next, pour this concoction into the flour mix and beat into a batter.

Heat a skillet and add the soy oil. Use a ladle to pour batter into pan. Brown both sides on medium heat. Serve with maple syrup. [MAKES 4-6 PANCAKES]

Blueberry Pancakes

Nothing quite compares to good, old fashioned blueberry pancakes.

MEASURE	INGREDIENT
1/2 cup	fresh blueberries
1 cup	*Basic Wheat Pancakes* batter
2 Tbsps	soy oil

Mix the fresh, washed berries with the pancake batter. Heat a skillet and add a little oil. Fry pancakes on medium, browning both sides. Cover pan during the first half of the cooking process for a better cooked berry.
[MAKE 4 LARGE PANCAKES]

Puff Pastry

This prepared dough is a very versatile substance for creating delicious and interesting baked goods, ranging from croissants to stuffed pastry pies.

MEASURE	INGREDIENT
2 & 1/2 cups	unbleached white flour
1 tsp	salt
1 cup	soy milk - preheated to 110°F
1 Tbsp	active dry yeast
1 Tbsp	raw sugar (or xylitol)
1 Tbsp	soy oil
1 cup	soy margarine - melted

Stir the flour and salt. and set aside.

Heat the soy milk to about 110°F and mix in the yeast and raw sugar. When the yeast has risen and the liquid has a foam on top, add the oil to the liquid. Now mix the liquid and salted flour mix together, knead and set aside, covered for about 45 minutes.

Punch down the expanded dough and knead until it becomes smooth and elastic. Cover the dough and refrigerate for half an hour. Remove dough and turn onto a floured board. Roll dough out into an oblong form, a 1/4 inch thick. Using a pastry brush, paint melted (not warmer than 70°F) margarine.

Fold one third of the dough into the center. Take the other end and fold that over the doubled side. You now have three layers. Roll this out again to the same dimensions as the first time. Repeat entire process a total of four times. The last time do not roll out but refrigerate folded. This refrigerated dough can be saved for future applications.

Whole Wheat Bread

Perfect bread is not difficult to make with this recipe. Adding vital wheat gluten is the key to successful whole wheat bread making.

MEASURE	INGREDIENT
4 cups	whole wheat flour
6 Tbsps	vital wheat gluten
1 Tbsp	salt
2 & 3/4 cups	water - preheated to 110°F
2 Tbsps	active dry yeast
2 Tbsps	raw sugar (or xylitol)
1/3 cup	soy oil

Sift and thoroughly combine flour with the vital wheat gluten and salt, into a large mixing bowl.

Mix the hot water with the yeast and raw sugar (or xylitol). Allow several minutes for the yeast water to become frothy, then add the oil. Pour this liquid into the center of the mixing bowl containing the flour mix. Stir well with a large rubber spatula, then finish and shape into a ball with your hands. Cover with a moist towel or inverted mixing bowl and let set in a warm room.

In about one hour the dough should have doubled in size. Punch this down and knead the dough for about two minutes. Cover dough and allow to rise again, about 30 minutes.

Punch down dough and knead about 30 seconds. Sprinkle a little flour on a board and cut dough in half. Roll each dough ball on the flour. Next, pick it up and hold the dough ball in you hands and begin to knead by drawing the dough underneath you fingers. This stretches the top while shaping into a loaf.

Grease two loaf pans and preheat oven to 400°F. Make loaves as described above and place in pans. Bake one hour or until loaf tops are firm. Remove from pans and let rest on their sides for ten minutes before slicing.

Whole Wheat Rolls
Delicious wholesome rolls for sandwiches or as dinner rolls, hot out of the oven.

MEASURE	INGREDIENT
(as needed)	***Whole Wheat Bread*** dough
1/4 cup	soy margarine - melted

Follow the directions for making whole wheat bread in this chapter. Instead of making bread loaves, however, form small balls about three inches in diameter for sandwich rolls, or two inches in diameter for dinner rolls.

Grease a cookie sheet and preheat oven to 375°F. Place balls on sheet with about one inch space around each ball. Bake about 25 minutes. Dough balls will expand and connect forming rolls. Brush tops with melted margarine after twenty minutes for a smooth, glazed finish.

White Bread
The use of organically grown and responsibly processed white flour makes this bread a nutritionally stable treat.

MEASURE	INGREDIENT
4 cups	unbleached white flour
2 Tbsps	vital wheat gluten
3 tsps	salt
2 Tbsps	soy flour (optional)
2 & 1/2 cups	water - preheated to 110°F
2 Tbsps	active dry yeast
2 Tbsps	raw sugar (or fructose, or xylitol, or Sucanat)
1/3 cup	soy oil

Sift and thoroughly combine flour with the vital wheat gluten, salt and soy flour (optional), then set aside.

Mix hot water with the yeast and raw sugar. When yeasted water froths up, pour the oil into the water. Mix this liquid thoroughly with the flour, forming a wet dough. Cover and set in a warm place to rise for one hour.

When dough has risen to twice its original size, punch it down and knead for two minutes. Cover and allow to rise again for 30 minutes.

Sprinkle a little flour on a board and cut dough in half. Roll each dough ball on the flour. Next, pick it up and hold the dough ball in you hands and begin to knead by drawing the dough underneath you fingers. This stretches the top while shaping into a loaf.

Grease two loaf pans and preheat oven to 400°F. Place loaves in pans and bake one hour or until top crust is firm. Remove from pans and let rest on their sides for ten minutes before slicing.

Vegan Meats

Introduction

In this chapter you will learn to perform a variety of techniques for transforming raw materials into high protein substances. Using only vegetable-sourced ingredients you will discover how to create 'working meats', suitable for sautés, casseroles, grilling and other applications.

The foods described in this chapter are the cornerstone of vegan home style cooking. Once you learn how to prepare and use these substances you will feel like the master of self sufficiency. No longer will you feel a slave to the American meat market. Your ability to become a vegetarian and to remain a vegetarian for the rest of your life may be based, to a good extant, on your interest in this chapter.

You will explore the wonderful power of soy and how to work with soy products. Discover how to prepare tofu or tempeh in interesting ways. An extensive section covering general usage of soy products is also included. Learn how to use TVP [Textured Vegetable Protein], in a variety of ways.

Everything you'll need to know about creating wheat meats is covered here. This chapter unveils the real power of wheat, the 'Staff of Life." Try the recipes for creating different versions of seitan, the ancient wheat meat of the Orient. Also included are some of the world's most original recipes for gluten steak and gluten products.

As you learn to produce these meats in your home, a broader understanding of the human condition will begin to grow inside of you. As you help to relieve the burden that farm animals have to bear as food commodities in our world, positive universal forces will come to your aid. The ripple effect of your evolved understanding and implementation of the recipes and principals in this book, will help to heal our world.

Soy Based Meats

Tofu

"...the other white meat". Made by curdling soy milk and then packing the curds like cheese, tofu is an ancient substance. First developed by the Chinese thousands of years ago, it has been a staple food in the Orient ever since. Introduced to the West by Chinese immigrants in the latter half of the nineteenth century, it took 100 years for the public to catch on. Today, however, many forms of tofu and tofu products flood American and European markets. With its health benefits and numerous applications, tofu has become an all world food.

Tofu is usually purchased at a local grocery or health food store. The two most common forms are basic tofu: available in soft, medium, firm or extra firm varieties; or silken tofu: also available in these grades. Silken Tofu is smooth with a very fine grain that lends itself well to preparations such as pies, cakes, sauces, condiments and thickeners. Silken Tofu is featured in a variety of recipes found in nearly every chapter in this book.

In this chapter, however, it is basic tofu and its application as a 'working meat' for sautés, soups, casseroles, grilled and broiled dishes that we'll be exploring. The grade of tofu recommended for this purpose is extra firm. Softer varieties of tofu don't hold up as well and can produce disappointing results.

Because tofu is bland in taste and weak of fiber, many unenlightened novices may think of tofu as inferior in nature. For the true master, however, it is these very qualities that provide a perfect medium for his or her art of transformation

Tofu Cooking Tips

1. The cut of tofu is of primary interest as this will define its role in the particular dish it is to be used in. Cubing tofu for sautés and casseroles, etc... is the most familiar form. Extra firm tofu is great for more interesting cuts such as fillets, steaks, triangles, cutlets and even special shapes made with cookie cutters. Thin, pan seared wafers' are another possibility. Learn to use the tip of your knife for more control in cutting out odd sautés meat pieces that resemble chicken breast or other cuts of meat.

Vegan Meats

2. Tofu can be marinated before using. Its spongy texture absorbs flavor well. Squeeze original water out of tofu block before immersing, completely in marinade.

3. Parboiling the tofu cutlets in water or stock will transform the texture from a crumbly consistency to a smoother, more flexible form. This rendering makes the tofu hold its form better. Steaming or simmering in a stew or sauté will achieve similar results.

4. As in other cooking applications, searing will help tofu surfaces to maintain their form. This quick frying in hot oil creates a microscopically thin skin that maintains the shape intended and seals in flavor. If sautéing with a small amount of oil, simply add the cuts to the sauté at an early stage and maintain medium heat. Flip pan or turn to sear all sides.

If you are preparing a larger meal or want to store these meats prepared for future use, skillet frying with non-stick cookware works well. Again, get pan hot first then reduce to medium heat. Sear all sides. If deep frying, fry 30 to 45 seconds, drain well.

5. Reverse marinating: sear tofu cuts as mentioned in rule 4, then boil in flavored stock for ten minutes.

6. When grilling tofu, preheat the tofu by heating in a pan with a little water, stock or marinade. This will help to prevent tofu from sticking on a hot grill. Brush the tofu with the desired grill glaze or with a little oil before placing tofu on the hot grill. Have grill surface temperature at medium hot and grill tofu long enough to create well defined grill lines.

7. When broiling tofu, have broiler set at 400°F. Grease a baking pan and place tofu and any vegetables desired together with the chosen sauce on the pan or tray. Baste well and broil for about 5 minutes, turn and baste a little more and broil another 5 minutes. Repeat this process until tofu and veggies are browned.

8. To sauté a scrambled mix of tofu and diced veggies, start the vegetables first with a little oil in a hot pan. Reduce heat to medium. After 5 minutes add the crumbled tofu and seasoning, cover and braise this for five minutes. Remove cover and stir mixture, then resume cooking another five minutes. Next, add liquid such as vegetable stock or citrus. Cover pan again and steam this all down

until liquid is reduced. This finished product is usually a stuffing, patty, scrambled mock egg or as a layer in casseroles.

9. To bread tofu for sautés, dredge the cuts, or slices, in flour and fry on both sides. One can substitute soy flour or a mixture of corn meal and cornstarch for wheat flour if desired.

10. To bread tofu for chicken fried applications, simply dredge piece in flour then soy milk then bread crumbs. Alternative method: soy flour or rice flour, rice milk, corn meal.   The above rules apply to all preparations of tofu as a meat substitute. To create cutlets or sauté meats and store for future use, simply use rules 2 and 3 or alternatively rules 4 and 5.

Tempeh

Tempeh is a soy bean food product produced by packing cooked, mashed beans and then fermenting for a given time period. Tempeh can be found fermented with other whole grains or vegetable bits for increased nutritional value and different flavors.

Creating tempeh at home is not recommended, it is readily available at local grocery or health food stores. Enjoying tempeh may be an acquired experience for many of us as it is has a peculiar nutty flavor. A good chef can learn to work with it, maximizing on its potential as a high protein natural foodstuff.

Like tofu, seitan or gluten, tempeh works well as sauté meat, in stews, casseroles or grilled. These are a few rules for cooking tempeh that should be observed

Tempeh Cooking Tips

1. Although possible, it is not recommended to marinate tempeh, if it is not very firm, before cooking. Tempeh may become mushy and fall apart. Reverse marinate -- sear first then soak.

2. Sear tempeh cuts. Pan fry on high heat briefly in a small amount of oil, browning all sides. Or, deep fry 45 seconds at 350°F. Drain well and use or refrigerate.

3. Keep tempeh refrigerated until using. Tempeh is firm and easy to work with cold. If tempeh is too warm it will become soft and fall apart easily.

4. To get the best flavor from tempeh, use thin slices, well seared in cooking applications. Tempeh absorbs flavor and keeps it shape if seared.

TVP

Textured Vegetable Protein (TVP) is a high protein food by-product manufactured from soy beans. Wheat and corn can also be used to produce TVP foods, though the term is usually applied to isolated soy protein products. Soy bean TVP is produced in large quantities and converted to a multitude of end use food products.

What we'll be exploring is TVP end products such as poultry or beef style chunks, TVP burger blend and soy meal or flour. These products are excellent raw materials for the vegan chef. One must, however, learn how to use them and this information is not readily available. In this section we'll look at different types of textured soy products and apply some basic rules for using effectively.

Textured soy protein is manufactured by utilizing the cracked, flaked and heated bean in the oil extraction process. The resultant meal is then emulsified and heat fused. The product is a fibrous substance that is higher in protein than beef, without fat or starch. The marketed products are usually infused with concentrated vegetable flavorings and convenient shapes for cooking applications.

Textured soy is also used as an ingredient together with wheat gluten, isolated soy protein, vegetable flavorings, herbs and spices to create the veggie cold cuts. These convenient, healthy and karma free foods are continually growing in variety and popularity. They can be found in most food markets.

Simplified, isolated soy protein is dehydrated, freeze dried tofu flakes ground into powder. Like tofu it is edible 'raw' and can be found as a main ingredient in body building protein drinks. It is also sold in capsule form as a health supplement. Other uses include silken tofu and as a binder in prepared foods.

Convenient dehydrated mixtures of these vegetable proteins are a boon for the creative vegan chef. With a variety of flavored protein mixes for specialized purposes, quick meals can be easily assembled.

In this section our main emphasis will be on the TVP burger blend. What a good vegan chef can do with raw soy burger that has similar properties as beef, is mind-boggling.   We'll examine a few recipes here, exemplifying the versatility of this substance.

Hopefully this chapter will shed some light on what these foods are and how to use them effectively. There is nothing to be afraid of. These are good, healthy protein substances that will add variety and enjoyment to your life. These products are fast becoming mainstream in our culture and will be a large part of the world's food supply in the near future.

TVP Chunks
These dehydrated soy meat chunks have been flavored with concentrated vegetable-sourced flavorings to resemble the taste of beef or chicken.

MEASURE	INGREDIENT
2 cups	TVP beef style (or TVP poultry style) [Textured Vegetable Protein]
4 cups	*Vegetable Stock* (or water)

To re-hydrate and use in sautés, salads, soups or casseroles, boil TVP chunks 3 minutes in stock or water. Cover pot and let stand about 15 minutes. Drain off any excess liquid and 'meats' are ready to use in soups, stews, casseroles or sautés. TVP will be moist and flavorful.
[MAKES ABOUT 4 CUPS OF PREPARED CHUNKS]

Vegan Meatloaf
The following recipe for vegan meatloaf is has similar characteristics to that of ground beef.

MEASURE	INGREDIENT
1 lb	TVP burger blend - dry mix
3 & 1/2 cups	ice cold water
1/4 cup	tomato paste
1 tsp	black pepper
1 Tbsp	thyme leaf
1 medium	onion - diced
1 tsp	salt
1 cup	bread crumbs

Mix the burger blend with the cold water, then refrigerate for at least 30 minutes, or more.

After sufficient set time, add all ingredients together and mix with your clean hands, by smooshing TVP through your fingers. It is the best way to thoroughly mix it, as the working material is extremely stiff.

Preheat oven to 400°F. Grease a bread loaf pan and push the mixture into the pan. Use wet hands to smooth the top over, then bake loaf in the oven for 55 minutes.

Allow to cool completely before using. Loaf should be cooled to 40°F before using. If you attempt to serve immediately from the oven, loaf will crumble badly.

To prepare loaf for serving, slice off desired number of pieces about a half inch thick from cold loaf. Heat up a skillet and add a small amount of oil. Brown each piece well on both sides. Serve with vegan gravy or other sauce or use cold in sandwiches with ketchup. [10 PORTIONS]

NOTE: A dinner made with slices of this loaf, mashed potatoes and vegan gravy is the single most popular item sold at Veggie Works. It is no wonder, as this vegan version beats out any meatloaf made with animal flesh, hands down. This loaf has tamed a great many carnivores since it was introduced in 1994, and if you learn to make correctly, you will convert many more.

Breakfast 'Sausage'
Great little mock sausage patties with lots of protein. Excellent accompaniment to *Mock Scrambled Eggs* and pancakes or muffins.

MEASURE	INGREDIENT
1 cup	TVP burger blend - dry mix
2 Tbsps	unbleached white flour (organic)
1 Tbsp	vital wheat gluten
1/2 tsp	salt
2 tsps	fennel seeds - crushed
1 pinch each:	cumin, thyme, coriander, savory, bay leaves - powdered
1 Tbsp	soy oil
2 & 1/2 cups	ice cold water

Mix all the dry ingredients, then set aside. Mix oil and water, then combine with dry ingredients and chill for 30 minutes. Wet hands and form 3-4 patties. Griddle fry, covered on medium heat. [MAKES 6-8 SMALL PATTIES]

Italian Sausage
With all the flavor, appearance and texture of the traditional pork and beef version.

MEASURE	INGREDIENT
3 Tbsps	fennel seeds - crushed
1 lb	TVP burger blend - dry mix
3 & 1/2 cups	ice cold water
1 tsp	allspice
1 tsp	salt
1 tsp	black pepper
3 Tbsps	soy oil
2 Tbsps	onion powder
1 Tbsp	garlic powder
1 cup	vital wheat gluten
1/4 cup	olive oil
1 cup	**Vegetable Stock**

Heat up a skillet (or saute pan), then dry roast fennel seeds until lightly browned.

Mix the burger blend with the cold water, then refrigerate for at least 30 minutes, or more.

Place the prepared burger mix in a large bowl and combine the roasted fennel seed, allspice, salt, pepper, soy oil, onion and garlic powders. Mix ingredients well.

Remove a small handful of the sausage mixture and form this into a one inch diameter by 4-5 inches long cylinder (using wet hands). Pour a small amount of the vital wheat gluten into a tray and proceed to roll the sausage in this flour. When sausage is coated, wet your hands again and gently hydrate the vital wheat gluten coating on the sausage. Repeat this procedure several times until a 'skin' develops. Use the same method to convert the rest of the TVP mixture into sausages.

When sausages are 'skinned', heat up a large skillet and add enough olive oil to cover bottom of pan. Pan fry sausages in the olive oil, turning to brown all sides. Remove sausages when well browned.

Next, pour off oil from skillet and add one-half cup of the vegetable stock. Place half the sausages in the pan, bring to a boil and then simmer until liquid is absorbed. Repeat this procedure with the rest of the sausages. Sausages can now be refrigerated for use in sautes, etc. [MAKE 15-20 SMALL SAUSAGES]

Taco-Style Ground 'Beef'
This method of preparing ground soy burger can be altered with spices to create authentic tasting ethnic meals.

MEASURE	INGREDIENT
1 lb	TVP burger blend - dry mix
3 & 1/2 cups	ice cold water
1 cup	onions - diced
2 Tbsps	garlic clove - crushed
1/4 cup	soy oil
1 tsp	salt
1/2 tsp	black pepper
2 tsps	oregano

Mix the burger blend with the cold water, then refrigerate for at least 30 minutes, or more. Fry onions, garlic and spices in oil, on medium heat, for 5 minutes. Crumble in raw TVP, add salt and oregano, cover pan and cook 3 minutes. Uncover, chop-up burger, mix into saute and brown 10 minutes. Makes about 3 pounds of seasoned taco style 'beef'.

Vegan Meatballs

Our Veggie Works brand of TVP burger blend, makes the best meatballs. It has been said that our meatballs are better than traditional meatballs made with animal flesh. Here are two recipes for meatballs, both delicious.

Italian Meatballs
With all the flavor, texture and protein of traditional Italian meatballs, this vegan version has no cholesterol and no saturated fat.

MEASURE	INGREDIENT
1 lb	TVP burger blend - dry mix
3 & 1/2 cups	ice cold water
1 small	onion - diced
3 Tbsps	garlic clove - crushed
1/4 cup	parsley - chopped
2 Tbsps	oregano
1-2 tsps	salt
1/2 tsp	black pepper
1 cup	bread crumbs
(as needed)	soy oil (for frying)

Mix the burger blend with the cold water, then refrigerate for at least 30 minutes, or more. After set time, toss all ingredients into the prepared burger mix and smoosh together with clean hands. Squeeze and push hands into mix letting it squeeze through your fingers. You can add a little cold water if it seems too dry.

Once mixed, use wet hands to form small round balls. Heat skillet and add oil (about 1/4 cup). Fry balls, turning to brown all sides. Remove to cook further in **Marinara Sauce** sauce. [MAKES ABOUT 30 MEATBALLS]

Swedish Meatballs
A Scandinavian favorite, during the holiday seasons.

MEASURE	INGREDIENT
1 lb	TVP burger blend - dry mix
3 & 1/2 cups	ice cold water
1 small	onion - diced
1-2 tsps	salt
1/2 tsp	black pepper
1 scant tsp	nutmeg
1 cup	bread crumbs
1/4 cup	parsley - minced
1 qt	*Swedish Meatball Gravy*

Mix the burger blend with the cold water, then refrigerate for at least 30 minutes, or more. Mix in other ingredients well, as described in above recipe for *Italian Meatballs*.

Fry balls the same as above meatball recipe. Finish meatballs by simmering in prepared gravy. [MAKES ABOUT 30 MEATBALLS]

Eggless Egg
Use in baking and to facilitate the rendering of recipes that usually include eggs, to healthy vegan recipes.

Note: The ratio is 1:1, or, 1 EGG = 1 EGGLESS EGG.

MEASURE	INGREDIENT
6-oz (1/2 package)	silken-firm tofu
2 tsps	*Egg Substitute*
1 tsp	powdered lecithin
3 Tbsps	water

Vegan Meats

Note: Do not attempt to use as breakfast eggs, i.e. scrambled. This is a baking agent only.

Blend ingredients with a blender or food processor and refrigerate for future use.

Egg Substitute
This powdered mixture of binding and leavening agents serves as a healthy replacement for eggs.

MEASURE	INGREDIENT
1 Tbsp	cornstarch
1/2 tsp	baking powder
1/4 tsp	baking soda
1 tsp	xanthum gum
3 Tbsps	water

Note: This recipe produces the equivalent of one baking egg.

Thoroughly combine all dry ingredients together, then mix into the water. Use as a substitute for one egg in baking recipes.

Mock Scrambled Eggs
This recipe works well as a scrambled egg substitute.
This recipe makes two average sized portions.

MEASURE	INGREDIENT
1 lb block	tofu - hand crumbled
1 Tbsp	onion powder
1/2 tsp	garlic powder
1/2 tsp	salt
1 pinch	black pepper
1 Tbsp	nutritional yeast

MEASURE	INGREDIENT
2 Tbsps	soy oil (or soy margarine)
1/2 cup	**Vegetable Stock**

Hand crumble the tofu into a mixing bowl. Mix in flavoring agents: onion powder, garlic powder, salt, pepper, and nutritional yeast. Heat up a skillet and add the oil or margarine. Reduce heat to medium. Have the tofu mixture close to room temperature and add it to the hot oil.

Use a wooden spatula or similar device to stir the tofu, lightly browning it. Next add the vegetable stock, cover and reduce liquid until tofu scrambled 'eggs' are moist, with no additional liquid. Scrambled tofu 'eggs' are now ready to serve. [2-4 PORTIONS]

Tofu Crabcakes
This excellent cake can be baked with a number of unique sauces to create different mock crab cake recipes.

MEASURE	INGREDIENT
3 Tbsps	soy oil
1/2	onion - minced
4	celery stalks - minced
1 cup	colored bell peppers - minced
2 lb packages	firm tofu - crumbled
1 Tbsp	Old Bay Seasoning
1 Tbsp	garlic powder
1 tsp	powdered thyme
1 Tbsp	salt
1/2 tsp	black pepper
1/3 cup	orange juice
1/2	lemon - juiced
1/2 cup	**Vegetable Stock**
1 cup	unbleached white flour
1/2 cup	bread crumbs

Vegan Meats

Heat a large skillet or pot and add the oil. Mince the onion, celery, bell peppers, then begin frying on medium heat. After frying for about 5 minutes, crumble the tofu into the pan and stir into sautéing vegetables. Add the Old Bay Seasoning, garlic powder, thyme, salt, black pepper, orange juice and squeezed juice from halved lemon, to the cooking mixture. Stir this around and simmer on low for about three minutes, covered. Next add the vegetable stock and simmer, covered, for another 5 minutes. This will reduce liquid and change the texture of the tofu.

Remove tofu mixture from heat and set aside to cool. When sufficiently cooled down, add the bread crumbs and half the flour. Mix together well and form cakes with your hands. You will need to keep wetting hands to prevent crab cake mixture from sticking to them.

Dredge crab cakes in the rest of the flour and fry on each side in a skillet with hot oil. Use medium heat and cover pan to cook evenly. Bake, covered with **Marinara Sauce** and smothered in soy cheese or serve with rice and steamed asparagus, topped with **Seafood Sauce**. [MAKES 10-12 CRABCAKES]

Baked Tofu Turkey
Recreate the flavor of turkey, by marinating a block of tofu, then baking it. A great centerpiece to a large meal.

MEASURE	INGREDIENT	
1 lb package	extra-firm tofu	
2 Tbsps	soy oil	
3 cups	Vegetable Stock	(for marinade)
1/2 cup	orange juice	(")
2 Tbsps	nutritional yeast	(")
1/2 tsp	powdered thyme	(")
1/2 tsp	powdered sage	(")
1 Tbsp	soy sauce	(")
1 tsp	sea salt	(")

With the exception of the tofu and soy oil, mix all other ingredients together, to create marinade. Use a small, deep plastic container or stainless steel bowl to place the tofu and pour in the marinade mixture. Make sure that the tofu is completely immersed. Cover container if necessary. Allow tofu to marinate several hours...or overnight.

Preheat an oven to 350°F. Place the marinated tofu into a baking pan or dish that is small, square and deep. Mix the soy oil into the marinade, then pour enough marinade into the baking pan to cover the tofu halfway. Cover the pan with aluminum foil and bake the tofu for 30 minutes.

Remove the pan from the oven and uncover it. Flip the tofu over and add more marinade to cover half the tofu. Bake another 10 minutes covered, then uncover and roast tofu for 20 more minutes, basting occasionally with remaining marinade. By this time liquid should have significantly reduced. Remove tofu and let rest several minutes before slicing. [4-6 PORTIONS]

Tempeh Bacon Strips

Use this clever recipe to create bacon-like flavor in thin strips of pan fried tempeh. An excellent side dish for breakfast, or *Bacon Lettuce & Tomato Sandwich*!

MEASURE	INGREDIENT
1/4 cup	***Vegetable Stock***
2 Tbsps	vegan-style bacon bits
1-2 pinches	black pepper
few drops	Liquid Smoke
1/4 cup	soy oil (for frying)
1 lb block	tempeh

Prepare the flavoring by simmering the vegetable stock with the bacon bits, black pepper and liquid smoke, for five minutes on low heat. Strain off and set aside liquid.

Heat up a skillet and add the oil. Cut the tempeh into thin, long strips and begin frying, on medium heat. Brown both sides of the tempeh then pour in the

Vegan Meats

strained stock. Reduce heat and simmer until liquid is absorbed. Move pieces around in the dry pan a few moments to firm up strips, then serve hot.
[4-6 PORTIONS]

Wheat Based Meats

Seitan

Proteins contain amino acids and these substances are the building blocks of life. 22 of these amino acids make up a complete protein, yet only 8 amino acids are considered essential amino acids. If a protein rich food has significant amounts of these 8 essential amino acids, the other 14 acids can be synthesized by the human body.

Most grain or legume-sourced protein lack a "perfectly balanced" ratio of these eight amino acids. Animal flesh is rich in essential aminos and this is the basis for belief that animal protein is superior to vegetable protein.

The truth is that, through a balanced vegetarian diet, all the essential amino acids can easily be obtained. Some grains and beans have higher concentrations of certain essential aminos that are found lacking in other grains and beans. A variety of fresh vegetables in your diet also contribute to boosting your essential amino acid levels. It is actually nature's way of telling you that you should eat a variety of vegan foods to live healthy.

The following includes a recipe that mimics animal flesh in its balance of essential amino acids. *Seitan Supreme* is fortified with wheat, soy and corn flours and presents itself as a "perfect" protein, as it contains a strong balance of all the essential amino acids. This illustrates the point that by combining natural plant based foods one can easily produce perfect protein products.

Rest assured that achieving a "perfect protein" is not necessary in your diet. A well balanced diet with fruit, vegetables, nuts, grains, beans and veggie meats (such as gluten steak, TVP, tofu, tempeh or basic seitan) provide all of the essential amino acids needed by your body.

Basic Seitan
**This is the basic formula for excellent homemade seitan.
Can be used as stew meat or 'beef' chunks in
sautes, soups, casseroles and more!**

MEASURE	INGREDIENT
1 cup	unbleached white flour
3 1/2 cups	vital wheat gluten
1 tsp	salt
3 cups	cold water
4 qts	*Vegetable Stock*

Thoroughly sift and combine the flour with the vital wheat gluten and salt, then add the water. Use your hands to mix into a firm dough. Allow dough to rest for at least 15 minutes.

After rest period, knead the dough with your hands as you would a bread loaf for about one minute. Allow dough to rest again for another 5-15 minutes.

After second rest period, knead dough as before but this time dig deeper with your fingers until dough thins at center. Continuing this motion, center will tear away, leaving a doughnut shaped rope of raw seitan.

Wet hands lightly and place rope on a cutting board. Cut rope at some point and then slice inch thick rounds off of seitan dough rope. Have stock boiling on the stove and commence tossing the seitan medallions into the pot, making sure that medallions don't stick to each other. Cover pot, reduce heat to medium and boil seitan for a minimum of 20 minutes.

When cooking period is finished, remove seitan chunks from stock pot using a small strainer to pick them out of the pot. Place cooked seitan in a bowl or container for cooling. Cooked seitan will not stick together so no need to worry about putting all the pieces together.

Seitan medallions are now ready for use, and can be used whole, chopped, or sliced. Prepared cuts should then always be pan seared in a small amount of oil before using in meals. Can be frozen. [MAKES ABOUT 30 MEDALLIONS]

Seitan Supreme

This recipe for seitan is fortified with corn and soy flours to create a meat-like substance with all 8 essential amino acids.

MEASURE	INGREDIENT
1/2 cup	unbleached white flour
3 cups	vital wheat gluten
1/4 cup	fine grain corn meal
1/4 cup	soy flour
1 tsp	baking powder
1 tsp	salt
2 & 3/4 cups	cold water
4 qts	***Vegetable Stock***

Prepare the seitan supreme exactly as in the recipe for **Basic Seitan**. Thoroughly sift and combine the flour with the vital wheat gluten, corn meal and salt, then add the water. Mix well and knead dough lightly. Allow to rest 20 minutes. Knead once more and let rest another 10 minutes.

Form into dough ring, slice up and cook in the vegetable stock. Produces 2 & 1/2 inch diameter medallions. See **Basic Seitan** recipe, for additional details. [MAKES 25-30 MEDALLIONS]

Seitan Deluxe

Another fortified seitan meat product. This one features minced vegetables for boosting nutrition and flavor. An interesting foodstuff that can be used in a variety of ways.

MEASURE	INGREDIENT
2/3 cup	unbleached white flour (organic)
2 cups	vital wheat gluten
1 tsp	garlic powder
1 tsp	baking powder
1 tsp	salt
1 & 3/4 cups	water
4 qts	***Vegetable Stock***
1 cup mixed:	carrots, onions, mushrooms, colored bell peppers - finely diced

Thoroughly sift and combine the flour with the vital wheat gluten, garlic powder, baking powder and salt. Drain the diced vegetables on a paper towel, then thoroughly combine them into the dry flour mix. Add the water and try to keep veggies well distributed while gently mixing. Allow dough ball to rest for 20 minutes.

After first rest period, knead dough gently. The diced vegetables make the kneading process a little tricky. Let dough rest another 10 to 20 minutes.

After second rest period, knead dough into dough-ring as described in the recipe for **Basic Seitan**. As an alternative you can pat or roll dough twice its size on a floured board and then cut into steaks. Cook as directed in Basic Seitan recipe. [MAKES 10-15 MEDALLIONS]

Perfect Gluten Flank Steak
Can be used in various recipes, just as one uses raw meat, and substitutes well for chicken, beef or veal. Extremely high in protein and similar in texture to animal flesh.

MEASURE	INGREDIENT
2 cups	vital wheat gluten
2 & 1/2 cups	cold water
2 qts	*Vegetable Stock*

NOTE: Carefully following directions, is imperative to the success of this recipe. Exact proportions and precise set time, determine the success of this process. The result is a thin steak with excellent texture, pliability and taste!

Sift then pour the measured vital wheat gluten into a mixing bowl. Next pour in the water and mix thoroughly, but briefly, then pat mass to flatten slightly. Do this in less than one minute and only with your hands.

Allow mass to set up for 60 minutes. Gluten should now appear to be glossy and will have expelled any unused water. Test mass by gently tugging on an edge. If gluten surface tears slightly and doesn't stretch well, wait an additional five minutes. Test also by running your finger over the surface of the mass. If the skin tears, it's not ready. If only an ounce, or more, of extra water is used, set time could increase to 90 minutes or more.

Cut gluten mass into 8 equal pieces. Using a rolling pin and a cool flat surface (such as a stainless steel table), carefully roll gluten piece into an almost paper-thin irregular shape.*

Have well flavored vegetable stock boiling on the stove. Drop each steak into the stock as soon as it is rolled out. Do not allow any set time after rolling out steak before cooking it. Any modifications to these instructions will result in a mushy steak, that easily breaks apart, or a rubbery - shoe leather - textured product.

Boil steaks in preheated stock, covered, for a minimum of ten minutes, or a maximum period of 30 minutes. Carefully remove steaks from stock pot with tongs or by straining off stock. Steaks should rest for 15 minutes or more before handling as they could easily tear while they're still hot. Allow them to gradually cool to room temperature. Don't attempt to plunge into cold water or cool rapidly! After this period, steaks are ready to be used as meat.

*NOTE: The explanation for this is simple, as there must be a minimum of protein fibers flowing in the same direction for producing a perfect, unleavened gluten flank steak. [MAKES 8 STEAKS]

New York Gluten Strip
Almost identical in appearance and flavor to a cut of beef, with high protein content. Don't forget those steak knives!

MEASURE	INGREDIENT
2 & 1/4 cups	**Vegetable Stock**
1 Tbsp	soy oil
1 lb package	soft tofu
2 1/2 cups	vital wheat gluten
1/2 tsp	salt
1 tsp	baking powder
1/2 cup	**Grill Goddess Sauce**

Have 2 & 1/4 cups of vegetable stock at (or below) room temperature, and mix the soy oil into this stock. Place tofu into food processor and begin processing while slowly pouring in prepared stock solution.

Thoroughly mix vital wheat gluten with salt and baking powder in a large mixing bowl. Now, quickly and evenly stir in strained tofu-stock liquid, into the dry flour mix. Pat mixture down with your hands or spatula and allow to set for one hour.

Grease a medium sized casserole dish and preheat oven to 450°F. Remove the ready gluten mass to a table or board and slice, as you would a pie, into 5-6 pieces. Carefully knead pieces by gently rubbing, tugging and twisting steaks. Brush a little oil on the bottom of each steak then place these strips into the greased dish and brush tops of steaks with Grill Goddess sauce. Cover with foil and roast for 35 minutes.

Vegan Meats

Remove foil and turn steaks. Baste with the additional Grill Goddess sauce and bake another 10 minutes uncovered. Remove from oven. Steaks should appear fairly dry and puffed up. Steaks are now ready to grill, broil or store refrigerated. Note: When re-cooking steaks, add plenty of vegetable stock, as this will restore them to a thick, juicy condition. [MAKES 5-6 STEAKS]

Southern Fried Gluten Cutlet

This recipe for Southern Fried Gluten is a great substitute for fried chicken. Great texture and great flavor highlight the result.

MEASURE	INGREDIENT
2 & 1/4 cups	vital wheat gluten
1 tsp	baking powder
1/2 tsp	salt
1 tsp	powdered thyme
1 tsp	powdered savory
1/2 tsp	powdered sage
1 Tbsp	soy oil
1 Tbsp	nutritional yeast
3 cups	*Vegetable Stock*
3/4 lb package	firm tofu
1 cup	unbleached white flour (or whole wheat flour)
1/2 cup	soy milk
1 cup	unseasoned bread crumbs

Thoroughly mix vital wheat gluten with baking powder and salt, then set aside. Mix the herbs, oil and nutritional yeast into the vegetable stock. Pour 1/2 cup of this stock into a separate cup and set aside for later use. Using a blender, mix remainder (2 & 1/2 cups) of vegetable stock (make sure this stock is at room temperature or cooler) with firm tofu. Combine (in a medium sized mixing bowl) tofu-stock liquid with the prepared gluten powder mixture. Mix well, but for only a few moments, as this can upset the texture. Pat down surface and allow to set for 45 minutes.

Grease an 8"x12" casserole dish and preheat oven to 425°F. When set, gently knead gluten mass, then place onto a clean surface and evenly slice into 12 pieces. Place gluten cuts into the casserole dish and baste with a little oil. Cover with foil and bake for 25 minutes.

Remove foil from baking dish from oven. Pour in the 1/2 cup of additional vegetable stock and use a metal spatula to loosen and turn pieces over. Bake another 10 minutes uncovered to dry out and 'set' gluten. Let gluten pieces rest and cool. Once cooled, add the remaining vegetable stock and allow oven dried gluten pieces to rehydrate.

When gluten pieces are cooled you can bread and fry them like chicken. Simply dredge first in the flour then the soy milk and finally the bread crumbs. Fry in a hot pan at medium heat, covered, until well browned. Serve hot or cold.

Note: This tasty gluten recipe follows the same basic rules as the recipe for New York gluten strip, the difference lies essentially with the flavorings and cuts. [MAKES 2 CUTLETS]

Chicken Fried Gluten Cutlet
These breaded cutlets can be used for a variety of purposes. Use them in sandwiches or sautes, with delicious results.

MEASURE	INGREDIENT
1/2 cup	unbleached white flour (or whole wheat flour)
1/4 cup	soy milk
1/2 cup	unseasoned bread crumbs
1	*Perfect Gluten Flank Steak* - cutlet (alternatively: tofu or tempeh cutlets)
(as needed)	soy oil (for frying)

Vegan Meats

Put the flour, soy milk and bread crumbs into individual bowls. Take steak or cutlets (whole or sliced into desired shapes and sizes), first dredge in flour, then dip floured pieces into the soy milk, and finally coat with bread crumbs.

Heat a skillet and add enough oil to coat the bottom of the pan. fry each breaded cutlet on both sides to brown evenly. Cutlets are ready to serve or incorporate into another dish. Cutlets breaded and fried can be stored refrigerated for several days before using. [MAKES 1 STEAK]

Gluten Roulade
An excellent example of the versatility of our gluten flank steak. This one excels over beef!

MEASURE	INGREDIENT
2 Tbsps	olive oil
1 cup	portabella mushroom - sliced
2 cups	raw spinach - shredded
3 tsps	garlic clove - minced
1/2 cup	fresh parsley - minced
2 pinches	salt and black pepper
1 large	*Perfect Gluten Flank Steak*
3 Tbsps	soy parmesan cheese - grated
1 cup	unbleached white flour
1/4 cup	soy oil
1 cup	*Marinara Sauce*
2 Tbsps	soy mozzarella cheese -grated (optional)

Heat a sauté pan (or skillet) and olive oil, then gradually add sliced portabella mushrooms, shredded spinach, minced garlic and fresh parsley, salt and pepper. Lay the flank steak on a flat surface and spread the cooked saute mixture evenly over entire steak. Sprinkle the soy parmesan cheese over this spread.

Starting with the side nearest you, begin rolling up the filled steak until you have a cylinder shape. Holding this together in your hands, carefully dredge roulade in the flour.

Heat a skillet and add the soy oil. Gently lay the roulade in the hot oil and lower heat to medium. Cover and fry for 3 minutes. Uncover and gently turn roulade to brown another of three total sides. As sides brown, roulade stiffens and begins to maintain its own shape. When all sides have been browned, remove roulade and transfer it to a small baking dish with a little marinara sauce covering the bottom. Cover roulade with more marinara and soy cheese (optional) and bake for 10 minutes in a 450°F oven. [1-2 PORTIONS]

Desserts

Introduction

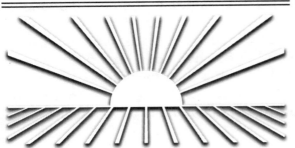

In this chapter we'll investigate the sweet world of desserts, cookies and confections. You will learn the fundamentals of vegan dessert making and the relationship of common elements. You'll discover that working without eggs or dairy can be easier than you thought, with great results.

Decades ago, people believed the more eggs and dairy you could put into something, the healthier it was. Good health was not equated with vitamins, enzymes, complex carbohydrates or clean proteins, but with sustaining power or, how well food "stuck to your ribs." Meat, dairy and eggs were good, vegetables and fruits were canned.

The health movement in America, spawned in the 1970's, has defined our current understanding of what healthy foods are. A movement that was once recognized for yogurt and goat cheese has evolved into a completely plant based movement with icons such as silken tofu and vegan meat analogs.

In this Chapter we'll examine a number of recipes from cookies to cakes and pies. You'll learn how to use egg substitutes for binding, silken tofu for body, and various natural sweeteners. Also included, basics for making great pie crusts, mixing wet and dry ingredients for cakes and cookies, and baking instructions.

As with all of the recipes in this book, those included in this chapter are intended inspire and teach. Once the dedicated chef understands his materials and has worked some examples, a world of possibilities for new creations will be at your command!

Apple Sauce Doughnuts

A great way to make vegan doughnuts with the autumnal flavors of apple and holiday spices.

MEASURE	INGREDIENT
1 cup	raw sugar (or fructose, or xylitol)
3 Tbsps	*Egg Substitute*
1 cup	apple sauce
1/4 cup	soy margarine - melted
4 cups	unbleached white flour
2 Tbsps	baking powder
1/2 tsp	salt
2 pinches	cinnamon
1 pinch	nutmeg

Beat the sugar with the egg substitute, apple sauce and margarine in a mixing bowl. Sift or mix flour, baking powder, salt and spices in another bowl. Next, fold the wet ingredients into the dry ingredients, carefully, with a few slow strokes. This is to prevent excess gluten development, resulting in a tough doughnut.

Turn the resulting dough mass onto a floured board and gently roll out the dough to 1/4 inch thickness. Next cut the doughnut shape with 2 round cookie cutters of unequal diameter or use a doughnut cutting tool. Place cut doughnut rings and doughnut balls on a lightly floured cookie sheet and let rest 15 minutes.

Heat a large cast iron skillet and add 1 cup of soy oil. If you are using a deep fryer have oil at 350°F. Begin frying doughnuts and doughnut balls, on one side for 2-3 minutes, turn and fry the other side another 2 minutes. Remove from fryer or skillet and allow to drain well. Decorate with cake icing or use as an interesting dessert. [MAKES 12-16 DOUGHNUTS]

Apple Pie

What's better than Mom's apple pie. This recipe is rooted in the great American homestyle tradition, yet is entirely vegan.

MEASURE	INGREDIENT
8	Granny Smith apples
1	lemon - juiced
1 tsp	allspice
1 tsp	cinnamon
1/2 tsp	ginger powder
2 Tbsps	raw sugar (or xylitol)
3 Tbsps	cornstarch
(as needed)	*Basic Pie Crust* dough

Peel, core and slice apples into thin wedges. Squeeze the lemon juice into a bowl with apple slices and mix well. This will prevent browning of the apples and adds zest to the flavor. Now mix in the spices, sugar (or xylitol) and cornstarch.

On a floured surface, roll out half the dough to a thickness of about 1/8 inch, then place into a greased pie dish or pan. Prick holes around crust and paint oil or melted margarine on surface.

Dump the apple mix into the prepared pie shell and then roll out other half of dough. Brush a little cold water around rim of pie shell and place top crust over apples. Using a fork, crimp down the edge around the pie, locking the two crusts together. Prick holes or cut slits into crust to release steam.

Bake in a 425°F oven for 45 minutes or until juice begins to ooze and pie crust is browned and firm. To prevent burning of the crust edge, crimp a thin strip of tin foil around edge while baking.

Baked Custard

Traditionally made with lots of eggs and milk, this vegan version tastes great, sets up well, and is actually good for you.

MEASURE	INGREDIENT
2 12-oz packages	silken-firm tofu
1/2 cup	soy milk (or fruit juice)
4 tsps	*Egg Substitute*
1/2 cup	raw sugar (or xylitol, or Sucanat)
1 tsp	xanthum gum

Blend all ingredients. Grease 6 custard cups and fill each one with mixture. Pre-heat oven to 350°F. Place cups in a pan with water and put this in the hot oven. Bake 30 minutes and test with a knife or toothpick. If toothpick comes out free of custard, it's done.

For an alternative usage, pour blended custard in a pie shell and bake 30 minutes. Scatter slivered almonds on top after 20 minutes in the oven.

Banana Cake

This cake is one of our customer favorites with its homespun flavor and light texture, it will become one of your favorites, too.

MEASURE	INGREDIENT
1/2 cup	raw sugar (or xylitol)
1/2 cup	soy margarine
1 tsp	vanilla extract
2 Tbsps	*Egg Substitute*
2 cups	unbleached white flour
1/2 tsp	salt
1 tsp	baking powder
1 tsp	baking soda

Desserts

MEASURE	INGREDIENT
2	ripe bananas - mashed
1/4 cup	soy milk
2 Tbsps	apple cider vinegar
1/2 cup	walnuts - chopped (optional)

In a large mixing bowl, blen sugar with margarine, vanilla and egg substitute. Sift 1 cup of the flour with salt, baking powder and baking soda into same mixing bowl. Cream this well together.

Next, blend in the ripe bananas with the soy milk and vinegar. When well blended, add the remaining flour and chopped nuts and mix to incorporate.

Pour batter into a well greased 9"x 13" baking pan and bake at 350°F for about 35 minutes. Test if done with a toothpick, cake wire or fork. When cooled, ice with **Mocha Frosting**. [8-12 PORTIONS]

Banana Flambe

An appetizing dessert, made with fresh bananas (or other tropical fruit). It's quick and easy, and an excellent way to top off a Pacific Rim or Meso-American dinner.

MEASURE	INGREDIENT
2	ripe bananas
2 Tbsps	soy margarine
1 shot	rum liquor (or cognac)

Peel and slice bananas into discs a quarter of an inch thick. Heat a skillet on the stove and add margarine. Dump in banana slices and toss pan frequently under high heat. After two minutes add rum or cognac and toss for another minute. CAUTION!!! Pan will flame up after alcohol is added.

Serve immediately on a dessert plate with a slice of orange. [1-2 PORTIONS]

Basic Pie Crust

This recipe is for an all-purpose wheat pie crust that is easy to make and goes well with most types of pie. From apple to berry, pumpkin or meringue, this crust stands up well, is light and tastes good.

MEASURE	INGREDIENT
1 cup	whole wheat flour
1 cup	unbleached white flour
1/4 cup	ice cold water
1 tsp	baking powder
2 Tbsps	raw sugar (or xylitol)
1/2 tsp	salt
3/4 cup	soy margarine (or soy oil)

Mix the flours in a medium-size bowl, then transfer a 1/4 cup of the mixed flour into a small bowl. Mix the cold water with this 1/4 cup of flour into a wet slurry or paste, and set aside.

Mix the remaining dry ingredients in a large mixing bowl. Making sure the soy margarine or oil is about 70°F, cut this into the dry mix, using a pastry cutter. Cut until mixture is granulated into small beads.

Next, evenly distribute the slurry over the cut flour mix and then mix it in thoroughly. Use your hands to knead dough for about one minute. Mold dough into a ball and refrigerate before using.

When ready to use for pie crust, remove dough from refrigeration and cut in half. Flour a board and roll one half of the dough into a 1/8 inch thick, large round disk. Grease a pie dish and lay dough inside. Paint pie crust with margarine or oil before adding filling and prick holes in it with a fork. Use other half of dough to roll out for pie's top crust.
[MAKES ENOUGH DOUGH FOR 1 LARGE PIE]

Basic Pie Crust II

**Another basic pie crust, this version is somewhat simpler to make.
This recipe is lighter than *Basic Pie Crust*, as it uses
only unbleached white flour.**

MEASURE	INGREDIENT
2 & 1/2 cups	unbleached white flour
1 tsp	salt
1 tsp	raw sugar (or xylitol, or Sucanat)
1 cup	soy margarine (chilled)
1/4-1/2 cup	water - ice cold

Put dry ingredients in the bowl of a food processor. Pulse to combine. Next combine the margarine by adding small amounts between more pulsing until all the margarine is combined. Mixture should now appear mealy.

Continue to pulse while adding the ice water slowly to the meal until the texture changes to a stiff dough. Be careful not to add too much ice water.

Chill dough well until ready for use then follow directions for rolling out dough and forming pie crusts as illustrated in the Basic Pie Crust recipe.

Bavarian Cream Pie

**With all the rich flavor and body of the classic dairy version,
this vegan recipe creates a light creamy, uncooked
filling for pies or stuffed pastries.**

MEASURE	INGREDIENT
1 & 1/4 cups	soy milk
1/2 cup	raw sugar (or xylitol, or Sucanat)
2 Tbsps	agar agar flakes
1/4 cup	cold water

MEASURE	INGREDIENT
1/2 tsp	vanilla extract
1 cup	**Whipped Cream**

Heat the soy milk and dissolve the sugar in it. Soak the agar agar in the cold water for several minutes, then add this to the heated milk. Slowly bring this to a boil then remove from heat and allow to cool, refrigerated.

When cooled down, but before it has completely set up, add vanilla extract and fold whipped cream into mixture. Use this finished cream filling in cooled pie crusts for refrigerated cream pies, or place in parfait glasses to chill until serving. Chill down to 40°F before serving. You can also put the Bavarian cream filling into a pastry decorating bag and fill pastries to make stuffed doughnuts or eclairs. [MAKES ENOUGH CUSTARD FOR 1 LARGE PIE]

Berry Pie
**Blueberry, cherry, strawberry or wild berry pies are
wonderful desserts, and easy to make too.**

MEASURE	INGREDIENT
4 cups	fresh berries (or frozen)
3 Tbsps	raw sugar (or xylitol)
3 Tbsps	cornstarch
(as needed)	**Basic Pie Crust** dough

If using frozen berries, thaw out berries and pour off some of the excess juice before adding the sugar and cornstarch. Roll the dough and prepare a pie shell for berry mixture. Fill prepared pie shell with berry mixture, then bake as instructed in recipe for **Apple Pie**.

Desserts

Birch Sugar Syrup

This easy syrup is tasty and useful for different applications. It's naturally clear in appearance, and can substitute for maple syrup.

MEASURE	INGREDIENT
1/4 cup	xylitol (birch sugar)
1/4 cup	water

In a small sauce pan stir together the xylitol and water while heating to a boil. Simmer to reduce until syrup has thickened but still flows. Use immediately, as syrup will set up as it cools (can be thinned with a little warm water). [MAKES 1/4 CUP SYRUP]

Brownies

Everybody loves brownies, especially kids. This recipe is entirely vegan but has all the flavor and richness as traditional brownies.

MEASURE	INGREDIENT
1 & 1/4 cups	unbleached white flour
1/2 tsp	baking powder
3/4 cup	cocoa
1/4 tsp	salt
1 Tbsp	*Egg Substitute*
1 cup	soy margarine
2 cups	raw sugar (or xylitol, or Sucanat)
2 tsps	vanilla extract
1 cup	non-dairy unsweetened chocolate chips

Combine and sift all dry ingredients together in a large mixing bowl, then set aside. Melt margarine and add to it the sugar and vanilla in another bowl. Combine this with one third of the dry mix until smooth. Repeat this procedure with the next third of dry mix. Then mix in the last third of the dry mix until batter is complete.

Next, fold chips into the batter then spread into a 9" x 9" baking pan. Bake at 350°F for 25-35 minutes. Test if done by poking with a fork or toothpick. If it comes out clean, brownies are done. Cool and cut into squares.
[MAKES 8-12 BROWNIES]

Brown Rice Pudding

This healthy dessert will forever be a staple of vegetarian cuisine. This is our restaurant version.

MEASURE	INGREDIENT
2 cups	*Brown Rice* - cooked
3 cups	soy milk
1 cup	raisins
1/4 cup	dark brown sugar
3 Tbsps	Sucanat (or xylitol, or brown rice syrup)
1/2 tsp	nutmeg
1/2 tsp	cinnamon
4 tsps	*Egg Substitute*
1/4 cup	cold water

Grease a small, deep casserole dish. Blend all ingredients and pour mixture into casserole dish. Bake at 350°F for 30 minutes. Allow pudding to cool and refrigerate before serving.

Brown Sugar Stars

Here is an interesting technique that produces delightful caramelized sugar patterns or pictures to decorate custard pies, cakes or parfaits.

MEASURE	INGREDIENT
(as needed)	vegetable oil spray (or soy oil)
1 piece	aluminum foil
(as needed)	brown sugar

Desserts

Heat oven broiler. Spray oil or paint over one side of the aluminum foil. Make sure the brown sugar is dark brown and is moist and crumbles easily.

Using your fingers mold the outline of a desired picture or pattern 1/4 inch thick on the greased side of the foil. Put the foil with patterns on a cookie sheet and place under the hot broiler. Leave the oven door open and keep close eye on the sugar patterns to watch for burning. When the sugar is caramelized, remove from oven and reverse the foil unto a cool surface. Once cooled, the sugar stars or patterns can be easily removed from foil. Refrigerate in wax paper until ready for use.

Chocolate Drop Cookies

This age old holiday cookie recipe is easily converted to vegan. These cookies distinguish themselves with both flavor and appearance.

MEASURE	INGREDIENT
1	*Eggless Egg* (or 2 tsps *Egg Substitute*)
3 Tbsps	water
1/2 cup	soy margarine
1/2 cup	dark brown sugar
1/2 cup	raw sugar (or xylitol)
1/2 tsp	vanilla extract
1 cup	unbleached white flour
1 tsp	baking soda
1/2 cup	nuts - chopped
1/2 tsp	salt
1/2 cup	non-dairy unsweetened chocolate chips

Preheat oven to 375°F and grease a large cookie sheet. Beat together the eggless egg (or egg substitute) with the 3 tablespoons of water in a bowl with the margarine (room temperature), sugars and vanilla.

In another bowl, combine the flour, baking soda, chopped nuts, salt and chocolate chips. Add the premixed eggless egg mixture into the dry mixture's bowl.

Beat this together and drop the resultant batter onto the cookie sheet with a teaspoon. Bake 10 - 12 minutes. Cool and serve. [MAKE 40-50 COOKIES]

Chocolate Mousse
**Can be served chilled in parfait glasses or in a baked pie shell.
The light texture is achieved by whipping the egg replacer
and folding it into the hot pudding before it has set.**

MEASURE	INGREDIENT
12 ozs	non-dairy unsweetened chocolate chips
2 12-oz packages	silken tofu
1 Tbsp	agar agar flakes
2/3 cup	raw sugar (or evaporated cane juice, or xylitol, or fructose)
1 Tbsp	cornstarch
1/2 cup	soy milk
2 Tbsps	*Egg Substitute*

Melt the chocolate chips and blend with the silken tofu, agar agar flakes, and sugar in a blender. Mix cornstarch with 1/4 cup soy milk and set aside.

Pour blended contents into a sauce pan and add cornstarch-soy milk mixture. Stir blend while heating slowly until mixture is hot enough to start to thicken. Meanwhile use an electric mixer to whip the egg substitute with 1/4 cup cold soy milk, into stiff peaks.

Next, transfer pudding to a mixing bowl and proceed to fold the whipped egg substitute mixture with the hot pudding. Pour prepared pudding into parfait glasses or baked pie shell and chill. Serve refrigerated.

Chocolate Peanut Butter Cheesecake
A delicious and wholesome dessert, full bodied and similar in texture to the lacto/ovo version. A piece of this pie has about the same nutrition as a sandwich.

MEASURE	INGREDIENT
1/2 cup	soy margarine
3 cups	chocolate flavored graham crackers - crumbled
2 cups	creamy - natural peanut butter
2 12-oz packages	silken-firm tofu
3 tsps	**_Egg Substitute_**
1/2 cup	Sucanat (or xylitol)
1 tsp	vanilla extract
2 lbs	non-dairy unsweetened chocolate chips

Melt the margarine and mix it into the crumbled graham crackers. Grease an 8 inch spring form and mold your cracker mix around the inside sides of the spring form and also the bottom to form the crust.

Pour half the oil out of the peanut butter jar and then combine the peanut butter, tofu, egg substitute, sucanat and vanilla into a mixing bowl. Melt the chocolate chips in a pan on a low flame until chips are melted then add melted chocolate to mixing bowl.

Transfer contents of mixing bowl to a blender or food processor and blend well. Pour this mixture into the spring form with molded cracker crust. Bake in a pre-heated oven at 400°F for 45 minutes. Allow to cool to room temperature then refrigerate. Serve cold decorated or undecorated.

Chocolate Tofu Icing

This great, creamy icing is made with a base of silken-firm tofu illustrating the versatility of this substance. A classic application is the Triple Chocolate Cake.

MEASURE	INGREDIENT
6 ozs	non-dairy unsweetened chocolate chips
1 12-oz package	silken-firm tofu

Melt chips in a skillet at very low flame until melted. An alternative method is to microwave at full power for 40 - 45 seconds.

Combine silken-firm tofu with melted chips in a food processor or blender and blend until smooth. Ice cake when cooled with this frosting, which should be kept cool as well. Recipe creates generous portion with plenty extra to fill cake between cake layers.

Christmas Logs

These happy little Christmas cookies are a hit for the holidays and great for decorating.

MEASURE	INGREDIENT
1 cup	soy margarine (room temperature)
2 tsps	vanilla extract
2 tsps	rum liquor
3/4 cup	raw sugar (or xylitol)
2	*Eggless Egg*s
3 cups	unbleached white flour
1 tsp	nutmeg

Cream the margarine, vanilla and rum in a mixing bowl. Gradually add in the sugar and cream well. Next beat in the eggless eggs. Sift the flour with the nutmeg and stir this into the wet mixture slowly while beating vigorously.

Desserts

Shape the dough into long, narrow rolls and cut into logs on the bias. Bake logs in a 350°F oven, on a greased cookie sheet, for 12 to 15 minutes. Decorate or serve plain. [MAKES 30-40 COOKIES]

Coconut Cream Pie
Simple and delicious pie with all the flavor and body of the more familiar dairy and egg version.

MEASURE	INGREDIENT
1 & 1/2 12-oz packages	silken tofu
1 cup	unsweetened coconut flakes
3/4 cup	raw sugar (or xylitol, or Sucanat)
1 cup	soy milk
1/3 cup	**Egg Substitute**
1 tsp	coconut extract
1 tsp	vanilla extract

Combine all ingredients in food processor and blend smooth. Pour into pre-baked pie shell and bake in a 350°F oven for 45 minutes. Cool and serve pie chilled.

Crust Cookies
Here's a homespun way to use extra pie crust for quick cookies. Kids love them.

MEASURE	INGREDIENT
fist-sized ball	**Basic Pie Crust** dough
1/4 cup	raw sugar

Roll out the pie dough to a thickness of about 1/8 inch. Use a cookie cutter to cut out desired shapes. Grease a cookie sheet and place cutouts on sheets. Sprinkle the sugar over the cookies and bake in a preheated oven at 400°F for about 15 minutes. [MAKES 12 COOKIES]

Egyptian Date Nut Candy

Here is a tasty raw food candy that packs alot of energy and nutrition. Kids love them...rolled in roasted sesame seeds, they are irresistible.

MEASURE	INGREDIENT
1/2 cup	sunflower seeds
1/2 cup	almonds
2 cups	pitted dates
1/2 cup	figs - chopped
1 cup	raisins
1/4 cup	water
1 cup	roasted sesame seeds
	(or unsweetened coconut flakes)

Combine the sunflower seeds and almonds into a food processor with chopping blade attachment. Pulse until seeds and nuts are coarsely ground. Remove this to a bowl.

Place the dates, figs and raisins in the emptied food processor and add the water. Process until mass is thick and pasty. Add this to the ground nuts and seeds and mash together well with clean hands. Form balls or small barrels from this mixture and roll these in the roasted sesame seeds (or coconut flakes). They are ready to serve and will keep well in the refrigerator. [MAKES 20-30 CANDIES]

German Chocolate Icing/Filling

This rich, chocolate cake icing combines the flavor of coffee and coconut. Makes a Great topping or filling between layers of your favorite Chocolate or *White Cake*.

MEASURE	INGREDIENT
1 & 1/2 12-oz packages	silken tofu
2/3 cup	maple syrup (or brown rice syrup)
1/4 cup	soy oil
2 tsps	vanilla extract
1 tsp	instant coffee
1/2 cup	pecans - chopped
1/2 cup	unsweetened coconut flakes

Combine tofu, maple syrup, oil, vanilla and coffee in a food processor and blend until smooth. Pour this mixture into a bowl. Fold in the chopped pecans and the coconut flakes. Allow this blend to cool down and then refrigerate. Use this chilled mix to ice and fill your favorite chocolate cake.

Ginger Bread Cookies

These tasty cookies are always a hit with children on the holidays, as they can be cut into different shapes and decorated. Traditional to Germany and America.

MEASURE	INGREDIENT
1/2 cup	dark brown sugar
1/4 cup	molasses
1/4 cup	water
1/3 cup	soy margarine (room temperature)
2 pinches	powdered cloves
1/2 tsp	cinnamon
1 tsp	ginger powder

MEASURE	INGREDIENT
1 tsp	baking soda
1/2 tsp	salt
3 & 1/2 cups	unbleached white flour

Beat the sugar, molasses and water with the margarine in one bowl and sift the spices, baking soda, salt and flour in another bowl. Mix the wet ingredients into dry ingredients in three stages forming a dough ball. Allow dough to rest, refrigerated for at least 15 minutes, then roll out the dough to about 1/8" in thickness. Use a cookie cutter to make shapes then bake cookies for 12 minutes at 350°F, on a greased cookie sheet. [MAKES 25 COOKIES]

Graham Cracker Pie Crust
This crunchy and flavorful crust is easy to make and very effective.

MEASURE	INGREDIENT
8 ozs	graham crackers
1/4 cup	soy margarine - melted
1 Tbsp	raw sugar (or xylitol)
1/4 cup	unsweetened coconut flakes (optional)

Crush graham crackers in a food processor. Add melted margarine and sugar and process until mixture is well combined. Press mixture into a greased pie pan. Add favorite your pie filling, custard or other, and bake.
MAKES ENOUGH CRUST FOR 1 PIE]

Desserts

Key Lime Pie

Anyone who has ever eaten Key Lime Pie will never forget its distinctive flavor! One bite of this vegan delight will almost transport you to the sunny atolls of the Caribbean.

MEASURE	INGREDIENT
3/4 cup	key lime juice
1 Tbsp	agar agar flakes
2 12-oz packages	silken tofu
3/4 cup	raw sugar (or xylitol)
1	*Graham Cracker Pie Crust* shell

In a sauce pan, heat key lime juice to a boil. Stir in the agar agar flakes. Reduce the heat to a simmer and continue to stir in the agar agar until it is completely dissolved. Set this aside.

Using a food processor, blend the tofu and sugar until it is smooth and creamy. Next add the key lime-agar agar blend to the contents of the processor and pulse this in. Pour this final mixture into a graham cracker crust shell and bake at 350°F for 20 minutes. Chill before serving.

Miso Mincemeat Pie

This interesting dessert is a great companion to pumpkin pie, or other holiday treat. With apples, raisins, nutmeats and miso, it mimics the flavor and body of the Colonial American version.

MEASURE	INGREDIENT
4	Granny Smith apples - cored & diced
1/2 cup	apple juice
1	orange - juiced
1	orange rind - grated
1 & 1/2 cups	raisins
2 cups	nutmeats (walnuts) - chopped
1/2 tsp	cinnamon

MEASURE	INGREDIENT
1/4 tsp	cloves
1/2 tsp	ginger powder
2 Tbsps	miso paste
1	**Basic Pie Crust**, or **Basic Pie Crust II**

Peel, core and dice the apples, then place them in a pot with the apple juice, orange juice, orange rind and the raisins. Heat this to a boil, then simmer for 30 minutes. Add the chopped nutmeats, cinnamon, cloves, ginger and miso and remove the pot from the stove.

Pre-bake the crust and then fill with the cooled contents from the pot. Cover pie filling with a lattice of pie crust strips. Bake pie for 45 minutes at 350°F.

Mocha Frosting

This delicious icing goes great with your favorite Chocolate Cake, *Banana Cake* or *Brownies*. This vegan frosting has a chocolate and coffee base for that special mocha flavor.

MEASURE	INGREDIENT
6 Tbsps	soy margarine
1 & 1/2 cups	raw sugar (or xylitol)
2 cups	powdered sugar
1 tsp	cocoa
3 Tbsps	brewed coffee (strong & hot)
1/2 tsp	vanilla extract

With margarine at room temperature, mix with sugar and cocoa in a medium-size mixing bowl until well incorporated. Add hot coffee and blend until smooth and creamy. Stir in the vanilla and allow to cool. Spread on cakes with a butter knife or small rubber spatula. When cake is completely iced you may sprinkle chopped nuts or vegan candy sprinkles for an additional touch. Keep iced cake covered or chilled, for best results.

Oatmeal Raisin Cookies

This cookie has all the flavor, richness, and texture of the original.

MEASURE	INGREDIENT
1 cup	soy margarine
1 cup	dark brown sugar
1/2 cup	xylitol (or brown rice syrup)
1 tsp	vanilla extract
2 Tbsps	**Egg Substitute** (or 2 **Eggless Egg**s)
1/4 cup	water
1 & 1/2 cups	unbleached white flour
1 tsp	baking powder
1/2 tsp	salt
1 tsp	cinnamon
1 cup	raisins
3 cups	rolled oats

Preheat oven to 350°F. Have margarine warmed to room temperature and combine with the brown sugar, xylitol and vanilla in a mixing bowl. In another mixing bowl, whisk the egg substitute with a 1/4 cup of water and then beat this into the margarine mixture.

Combine the flour, baking powder, salt, cinnamon, raisins and oats together in a third bowl. Make a well in the center of this dry mix and pour in the contents of the bowl with the margarine. Mix this well with a rubber spatula to form a stiff batter.

Grease a cookie sheet or baking pan and drop spoon sized dollops onto the sheet. Bake 10 to 12 minutes until lightly browned. Cool a few minutes and serve. Makes 40 - 50 cookies.

Old Fashion Chocolate Fudge
**Crave fudge, but want it without the excess fat and cholesterol?
This recipe produces a smooth-rich candy that everyone
can enjoy. Great for cake frostings, too!**

MEASURE	INGREDIENT
2 cups	raw sugar (or xylitol, or Sucanat)
3/4 cup	soy milk
2 ozs	non-dairy unsweetened chocolate chips
1 tsp	maple syrup (or malt syrup)
2 Tbsps	soy margarine
1 tsp	vanilla extract

Grease sides of a two quart sauce pan. Combine sugar, milk, chocolate and maple or malt syrup. Stir over medium heat until sugar dissolves and mixture comes to a boil. Continue heating past boiling point to about 230°F. Remove pan from heat. Add margarine and cool mixture to room temperature.

Add vanilla to the cooled mixture and beat vigorously with a hand whisk or electric mixer until fudge thickens and loses its gloss. Grease a shallow 9"x 9" baking pan and spread fudge evenly over bottom. Score surface for cutting into pieces while fudge is still warm. Cut into pieces after fudge is thoroughly cooled.

As an addition to the basic recipe, a 1/2 cup of chopped nuts may be added to the bottom of the baking pan and the fudge spread over top.

Peanut Butter Chip Brownies
Another kind of brownie...with crunchy peanut butter!

MEASURE	INGREDIENT
1 cup	unbleached white flour
1/2 cup	non-dairy unsweetened chocolate chips
1 tsp	baking powder
1 Tbsp	*Egg Substitute*

Desserts

MEASURE	INGREDIENT
1 & 1/2 cups	raw sugar (or xylitol, or Sucanat)
1 cup	crunchy - natural peanut butter
1/2 cup	soy margarine

Combine and sift dry ingredients into a mixing bowl, then set aside. Using a food processor, cream the sugar, peanut butter and soy margarine until smooth and fluffy. Add dry ingredients in two shifts, incorporating fully between each shift. Remove from food processor to a mixing bowl, and then fold in the chips. Pour batter into a greased 9"x 9" baking pan. Bake for 25-35 minutes. Test for if done with a fork or toothpick. Cut and serve chilled. [MAKE 8-12 BROWNIES]

Pumpkin Pie

What could be more traditional than pumpkin pie on the holidays. This recipe will provides all the joy and memories of Mom's...vegan style!

MEASURE	INGREDIENT
2 cups	pumpkin - cooked
1 cup	soy milk
1 tsp	vanilla extract
1/2 cup	dark brown sugar
1/4 cup	raw sugar (or xylitol, or Sucanat)
4	*Eggless Egg*s
1/2 tsp	salt
1 tsp	cinnamon
1/2 tsp	ginger powder
1/2 tsp	allspice
1 pinch	cloves - powdered
1	pie shell - prebaked - using either *Basic Pie Crust*, or *Basic Pie Crust II*, or *Graham Cracker Pie Crust*

Start by obtaining a medium sized pumpkin. Cut pumpkin in half and scoop out the seeds and stringy seed net. Next, slice the pumpkin into manageable pieces and begin removing the soft inner flesh from the tough outer skin. The best way to do this is by scoring the surface of the inner flesh into a 1-2 inch matrix, then slicing off the 'cubes' from the outer skin.

Place the pumpkin cubes into a steamer and steam until soft (about 15 minutes). Next place steamed pumpkin in a food processor and blend with all other ingredients.

Pour mixture into the prebaked pie shell and bake pie at 400°F for 45 minutes. Serve cooled, plain or with vegan whipped cream

Ranger Cookies
These tasty cookies are great for the holidays. Plain or decorated, they're always a hit...with kids of all ages!

MEASURE	INGREDIENT
2	*Eggless Egg*s
1 cup	brown sugar
1 cup	raw sugar (or xylitol)
1 tsp	vanilla extract
1 cup	soy margarine (room temperature)
2 cups	unbleached white flour
1/2 tsp	baking powder
1 tsp	baking soda
2 cups	rice crispies
2 cups	rolled oats
1 tsp	salt
1 cup	chopped nuts

Desserts

Beat the eggless eggs with the sugars, vanilla and margarine in one bowl. In another bowl mix the flour, baking powder, baking soda, rice crispies, oatmeal and salt.

Fold the wet mixture into the dry mixture and add the nuts. Grease a cookie sheet and drop batter onto sheet with a table spoon. Bake cookies in a 350°F oven for 30 minutes or until golden brown.

Serve with **Whipped Cream** or vegan-style ice cream.
[MAKES 30-40 COOKIES]

Southern Style Fruit Cobbler
This homestyle delight is a seasonal dessert; enhanced with freshly picked (or flash frozen) berries.

MEASURE	INGREDIENT
1/4 cup	soy margarine
4 cups	berries (or peeled and sliced fresh fruit)
1 cup	raw sugar (or xylitol)
1 & 1/2 cups	unbleached white flour
4 tsps	baking powder
1 & 1/2 cups	soy milk

Preheat oven to 375°F. Place margarine in a 2-quart capacity casserole dish and melt the margarine in the oven. Remove the baking dish when the margarine is melted.

Mix berries (or sliced fresh fruit) with the half the sugar or xylitol in a bowl and set aside. In another bowl, mix the flour, baking powder and the rest of the sugar together.

Make a well in the center of the flour mixture and pour in the soy milk. Mix gently by folding, into a batter and then pour this batter into the casserole dish with the melted margarine. Bake about 45 minutes and test if done with a toothpick, fork or cake tester. [SERVES 8-12]

Soy Milk Doughnuts
Yes, even these decadent treats can be rendered vegan...with great results!

MEASURE	INGREDIENT
1 cup	raw sugar (or fructose, or xylitol)
3 Tbsps	*Egg Substitute*
1 cup	soy milk
1/4 cup	soy margarine - melted
4 cups	unbleached white flour
2 Tbsps	baking powder
1/2 tsp	salt
2 pinches	cinnamon
1 pinch	nutmeg

Beat the sugar with the egg substitute, soy milk and margarine in a bowl. Sift or mix flour, baking powder, salt and spices in another bowl. Next, fold the wet ingredients into the dry ingredients, carefully, with a few slow strokes. This is to prevent excess gluten development resulting in a tough doughnut.

Turn the resulting dough mass onto a floured board and gently roll out the dough to 1/4 inch thickness. Next cut the doughnut shape with 2 round cookie cutters of unequal diameter or use a doughnut cutting tool. Place cut doughnut rings and doughnut balls on a lightly floured cookie sheet and let rest 15 minutes.

Heat a large cast iron skillet and add 1 cup of soy oil. If you are using a deep fryer have oil at 350°F. Begin frying doughnuts and doughnut balls, on one side for 2-3 minutes, turn and fry the other side another 2 minutes. Remove from fryer or skillet and allow to drain well. Decorate with cake icing or use as an interesting dessert base. [MAKES 12-20 DOUGHNUTS]

Stewed Pears

Easy to make and is a good way to use-up ripe fruit. Stewing pears also renders them more digestible when consumed with other foods.

MEASURE	INGREDIENT
2 (or more)	pears - ripe
1/4 cup	water
1/4 cup	fruit brandy (or cognac)
1/4 cup	raw sugar (or evaporated cane juice, or xylitol, or fructose)

Peel the pears, core them and slice the pears in half lengthwise. Mix the water, brandy or cognac and sugars and pour this into a large, deep skillet.   Place the pear halves in the skillet and bring this to a boil. Cover skillet, reduce heat and simmer for 10 minutes. Pears should be soft and liquid should be thickened like syrup. Serve halves individually in small bowls with a few tablespoons of the syrup.

Strawberry Shortcake

Traditional Spring dessert with fresh strawberries and vegan whipped cream.

MEASURE	INGREDIENT
2 cups	unbleached pastry flour
4 tsps	baking powder
1/2 tsp	salt
4 Tbsps	raw sugar (or brown rice syrup)
1/2 cup	soy margarine
3/4 cup	soy milk
4 cups	strawberries - chopped (sweetened)
1/2 cup	raw sugar (or brown rice syrup)
2-3 cups	**Whipped Cream**

Mix dry ingredients and cut in margarine as shown in pie crust recipes. Stir in soy milk and form dough ball with very little kneading.

Lightly flour a board and gently roll dough out to a one inch thickness. Grease a baking pan or dish of the appropriate size and place dough inside, patting down lightly to distribute dough evenly.

Bake in a 450°F oven for 15 to 20 minutes. Test if done with a toothpick. If toothpick comes out clean its probably done.

Slice the cake into squares and leave cake in pan. Mix strawberries with raw sugar, then spoon over the cake and serve with whipped cream.

Triple Chocolate Cake
A very popular vegan chocolate cake, with the flavor, texture, and richness of typical dairy and egg based cakes. You won't believe how good this is.

MEASURE	INGREDIENT
3/4 cup	soy margarine
2 Tbsps	*Egg Substitute*
1 & 3/4 cups	raw sugar
1 tsp	vanilla extract
2 cups	unbleached white flour
2 Tbsp	vital wheat gluten
3/4 cup	cocoa
1 tsp	baking soda
1/2-1 tsp	baking powder
1/2 tsp	salt
1 cup	water

Have the margarine at room temperature (soft) and cream it with egg substitute, raw suger and vanilla until smooth in a small mixing bowl.

Desserts

In another bowl, thoroughly combine flour, with vital wheat gluten, cocoa, baking soda, baking powder and salt, then sift this into creamed margarine mixture. Use an electric mixer and slowly pour in the water while mixing. Beat well until batter is smooth and glossy.

Pour batter into two 9" greased cake pans and bake at 350°F for 30 to 35 minutes. Test if done with fork, toothpick or cake wire. Stack two cakes with a layer of your favorite icing in between, and frost entire cake with remainder of icing.

Whipped Cream
Looks and tastes similar to the high fat and cholesterol dairy version...only, it's vegan!

MEASURE	INGREDIENT
1 tsp	agar agar flakes (dissolved in 3 Tbsps water)
2 Tbsps	soy milk
1/2 cup	raw sugar (or xylitol)
1 12-oz package	silken-firm tofu
2 tsps	soy oil

Heat the agar agar flakes and water to a boil, while stirring. Remove from heat then combine agar agar solution with all other ingredients in a food processor and blend for 2-3 minutes. Pour blended mixture into a small mixing bowl. Put blended mixture back in refrigerator to chill. Before serving, beat with an electric mixer, then spoon on dessert as a topping.

White Cake

A wonderful, all-purpose recipe for any occasion. Light and delicious, ice with your favorite vegan frosting.

MEASURE	INGREDIENT
2/3 cup	soy milk
1/2 tsp	vanilla extract
1/2 tsp	almond extract
1/2 cup	soy margarine
1 cup	raw sugar (or xylitol)
2 cups	unbleached pastry flour
3 tsps	baking powder
5 Tbsps	*Egg Substitute*
1 cup	water
1	lemon rind - grated

Mix soy milk with vanilla and almond extracts, then set aside.

Have margarine at room temperature (soft) and cream with the sugar (or xylitol). Sift flour with baking powder into a large mixing bowl, then combine sweetened margarine, alternating with the flavored soy milk mixture. Beat batter vigorously until smooth.

Use an electric mixer and beat the egg substitute and grated lemon rind, with the water, until it stiffens into peaks. Carefully fold stiffened egg substitute into batter. Pour batter into a 9" x 13" pan and bake at 375°F for 30 minutes.

Baby Food

Introduction

You might be wondering, why a chapter on baby food? Well, if you a have a small child, this section will be of special interest to you. Balanced nutrition is essential and fortified soy milk is highly recommended to supplement protein and vitamin requirements. Although babies and small children don't usually care for certain flavors or spicy food, they don't like their food bland either. Just like adults, they want their flavors balanced and their food cooked right. The following is a complete diet for small babies.

Included in this chapter are a few basic vegan recipes that can can get you jump started towards raising your child vegan. A better title for this chapter might be "A child's First Foods' because the simplest foods should be the first food a child eats after breast feeding. At the end of the chapter is a list of recipes found throughout the book, that are suitable as baby foods.

Combining Baby Foods

Proper food combining for best digestion is an art seldom practiced by adults, and babies are usually subjected to the same treatment. Mixing fruit with vegetables (especially raw) can result in vomiting and flu sometimes. Cooking foods generally render them easier to digest. A meal consisting of complex carbohydrates, fat, starch and protein is not difficult to digest when cooked together. The same meal is almost impossible to digest and assimilate if eaten raw. A good rule of thumb is to eat raw fruits, vegetables or nuts separately, allowing plenty of time between meals for digestion.

Baby's Fruit

Fruit is nature's perfect energy food. It contains Vitamin C, compounds, enzymes, cellulose roughage and carbohydrates. Baby's first foods can be pureed fruit or vegetables.

MEASURE	INGREDIENT
1 cup	fruit - soft (Avoid excessive citrus or too much sweet fruit, such as soaked raisins.)

Blend fruit well in food processor if feeding a small baby.

Baby's Grains

Babies can begin eating cooked grains that are mild and pureed, at only a few months of age.

MEASURE	INGREDIENT
1 cup mixed:	*Brown Rice*, *Millet*, rolled oats, farina, *Quinoa*, *Barley* and *Couscous* - precooked
1 Tbsp	maple syrup
1 tsp	flax seed oil
1 pinch	sea salt (finely ground)
1/4 cup	soy milk

Blend precooked grains with maple syrup, flax oil, salt and soy milk in a blender or food processor. Serve luke warm.

An alternative recipe would be to omit the maple syrup. This would allow the grain mash to be blended with steamed vegetables for another balanced baby dinner.

Baby's 'Jello'

This recipe enables you to create a tasty and nutritious vegan gelatin or 'jello', from agar agar, a sea vegetable.

MEASURE	INGREDIENT
3/4 cup	water
2 Tbsps	agar agar flakes
1 Tbsp	xylitol
1 cup	pure fruit juice
1/4 cup	fruit - chopped

Heat the water in a small sauce pan and stir in agar agar flakes. Bring this to a boil and then reduce heat. Simmer 3 minutes and then remove from heat.

Stir the xylitol into the agar agar water while the liquid is stir warm. Next add the fruit juice and and place mixture in a refrigerator to chill and set up. After 20 minutes, or when 'jello' begins to stiffen, add the chopped fruit. Pour into a mold or leave it in the same bowl and chill 2-4 hours before serving.

Baby's Nut-Seed Milk

This nutritious beverage is easy to make and children love the flavor.

MEASURE	INGREDIENT
1 cup	seeds or nuts - raw
2 cups	pure water
1 Tbsp	barley malt syrup (or xylitol)

Use only raw sunflower or sesame seeds, almonds, cashews. Soak seeds in three cups water 6-8 hours. Pour off this water and rinse seeds. Add 2 cups pure water and 1 Tablespoon barley malt syrup. Blend in blender. Strain off soy milk through a fine sieve and serve.

Baby's Pudding
Simple flavored pudding can be an excellent dessert or snack for a young child or baby. Easily digestible after it's pureed and cooked.

MEASURE	INGREDIENT
1 cup	soy milk
2 Tbsps	malt syrup (or xylitol)
2 Tbsps	cornstarch
1 12-oz package	silken tofu
1/2 tsp	vanilla extract

Blend all ingredients in a blender or food processor. Pour contents into a saucepan and heat slowly on medium. Stir frequently until mixture starts to thicken and almost boils. Remove from heat and chill for several hours before serving.

Baby's Salad
Babies and small children can enjoy raw vegetable salads, as long as they are mild in flavor, and well blended.

MEASURE	INGREDIENT
2 cups	greens - raw (don't use bitter greens or too much raw spinach) fresh rinsed - sprouts are ok
1 tsp	virgin olive oil
1 tsp	dulse seaweed - powdered
1	cucumber - seeded

In a food processor (works better than a blender for this recipe) blend all ingredients well and serve. Don't ever attempt to feed baby too much, a few small bites is all that is necessary. If baby wants more ok but don't overfeed.

Baby's Soy Milk

Fortified soy milk in a baby bottle twice a day. Once before nap again before bedtime. 6 months and up.

MEASURE	INGREDIENT
8-10 ozs	fortified soy milk
1 tsp	flax seed oil
1 tsp	liquid baby vitamins
	(!!!**ONCE A DAY ONLY**!!!)

Baby's Steamed Vegetables

Steaming vegetables render them easy to digest, with most of the nutrients preserved. Babies naturally love them.

MEASURE	INGREDIENT
2 cups mixed:	vegetables - raw (carrots, yams, potatoes, broccoli, cauliflower, peas, asparagus, etc.) in any combination
(as needed)	sea salt to taste (finely ground)
1/2-1 tsp	flax seed oil
1/4 cup	*Vegetable Stock*

Steam by putting veggies in a small sauce pan with a small amount of water. Cover sauce pan and bring to a boil and simmer until soft. If using a combination of vegetables, steam the harder root veggies for a few minutes before adding the softer veggies.

Place steamed vegetables in a food processor. Add a pinch of salt and half a teaspoon of flax seed oil. Pulse processor to reduce bulk then puree mixture while dribbling 2-4 tablespoons of vegetable stock. Finished blend should not be too thick or too thin, adjust by adding stock to blend slowly.

Suggested Baby Foods

There are a number of delicious and suitable recipes that you can feed your baby or small child that are listed in other chapters of this book. Here are some possibilities that you can choose from for quick meals or for designing weekly menus. Some of the listed recipes should be pureed (mashed) for small babies.

Cold Broccoli Salad
Elbow Macaroni Salad
Hummus
Garden Pasta Salad
Mediterranean Potato Salad
Pasta Salad with Fresh Basil
Raw Food Paté
String Bean Salad
American White Bean Soup
Autumn Moon Soup
Country Lentil Soup
Cream of Broccoli Soup
Cream of Tomato Soup
Escarole & Bean Soup
Miso Soup
Moonlight Sonata Soup
Mock Chicken Noodle Soup
MultiBean Soup
New World Lima Bean Soup
Pasta Fagioli Soup
Split Pea Soup
Vegetable Barley Soup
Vegetable Noodle Soup
Zucchini Rice Soup
Brown Gravy
Cheese Sauce
White Sauce
Marinara Sauce
Baked Cauliflower
Baked potato, Squash or Yams
Baking Powder Dumplings
Barley
Brown Rice

Baby Food

Sautéed Spinach
Sugar Glazed Beets or Carrots
Vegetable Medley
Polenta
Pot Pie
Shepherd's Pie
Tofu 'Tuna' Casserole
Vegan Meatloaf
Mashed Potatoes
American Stew
Gypsy's Fortune
Leonardo's Vision
Southern Comfort
Baking Powder Biscuits
Corn Bread
French Bread
Oatmeal Pancakes
Whole Wheat Bread
White Bread
Baked Custard
Crust Cookies

Meal Planner & Themes

Introduction

This is a fun chapter as it provides lists of compatible meal combinations and accompaniments for multi-course dinners based on themes such as holidays or world regions. There are also some daily menu examples for the individual, designed with nutritional balance in mind. All the suggested recipes can be found in the Table of Contents or Index.

In keeping with the style and format of this book all the lists compiled here represent compatible suggestions. There are numerous possible combinations for the themes found in this chapter, from other recipes found in this book. Perhaps you would like to use some of the recipes found in this book together with some of your own favorite recipes to create a theme. In any case, the suggested ideas conveyed here should help you to structure your next banquet --- or maybe just today's menu.

Themes

Christmas

Fruit & Nut Salad
German Potato Salad
Cold Broccoli Salad
French Onion Soup
Cream of Mushroom Soup
Mock Chicken Noodle Soup
Vegetable Barley Soup
Au Gratin Vegetables
Sugar Glazed Beets or Carrots
Baked Cauliflower

Candied Yams
baked squash
Mashed Potatoes
Brown Gravy
New World Stuffed Peppers
Vegan Meatloaf
Baking Powder Biscuits
Whole Wheat Bread
Nordic Rye Bread
Ranger Cookies
Christmas Logs
Bavarian Cream Pie
Chocolate Drop Cookies
Chocolate Peanut Butter Cheesecake

Thanksgiving

Green Salad
with Creamy Ranch Dressing
Mushroom Barley Soup
Cream of Broccoli Soup
Cream of Tomato Soup
Holiday Pumpkin Soup
Candied Yams
Vegetable Medley
Baked Cauliflower
Pilaf
Mashed Potatoes
Brown Gravy
Baked Tofu Turkey
Bread & Cornbread Stuffing
Cranberry Sauce
Pumpkin Pie
Berry Pie
Apple Pie
Miso Mincemeat Pie

Meal Planner & Themes

Cinco De Mayo

Mexican Corn & Bean Salad
String Bean Salad
Salsa
Guacamole
Corn Bread
Corn Chowder
Jalapeno Poppers
Nachos
Mexican Quesadilla
Tofu Tamales
Grilled Mexican Fajitas
Chimichanga
Mexican Pinto Bean Soup
'Beef' & Bean Burrito
'Beef' Enchiladas

South Pacific Feast

Fresh Fruit
with Fresh Fruit Salad Dressing
Fresh Fruit Salad
with Sunrise Seed Sauce
Thai Sweet Potato Soup
Brown Rice
Teriyaki Tempeh
Polynesian Tofu & Vegetables
Polynesian Seitan Medallions
Singapore Sunset
Gado Gado
Banana Flambe

Middle Eastern Party

Leek Salad
Mediterranean CousCous Salad

335

Babaganouj
Hummus
Tabouli
String Bean Salad
Falafel
Grilled Portabella Orzo Salad
Ispanakli Borek
Mediterranean Pasta Toss
Imam's Delight
Egyptian Date Nut Candy

Himalayan Rim Dinner

Curried Root Soup
Three Bean Salad
Indian Samosas
Corn or Vegetable Fritters
Chutney
Curried Lentil Soup
Indian Vegetable Curry
Curried Enlightenment
Vegetable Kebabs with
Creamed Curry Sauce
Tantric Dumplings
Stewed Pears

Oriental Banquet

Japanese Sesame Kale with Miso
Oriental Lo Mein Salad
Chinese Cabbage Spring Roll
Daikon Radish Soup
Miso Soup
Garlic Sesame Tofu
Oriental Stir Fry
Teriyaki Tempeh Strips

Meal Planner & Themes

Roman Feast

Cold Broccoli Salad
Mediterranean Potato Salad
Pasta Salad with Fresh Basil
Minestrone Soup
Pasta Fagioli Soup
Portabella Orzo Soup
Penne Pasta with Pesto Sauce
Italian Sausage & Italian Meatballs
with Marinara Sauce
Tuscan Toss
Pasta Primavera
Gluten Diablo
Eggplant Parmigiani
Lasagna
Stromboli
French Bread
Dessert

Nordic Smorgasbord

German Potato Salad
Lefsa
Nordic Rye Bread
Chicken Fried Tofu Sandwich
Swedish Meatballs
with Swedish Meatball Gravy
Baked Tofu Turkey
Neptune's Gift
Morning Coffee Cake
Apple Sauce Doughnuts
with Birch Sugar Syrup

American Sunday Picnic

Eggless Egg Salad
Garden Pasta Salad
Mock Chicken Salad
Elbow Macaroni Salad
Three Bean Salad
Raw Food Paté with crudite
Gazpacho Soup
Avocado & Hummus Sandwich
Bacon Lettuce & Tomato Sandwich
Chicken Fried Gluten Sandwich
White Bread
Strawberry Shortcake

All American Barbecue

Roasted Red Peppers
German Potato Salad
Spinach Quesadilla
Portabella Mushroom Burger
Veggie Burger
Grilled Perfect Gluten Flank Steak
with Basic Barbecue Sauce
Grilled New York Gluten Strip
Vegetable Kebabs
Grilled Corn on the Cob
Fruit Cocktail
with Fresh Fruit Salad Dressing

Meal Planner

Table 1: Day One

TIME OF DAY	SUGGESTED RECIPES
BREAKFAST	**Mock Scrambled Eggs**, whole wheat toast, **Home Fries**, fruit juice
LUNCH	**Cold Broccoli Salad** with **Creamy Cucumber Dressing**, **Avocado & Soy Cheese Sandwich**, **French Fried Potatoes**, **Banana Cake**
DINNER	**String Bean Salad**, **Vegan Meatloaf** and **Brown Gravy**, **Mashed Potatoes**, **Bavarian Cream Pie**

Table 2: Day Two

TIME OF DAY	SUGGESTED RECIPES
BREAKFAST	**Matzoh Cracker Pancakes**, **Hash Browns**, fresh fruit, maple syrup or **Birch Sugar Syrup**
LUNCH	**Harvest Burger**, **American White Bean Soup**, **Escarole**, **Whole Wheat Rolls**
DINNER	green salad with **Euro-Asian Vinaigrette**, **Pilaf**, **The Olympian**, **Triple Chocolate Cake**

Table 3: Day Three

TIME OF DAY	SUGGESTED RECIPES
BREAKFAST	fresh fruit with **Sunrise Seed Sauce**, **Waffles** with maple syrup
LUNCH	**Vegetable Barley Soup**, **Bacon Lettuce & Tomato Sandwich**, **Peanut Butter Chip Brownies**
DINNER	green salad with **Oriental Sesame Dressing**, grilled **New York Gluten Strip** with A-1 sauce, baked potato with **Sour Cream**, **Vegetable Medley**, **Key Lime Pie**

Table 4: Day Four

TIME OF DAY	SUGGESTED RECIPES
BREAKFAST	**Morning Coffee Cake**, fortified soy protein shake
LUNCH	**Country Lentil Soup**, **Whole Wheat Bread**, **Spinach Quesadilla**
DINNER	green salad with **French Dressing**, **Lasagna** with **Italian Meatballs** and **Marinara Sauce**, **Chocolate Mousse**

Table 5: Day Five

TIME OF DAY	SUGGESTED RECIPES
BREAKFAST	**Blueberry Pancakes** with maple syrup, **Home Fries**, **Tempeh Bacon Strips**
LUNCH	**Elbow Macaroni Salad**, **Mediterranean Potato Salad**, **New World Lima Bean Soup**, **Tofu Burger**
DINNER	**Hummus** and **Babaganouj** with crudite, **Ispanakli Borek**, **Egyptian Date Nut Candy**

Table 6: Day Six

TIME OF DAY	SUGGESTED RECIPES
BREAKFAST	fresh fruit, **Corn Muffins**, **French Toast** with **Birch Sugar Syrup**, **Breakfast 'Sausage'**
LUNCH	**Pizza**, **Artichokes Italian Style**, **Chocolate Drop Cookies**
DINNER	green salad with **Creamy Ranch Dressing**, **Old World Leek Soup**, **Tofu 'Tuna' Casserole**, **Stuffed Baked Tomatoes**, **Apple Pie**

Meal Planner & Themes

Table 7: Day Seven

TIME OF DAY	SUGGESTED RECIPES
BREAKFAST	*Potato Pancakes*, apple sauce, *Sour Cream*, vegan-style canadian bacon, fresh squeezed orange and grapefruit juice
LUNCH	green salad with *Bulgar Wheat* and *Tahini Vinaigrette*, *Sonoran Black Bean Soup*, *Whoopie Wrap*
DINNER	*Coleslaw*, *Hot Cross Buns*, *Chicken Fried Gluten Cutlet*s with *Mashed Potatoes* and *Brown Gravy*, *Baked Beans*, *Sautéed Spinach*, *Chocolate Peanut Butter Cheesecake*

Glossary

Introduction

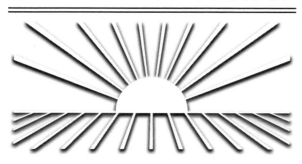

If you're new to cooking and vegan cuisine, you should take the time to read this section in its entirety. The following has been included to assist the reader in developing their knowledge-base in Vegan cuisine. It is alphabetically ordered and is also the destination of many of the hyperlinked references throughout the electronic version of this publication.

This glossary is an extremely important section! Not only does it serve to assist the reader in understanding materials and terms used throughout this book, the reader is also directed - at the end of these entries - to a product distributor catagory within the Resource Directory chapter. To assist the reader with the acquisition of recommended food products, this directory lists related business addresses, telephone numbers and Internet web site addresses.

agar agar

A translucent sea vegetable; when dried and reconstituted, is a vegan substitute for animal-based gelatin.

[see: Misc Grocer]

allspice

The whole or ground, dried berry of the pimento tree native to Jamaica. So named because its flavor resembles the combined flavors of many spices. Use in cakes and pies, desserts, Middle Eastern and Island cuisine such as stews, soups and sauces. Allspice is a global spice and is

included in fusion cuisine throughout the world today.
        [see: Herb, Spice, Seasonings]

almond

The nut of the sweet almond tree. The almond is used in a full range of cooking applications from sautés to dessert and candy. Almond milk is very nutritious. Almonds originally grew in western Asia but today they grow in the coastal regions of the Mediterranean. Almonds are a member of the rose family of plants.
[see: Beans, Nuts, Seeds & Grains]

anise

The whole or ground seed of the anise plant native to Egypt and the Mediterranean. Today, anise is cultivated in Germany and other countries and is used for flavoring in licorice, cookies and candy. The star shaped seed is also used in Asia for soups and stir-fry. Often mixed with other spices such as the commercially marketed Five Spice Powder.
        [see: Herb, Spice, Seasonings]

arrowroot

A starchy powder from the root of a tropical plant. It is usually less processed than cornstarch and is a one to one replacement, i.e. 1 tsp. cornstarch = 1 tsp. arrowroot
[see: Sweeteners & Baking Agents]

Glossary

artichoke A thistle like garden vegetable whose starchy edible parts are the heart and inner leaves. Usually served baked and stuffed, or steamed with a dipping sauce.

[see: Produce]

asafetida Available from Indian food markets, asafetida is a pungent, concentrated flavoring produced from the resin of a species of fennel. Substitute for onions and garlic.

[see: Herb, Spice, Seasonings]

au gratin Baked dishes covered with breadcrumbs and melted cheese or cheese sauce.

avocado A fruit of the tropics distinguished by its high unsaturated fat content and nutty flavor, like the tomato it combines well with raw fruits or vegetables. High in B vitamins and minerals.

[see: Produce]

bake To cook something in an oven, without basting.

balsamic vinegar A sweet Italian vinegar made from white Tribiano grapes aged in wooden barrels. Distinctive flavor, used in raw vegetable salads and sauces.

[see: Misc Grocer]

---

banana Fruit grown in the tropics, through intensive cultivation has become a worldwide crop. Sweet bananas are usually eaten raw and contain high amounts of potassium and vitamins A, B and C.

[see: Produce]

---

barbecuing to roast or grill food on skewers or grate while basting with a spice sauce over an open flame.

---

barley Barley was one of the first grains cultivated be man. Originating some 11,000 years ago and cultivated in Asia and the Middle East by 5000 BC, barley has been a staple grain of Western Civilization. Used predominantly in soups, stews, brewing, cereals and making malt syrup.
[see: Beans, Nuts, Seeds & Grains]

---

barley malt syrup A sweet syrup made by malting barley. Less sweet than honey, a more complex carbohydrate.

[see: Sweeteners & Baking Agents]

---

basil Common or sweet basil, native to Europe and America is used to flavor soups, sauces, casseroles, stews and

Glossary

sautés. Used predominantly in Italian cuisine.

[see: Herb, Spice, Seasonings]

---

basmati rice

Long grain brown or white rice from India and Asia that has been aged to create an aromatic flavor.

[see: Beans, Nuts, Seeds & Grains]

---

baste

to pour hot, flavored liquid over roasting or broiling foods.

---

bay leaves

Whole leaves from the Mediterranean or the coasts of North America used to flavor soups and stews. From the bay tree.

[see: Herb, Spice, Seasonings]

---

bean sprouts

Usually mung beans are used but soy, lentil, black or any other bean or seed will work. The dried bean is first soaked for 6 to 12 hours. Beans are then drained well and placed in a transparent container. This container is then exposed to sunlight for up to 3 days. Beans are rinsed several times a day to prevent spoilage. When tiny leaves appear and start to turn green, remove sprouts from sunlight, place in cold water and refrigerate. Sprouting converts starches to sugars and sprouts are rich in enzymes.

[see: Produce]

beans

Beans or legumes are one of the most important farmed products in the vegetable kingdom. Not only are beans excellent sources of protein, but they fix nitrogen from the air and help to fertilize the ground. The soybean is the source for tofu, tempeh and textured soy products. Beans vary in starch and protein content. Some beans such as kidney are high in protein while others such as garbanzo are high in starch. Every region of the world has its indigenous varieties or bean. Mung and red beans from the orient, pinto and kidneys from the Americas. Fresh, undried beans that are eaten raw or cooked include string and wax beans.
[see: Beans, Nuts, Seeds & Grains]

black pepper

Aromatic and pungent dried berry of the peppercorn plant, native to India and Southeast Asia. Milled or ground black pepper is used to enhance flavor in foods. It is combined in small amounts with other herbs and spices to flavor foods around the world. From the middle ages to the present time it remains one of the worlds most sought after spices. Almost always used with salted, other than sweetened foods. Whole peppercorns are used in consumes and for pickling. Black pepper has medicinal value by increasing blood circulation and improving digestion.
[see: Herb, Spice, Seasonings]

Glossary

blanch — To dip into boiling water for a short duration. Purposes are to loosen skin of vegetables such as tomatoes for peeling, or to whiten or brighten vegetables or to sterilize for freezing or canning.

boil — To heat liquids to 212 degrees Fahrenheit. Used in cooking to render starchy vegetables, beans and grains edible. Boiling liquid also blanches, sterilizes and creates steam for steaming.

bok choy — Member of the cabbage family grown extensively in the Orient and is used in many preparations, from soups to stir-fries.

[see: Produce]

Bragg's Liquid Aminos — A soy sauce substitute made wheat free with soy amino acids.

[see: Misc Grocer]

braising — Braising is the process of searing foods with a small amount of oil and then allowing food to simmer, covered, in its own juices or small amount of liquid.

broccoli

Originating in southern Europe and Italy, broccoli has become a staple vegetable of North America and can be found in most of the world's cuisine today. Related to cauliflower. The flowering buds and stalks make up the whole plant. Used in hot and cold dishes. Requires light to medium cooking or steaming. Contains chlorophyll, Vitamins A, B, C and cancer-fighting compounds.

[see: Produce]

---

broth

The liquid in soup, stock or consommés.

---

brown rice

Natural, unpearled whole grain complete with bran, starch and endosperm. Brown rice is a balanced food with substantial amounts of protein, carbohydrates and B vitamins. With origins in Asia and India, rice arrived in Greece and the Mediterranean region by 300 BC. Cultivated in Spain by the Moors in the eighth century, it was introduced to Europe and the Americas by Spanish explorers in the 1500s.

[see ***Brown Rice*** recipe]
[see: Beans, Nuts, Seeds & Grains]

---

brown rice syrup

Somewhat like dark honey but less sweet, it has a full flavor and can be used as a substitute for honey, corn syrup, or maple syrup.

[see: Sweeteners & Baking Agents]

Glossary

bulgar wheat

Cracked dried wheat berries, boiled and used in salads, pilafs, stews and various Middle Eastern cuisine.

[see: Beans, Nuts, Seeds & Grains]

butternut squash

Large, tough skinned yellow squash yielding a delicious starchy meat when baked.

[see: Produce]

cajun spice blend

A spice combination used to 'blacken' foods in Cajun cuisine consisting of chilies, black pepper, cayenne, onion and garlic powders. Use in small quantities as a flavor enhancer, in larger amounts to increase 'heat'.

[see: Herb, Spice, Seasonings]

canapé

A blended or creamed food that is served on crackers.

cantilini beans

White kidney beans.

[see: Beans, Nuts, Seeds & Grains]

canola oil

A mono and poly unsaturated fat - cold pressed oil.

[see: Oils & Butters]

capers

A pickled bud of the caper bush that grows in Europe and North America. Use in salads, sauces and sautéed pasta tosses.

[see: Misc Grocer]

caraway

The seeds and leaves are used to flavor soups, salads and stews. The seeds give rye bread its distinctive flavor.

[see: Herb, Spice, Seasonings]

cardamom

The fruit of a plant from India, is usually ground and used as a spice. The plant is quite large reaching a height of 15 feet and belongs to the ginger family. Cardamom has a distinct, aromatic flavor and is used in curries and spice mixes in both salty and sweet foods.

[see: Herb, Spice, Seasonings]

carob

The ground bean of the St. John's Bread tree. Used in baking as a flour, as well as a chocolate substitute. Tamarind is the pulpy sweet flesh of the bean. Native to Southern Asia, the tree is so named because it was supposed to have nourished John the Baptist while he was in the wilderness.

[see: Sweeteners & Baking Agents]

Glossary

carrot

Common root vegetable eaten raw or cooked, can be found in almost every culture and in every type of cuisine. Belonging to the parsley family, carrots are and important source of carotene, B vitamins vitamin A and C. Carrots are very health giving and are frequently used as a base for vegetable juice.

[see: Produce]

casserole

A baked tray of food bound together with cheese or sauce that serves several people.

cauliflower

White flowering bud garden vegetable belonging to the mustard family and closely related to broccoli. Found world wide it is usually cooked but can be eaten raw. Large amounts of Vitamin C, sulfur, vitamin A and phosphorus.

[see: Produce]

cayenne

Hot red pepper used to spice foods. Very hot, high frequency spice. Contains capsium, a medicinal compound.
[See Hot Pepper Chart]

[see: Herb, Spice, Seasonings]

celery

Belonging to the parsley and the turnip families, celery is used to flavor soups, stocks, and stews. The stalk and leaves are used for cooking, the seeds for spice.

[see: Produce]

---

chapati   A flat, unleavened bread from India.

---

chickpeas   Also known as garbanzo beans, this starchy bean, an important crop in the Middle East and Northern Africa, it is used in such preparations as falafel and hummus.
[see: Beans, Nuts, Seeds & Grains]

---

chili   A slang word describing a soup made with beans, vegetables and meat.
[see Vegan Meats chapter]

---

chili peppers   Various kinds of hot peppers each with different flavors, grown in Mexico. "chili" in Spanish means 'red pepper'. [See Hot Pepper Chart]
[see: Produce]

---

chili powder   A blend of cumin and mild to medium chili peppers.
[See Hot Pepper Chart]

[see: Herb, Spice, Seasonings]

---

chlorophyll   A complex carbohydrate created by plants from sunlight in a process called photosynthesis. This process includes water and carbon dioxide and produces oxygen as a byproduct. This is the green in green vegetables.

Glossary

High levels of chlorophyll in your diet are essential for good health.

chocolate

A dark, bitter resin from the seeds of the tropical cacao tree, which is processed into hard cakes with more of the cocoa butter than cocoa. Chocolate is a natural stimulant and is high in energy producing complex carbohydrates. Chocolate is usually considered a dessert ingredient but can be used in some salty dishes as well adding distinctive flavor.
[see: Sweeteners & Baking Agents]

cilantro

Green leaves of the coriander plant. Adds a fresh aromatic flavor to Asian and Mexican cuisine. Sometimes called Chinese parsley.
[see: Herb, Spice, Seasonings]

cinnamon

Aromatic spice used worldwide in candies, cookies, cakes, pies, soups, sauces, etc...Grown in the tropics, from the bark of the cinnamon laurel tree.
[see: Herb, Spice, Seasonings]

clove

The flower buds of the clove tree, and evergreen native to the Moluccas Islands. Used in curries and spice combinations in vegan cuisine. Strong aromatic and pungent flavor. The oil of clove is used as a medicine.
[see: Herb, Spice, Seasonings]

cocoa   Made from the cacao bean in the same process as chocolate, except with less of the cocoa butter. Cocoa is usually ground into a powder and used in beverages and baking.
[see: Sweeteners & Baking Agents]

coconut   The fruit of the coconut palm, probably the most important plant in the tropics. The tree, and fruit are used for everything from food to shelter and clothing. Dried shredded coconut is used in desserts throughout the world, coconut milk is used in cooking soups, sauces, sautés, and stews. The oil from the coconut is used in cooking as well as cosmetics. Hearts of palm are the tender young shoots and are used in salads.
[see: Produce]

consommé   In vegan cuisine, a clear vegetable broth.

coriander   An annual herb native to the Mediterranean. Leaves are cilantro. The ground seeds are called coriander and are used as spice in cooking throughout the Middle East and Central Asia. In Europe and America, coriander is used in cookies and candies.
[see: Herb, Spice, Seasonings]

Glossary

 corn   Probably the most valuable crop in the Americas, corn is eaten in a variety of ways. From soups to succotash, from oil to syrup. Cornstarch, popcorn, tamales and cornbread. Other products include glues, soaps, solvents, explosives, ether and ethyl alcohol. First discovered by the Western World in the 15th century, it has been cultivated in the Americas for over 10,000 years. Corn is a grain, and belongs to the Gramineae family of grasses. The nutritional value of corn comes in way of complex carbohydrates and sugars for energy for the most part and to a lesser degree, protein, vitamins and roughage.

[see: Produce]

 corn oil   Oil derived from corn. Used for salad dressings, frying, and other forms cooking and baking.

[see: Oils & Butters]

 corn syrup   Syrup made from the sugars in corn.

[see: Sweeteners & Baking Agents]

 cornstarch   Pure starch derived from corn. Used in cooking to thicken sources, soups, stews, pies, sautés and casseroles.

[see: Baking Mixes, Flours, Pastas & Cereals]

couscous A granular semolina pasta made from steaming, drying and cracking durham wheat. Used extensively in North African and Middle Eastern cuisine's. Uses include salads, sautés and as pie crust.
[see: **Baking Mixes, Flours, Pastas & Cereals**]

cracker A wheat or grain flatbread that is baked crisp and served as snacks, or with canapé.

[see: **Misc Grocer**]

cream, to Creaming is the process of beating with a whisk or electric mixer, a food mixture which is, at least in part, liquid. A secondary meaning is: to thicken with white sauce.

croutons Toasted bread cubes, often seasoned.

[see: **Misc Grocer**]

crudite Crudite, pronounced cru-di-tay, is a French word for sliced, finger sized raw vegetables intended for dipping into sauces.

cucumber Native to Southern Asia the cucumber is a staple of the raw vegetable salad of America. Cucumbers are a mem-

Glossary

ber of the gourd family. Usually eaten raw, cucumbers are good blood cleansers and alkalinizers. Preserved cucumbers in brine are called pickles

[see: Produce]

cumin

Spice used extensively throughout the world with emphasis on Mexican and Middle Eastern cuisine.

[see: Herb, Spice, Seasonings]

curry paste

A blend of dried spices and fresh herbs.

[see: Misc Grocer]

curry powder

A blend of dry herbs and aromatic spices. Used in Indian and Asian cooking. Very distinct flavor for soups, sautés, stews and sauces. Flavor and spice heat is adjustable by adding or subtracting spices. Best curries include fenugreek as a main ingredient.

[see: Herb, Spice, Seasonings]

custard

In vegan cuisine, a custard is a thickened sweet pudding made with tofu, sweeteners, binders, soy milk and flavorings. Used in pies, cakes and puddings.

dandelion — Tender young leaves from the common weed are edible (providing that they grow in ground untreated with chemicals).

[see: Produce]

dates — Very sweet, dried fruit of the date palm tree, found in the Southern Mediterranean region including North Africa. Date sugar is a very potent sweetener.

[see: Misc Grocer]

deep frying — To immerse food into oil at a temperature of around 350 degrees.

defrost — To thaw out frozen foods

deglaze — To loosen and wash out the pan juices and flavoring with wine, stock or water, while sautéing.

dijon mustard — A prepared mustard condiment made with spicy brown mustard seeds, white wine and vinegar as main ingredients.

[see: Misc Grocer]

dill — Both the leaf and the seed are used. The leaves are used fresh or dried in salads as well as some Turkish and eastern European cooked dishes. The

Glossary

seeds are used in salads, potatoes and vinegar.
[see: Herb, Spice, Seasonings]

dredge To coat with flour, generally before frying.

dumplings usually consisting of flour and potatoes or flavorings, dumplings are light pastries slow cooked on the tops of soups and stews.

edamame Frozen immature soy beans that can be steamed and eaten.

[see: Produce]

eggplant The large, black skinned fruit produced by the garden bush belonging to the nightshade family. Also called Aubergine, it is native to northern India but spread to the rest of the world thousands of years ago. Used extensively in Italian and Mediterranean cuisine. In Macrobiotic cuisine, eggplants are considered extremely Yin.

[see: Produce]

endive A leafy vegetable closely related to chicory. Sharp flavor, eaten raw in salads. Belongs to same family as escarole. High in vitamins A, B, and C and calcium. French endive is grown in low sunlight producing a light green, tight leafed plant used in cooking.

[see: Produce]

 escarole A leafy green vegetable whose tough leaves require cooking to tenderize. Escarole has a delicious flavor with lots of vitamins and minerals.

[see: Produce]

 fennel A celery like plant that has the flavor of anise. Use sparingly in place of celery in cooking. The Italian fenocchio - or bulbous white stalk - is the edible portion or the plant.

[see: Produce]

 fenugreek A plant native to Europe and Asia whose seeds are used in curry powders and medicinal teas.

[see: Produce]

 figs A fresh or dried sweet fruit from a tree native to Asia and the Middle East, but grown in all sub-tropical climates today.

[see: Produce]

 file powder A Creole spice mix consisting of dried and powdered sassafras leaves, powdered dried okra, coriander, allspice and sage. Used to thicken stews or gumbos.

[see: Herb, Spice, Seasonings]

Glossary

fillet   A thin slice of food.

flax seed oil   Cold pressed oil from the Flax plant. One of the oldest cultivated plants used by man for making linen and paper products. Flax seed oil contains essential omega 3 and 6 fatty acids.
[see: Oils & Butters]

fold, to   To gently mix foods without disturbing the air bubbles in the concoction. This is done by placing the lighter ingredient atop of the heavier ingredient and lifting the heavier material from the bottom of the bowl over the top of the lighter material until the foods are well mixed. An example is muffin making.

fricassee   To braise vegetables and vegetable meats then cook slowly in stock, gravy or sauce.

fritter   A fried cake with corn or vegetables made from a stiff batter.

fructose   The sugar in fruit.

garlic   One of the great, universal flavor enhancing plant foods, garlic is used in various degrees in cuisine throughout the world. The clove of bulb is used chopped, sliced or crushed.

Garlic is also well respected for its medicinal value.

[see: Produce]

ginger

A spice from the root of a kind of lily, native to Southeast Asia, now grown in Jamaica, South America, Japan and elsewhere. Used in Asian and Oriental cuisine's as well as Island cuisine of the Caribbean and in the South Pacific. Ginger that is candied is popular in the Orient.

[see: Produce]

glaze

A glaze is a thickened, flavored or spiced sauce that is applied (brushed) over cooking foods (i.e. open grill barbecuing).

glucose

The sugar from starch produced by plants.

gluten

Isolated gluten is used to make vegan meats such as steaks, seitan, and is also mixed with other vegetable-based food stuffs, to simulate animal meats, such as ham or turkey.
[see Vegan Meats chapter]

goulash

A heavily spiced Hungarian stew flavored with paprika.

gramineae

The family of grasses that include all the world's great grains such as

Glossary

wheat, barley, rice, corn and rye. This family of grasses, and their emergence on the scene about 11,000 years ago marked the beginning of agriculture and civilization.

grapefruit Citrus fruit, very juicy, slightly bitter-sweet.

[see: **Produce**]

gravy A sauce made with a rue of flour and oil and usually a flavored stock as a liquid.

grits Boiled white corn hominy.

[see: **Baking Mixes, Flours, Pastas & Cereals**]

guacamole A Mexican avocado dip.

gumbo A Cajun or Creole soup, thickened with file powder.

habenero Some of the hottest peppers in the world, grown in Mexico. Grown in Jamaica it is called Scotch Bonnet. To understand how hot: if a bell pepper is zero heat units, the dried Habenero can be as high as 200,000 heat units. [See Hot Pepper Chart]

[see: **Herb, Spice, Seasonings**]

hazelnut Hard shelled small nut also called a Filbert.

[see: Beans, Nuts, Seeds & Grains]

hoisin paste A Chinese soybean paste flavored with chilies, garlic and spices. Use in small quantities to flavor sauces and stir frys, distinctive flavor.

[see: Misc Grocer]

hominy Corn kernels whose husk and germ have been removed. This process is traditionally accomplished by soaking corn in slated lime. Grits are the broken up hominy.

[see: Beans, Nuts, Seeds & Grains]

honey A thick liquid sweetener produced by the action of enzymes of the honeybee's stomach on flower pollen ingested by the bee. The bee regurgitates the honey. Since beekeeping is essential for the pollination of plants, the symbiotic relationship between humans and bees has improved our control of food production in the environment. Although not a direct product of the bee, vegans find honey unacceptable as a food product.

[see: Sweeteners & Baking Agents]

hors d'oeuvres Hors d'oeuvres are small, prepared finger foods that are served with

Glossary

drinks. Unlike the Canapé, which sit on top of a cracker, hors d'oeuvres are stand alone concoctions that can be eaten with a cracker.

horseradish		A bitter, pungent root made into a mustard-like condiment. [see: Misc Grocer]

jalapeno		A medium hot Mexican pepper. [See Hot Pepper Chart] [see: Produce]

jerk sauce		A Jamaican spice sauce or glaze made with molasses, as a base. [see: Misc Grocer]

kale		A leafy green vegetable high in vitamins A and C as well as chlorophyll, enzymes, calcium and magnesium. [see: Produce]

kasha		Cooked buckwheat groats. [see: Baking Mixes, Flours, Pastas & Cereals]

kebab   A skewer of food usually intend for grilling or broiling.

 ketchup   A generic, slang name for a popular spiced tomato condiment. It's been theorized that the use of ketchup at dinner time, led to the pronunciation as "catsup".

[see: Misc Grocer]

knead   To massage or 'work' a dough in order to activate its gluten formation.

 lavender   The flowers are dried and used for seasoning, adding an aromatic, pungent and perfume like flavor to foods.

[see: Herb, Spice, Seasonings]

 leeks   Related to the onion in family and flavor, the leek is prized as a soup vegetable.

[see: Produce]

 legumes   Dried beans.

[see: Beans, Nuts, Seeds & Grains]

Glossary

lemon Sour citrus fruit used in all forms aspects of cooking. Native to Southeast Asia.

[see: **Produce**]

lemon grass Grass native to the tropics noted for its lemony taste and odor. Lemon grass is steeped in soups and sauces in Thai and Southeast Asian cuisine.

[see: **Produce**]

lentil Belonging to the pea family, the lentil is one of the oldest known legumes. Native to Egypt and Asia. Usually used in soups, lentils are high in protein.

[see: **Beans, Nuts, Seeds & Grains**]

lettuce Native to Middle East, lettuce has been cultivated for several thousand years and today is the most popular raw salad food in the world. Lettuce belongs to the composite family. The greener the leaf, the more nutritious the lettuce.

[see: **Produce**]

lima beans Native to North America, this bean is the most nutritious member of the pea family. Use dried beans in soups, fresh in stews.

[see: **Produce**]

lime Limes are closely related to lemons. A sour, citrus fruit with a skin and shape similar to lemons but green. Origins are from India.

[see: Produce]

 Liquid Smoke Bottled hickory smoke flavoring (vegan).

[see: Misc Grocer]

 macaroni Another word for pasta, usually associated with small noodles such as elbows.

[see: Baking Mixes, Flours, Pastas & Cereals]

 mace The dried, ground outer fruit of the Myristica Fragans. The same fruit produces nutmeg, and mace is a milder version of the same flavor.

[see: Herb, Spice, Seasonings]

 mango Tropical fruit noted for its sweet orange colored flesh under a tough outer skin. High in vitamin C.

[see: Produce]

 marinate To soak in a flavored liquid for a period of time so as to impart the same flavor to the food, which is then cooked.

Glossary

marjoram
A mild herb, excellent in soups, sautés and salad dressings. Marjoram is a member of the mint family.

[see: Herb, Spice, Seasonings]

masa harina
Mexican corn flour used in making tortillas. Made from dried and ground, lime soaked hominy.

[see: Baking Mixes, Flours, Pastas & Cereals]

mash
To crush a food such as boiled potatoes until it is smoothed and beaten, but not whipped.

matzoh meal
From ground, unleavened matzoh crackers. Used to thicken soups and dredge foods.

[see: Misc Grocer]

meat
The protein of a life form. Vegan 'meat' is a first-source food, and designates a TVP, tofu, tempeh, seitan or vital wheat gluten food product. These products are derived from vegetable, grain and nut protein combinations.
[see Vegan Meats chapter]

[see: Vegan Meats]

mesclum mix
An assortment of fresh field greens such as sorrel, radicchio, dandelion,

Glossary

frisee, arugala, oak leaf, mache and
mizuma used in raw salads.
[see: Produce]

 millet Small, granular grain with a yellow
color grown as a staple in Eastern
Asia. Cooks quickly and easily. Millet
is high in alkaline minerals.
[see: Beans, Nuts, Seeds & Grains]

mince, to To chop even finer than dicing.

 mint Many varieties of this herb grow
worldwide. Uses include raw and
prepared salads and Middle Eastern
dishes. Mint is used in many products
from candy and breath fresheners to
herbal teas. A variety of herbs come
from the mint family of plants.
[see: Herb, Spice, Seasonings]

 miso paste A fermented soy bean paste that
comes from the Far East, used to flavor soups and sauces. Varieties
range from light to dark. Dark miso
is stronger and saltier.
[see: Soy Products]

 molasses The thick syrup produced by boiling
the sugar cane. Molasses is the product of the first step in making sugar.
Used in desserts and sauces.
[see: Misc Grocer]

Glossary

mole   Mexican paste or sauce made with chilies, tomato, spices and chocolate.

mung bean   An oriental bean usually grown into 'bean sprouts'. Also ground into four to make noodles in the Orient.

[see: Produce]

mustard   The dry powder, or seed, used in preparations of vinegar and wine to make prepared pastes. The French Dijon variety or Louisiana mix is milder that the hot Jamaican or sharp yellow English varieties. Mustard powder is also used in salad dressings, soups and sautés.

[see: Misc Grocer]

mustard greens   Excellent nutrition and flavor when properly cooked. Tough leaves can't be eaten raw. Old fashioned Southern cuisine is fond of these greens.

[see: Produce]

nappa   Chinese cabbage.

[see: Produce]

nutmeg   Ground spice, made from a - fragrant - hard seed of an East India tree.

[see: Herb, Spice, Seasonings]

nutritional yeast

Similar to Brewer's Yeast but better flavored. Lends a distinctive cheesy, nutty flavor as a seasoning. High in essential aminos and B vitamins.

[see: Misc Grocer]

oats

Oats are a very nutritious cereal grain that is used as a breakfast cereal and for baking. Oats belong to the same family of grasses as do wheat, barley, corn, rye and rice, the family gramineae. Although a wild ancient grain, oats were not widely cultivated until the Middle Ages. The cereal is referred to as rolled oats or oatmeal.

[see: Beans, Nuts, Seeds & Grains]

olive

First grown in the Eastern Mediterranean region, the olive soon grew wild throughout the Middle East, Italy, Greece, Spain and Northern Africa where it has become a staple since ancient times. Prized for its oil, the olive is also canned in brine or pickled in vinegar.

[see: Misc Grocer]

olive oil

An excellent cooking or salad oil. Olive oil is pressed out of fresh olives and is a good source of mono-unsaturated fat. It congeals if refrigerated.

[see: Oils & Butters]

Glossary

 onion   Native to Central Asia, onions were brought to America by its earliest settlers. Strong, pungent flavor marks the use of the onion in cooking. The natural compounds in onions have medical value. Onions are also eaten raw and powdered for use as a flavoring agent.

[see: Produce]

 orange   Citrus fruit of the tropics its sweet orange juice is served as a beverage all over the world. Rich in vitamin C and antioxidants, the orange is also used in soups, sauces and desserts.

[see: Produce]

 oregano   Mild herb with a distinctive flavor used in Italian and Mexican cuisine. Belonging to the mint family.

[see: Herb, Spice, Seasonings]

 orzo   Small, seed like pasta used for soups and salads.

[see: Baking Mixes, Flours, Pastas & Cereals]

 **oyster mushroom**   White, fan shaped mushroom with a peppery flavor.

[see: Produce]

papaya A tropical fruit that is sweet and fleshy covered by a thick. tough skin. Besides being good sources of vitamin C and bioflavanoids, Papaya contains an enzyme called papain that digests protein. In the South Pacific, Papaya is eaten before a protein meal.

[see: Produce]

paprika A mild bright red pepper that has been dried and ground into a powder. The flavor of paprika is distinctive and is used in Spanish and Eastern European Cooking.

[see: Herb, Spice, Seasonings]

parsley Native to Southern Italy, the mild flavored green is treated more as an herb than as a vegetable although its nutritional value is quite high. Parsley is a good source of vitamins A and C and minerals such as Iron.

[see: Produce]

parsnip A hearty root vegetable related to the carrot and dill. Parsnips are shaped like carrots but yellowish white in color. A starchy vegetable that requires cooking, it is high in calories, vitamins A and C. Parsnips are native to Europe.

[see: Produce]

Glossary

PDF Advanced electronic publication format, developed by Adobe(tm) Systems Incorporated. Defined as *Portable Document Format*, these files are platform independent and multimedia capable.

peanuts Native to South America, early colonialists grew peanuts in America. An excellent source of protein peanut butter is has more protein and energy giving calories than beef. Peanuts have hundreds of industrial and commercial uses. Peanuts are a type of pea that grows in a pod underground. Peanuts are grown in South East Asia and are an important part of their cuisine.

[see: Beans, Nuts, Seeds & Grains]

pears Originally from southern Europe, Asia and China, pears are grown extensively in the United States. Pears are grown on trees in orchards. They are high in Vitamins and minerals. Pears can be eaten raw or stewed.

[see: Produce]

peas Edible round-shaped seeds from long green pods, which grow from a climbing vine-like plant.

[see: Produce]

pepper Family of vegetable fruits belonging to the Nightshades and ranging from sweet to hot in flavor. Heat spice in foods is usually created and controlled with peppers. Sweet bell peppers are an excellent source of vitamin C.

[see: Produce]

 pickle Usually refers to cucumbers that have been pickled, or preserved in brine and or vinegar.

[see: Misc Grocer]

 pine nuts Pine nuts (or pignoli nuts) are really the seeds of the pinon pine of the Southwestern United States. A staple food of Western Indian tribes; they are high energy foods with good protein content.

[see: Beans, Nuts, Seeds & Grains]

 pinto beans Mexican red beans used in refried beans. Staple of Mexico, high in protein and B vitamins.

[see: Beans, Nuts, Seeds & Grains]

poach, to Poaching a food such as dumplings, is to float the food on top of a boiling or simmering liquid, while basting the top of the food with the same liquid.

Glossary

 poblano chili Medium hot, long and fairly wide, used to stuff rellenos.

[see: Herb, Spice, Seasonings]

 polenta Polenta is a cornmeal mash that can be spread and cooled, then used as a pizza crust or cut into pieces and grilled. Polenta is a staple food of Northern Italy.

[see: Baking Mixes, Flours, Pastas & Cereals]

 pomegranate An ancient fruit that once grew wild on bushes in western Asia and India. A tough, leathery red skin covers a seed laden, juicy interior. A refreshing taste similar to sweetened cranberry.

[see: Produce]

 portabella mushroom Large capped Italian Mushroom whose flavor when grilled, is noted for its similarity to beef steak. Very versatile, great tasting grilled, or in sautés or soups.

[see: Produce]

 potato A tuber, the potato is grown all over the modern world. An important source of energy, the potato is surprisingly low in calories. Potatoes are a good source of B vitamins and minerals. A great cold weather vegetable, potatoes were first grown in the Andes Mountains of Peru and Bolivia.

Spanish explorers introduced the potato to Europe c.1550.

[see: Produce]

---

puff pastry

A commercially prepared pastry dough, made with multi-layered oiled dough. When baked, produces a puffed layered textured bread that can be stuffed.

[see: Baking Mixes, Flours, Pastas & Cereals]

---

pumpkin

Pumpkins are large orange, edible gourds native to North America and American Cuisine. Usually recognized for their use as carved 'Jack O' Lanterns' on Halloween. Pumpkin pie is a traditional Thanksgiving dessert.

[see: Misc Grocer]

---

quinoa

Pronounced keen-wah. This ancient grain was the only grain that could grow in the high Andes mountains and served as a staple for the Incas. High in protein and B vitamins, a very fine grain rediscovered only recently by the modern world. Quinoa grains are naturally coated with saponin, a resin that acts as an insect repellant, and must be rinsed well before cooking to remove its bitter flavor.

[see: Beans, Nuts, Seeds & Grains]

---

radish

A pungent garden vegetable that is usually eaten in salads but can also

Glossary

be found pickled. White radishes make good soup vegetables.

[see: Produce]

---

ragout   A highly seasoned stew.

---

raisin   Raisins are sun dried grapes. Black raisins are from red grapes and yellow raisins are from white grapes. Raisins are a good source of minerals such as iron and copper as well as vitamins A and G and are considered blood builders. They alkalinize the blood.

[see: Misc Grocer]

---

raspberry   Raspberries are little red or black berries that grow on thorny bushes in North America. Excellent in pies or torts, also eaten raw or the juice extracted. Raspberries belong to the rose family.

[see: Produce]

---

ravioli   An Italian dough pocket, stuffed with cheese and just about anything. Raviolis are usually boiled and served with a sauce.

---

rice   The 'Staff of Life' for most Asians, rice is a versatile, almost perfectly balanced grain that is grown in 'rice patties' or shallow water lakes. Rice was first grown in Asia and India thousands of years ago and first intro-

duced to the West by Alexander the Great in 326 BC. Brought by the Moors to Spain in the eighth century AD, the Spaniards first cultivated rice in South America in the 1600's. Brown rice, or unmilled rice contains a balanced mix of starch, protein and B vitamins as well as minerals. Rice is a member of the grass family gramineae.
[see: Beans, Nuts, Seeds & Grains]

rice syrup A complex carbohydrate sweetener derived from brown rice and sprouted barley.

[see: Sweeteners & Baking Agents]

risotto Risotto, or Italian rice, is really is a rice shaped pasta used in soups, casserole or sautés.

[see: Baking Mixes, Flours, Pastas & Cereals]

roast, to Roasting is to cook or bake a food preparation or whole food in an oven, basting with seasoned liquid frequently.

romaine lettuce A type of lettuce plant whose edible salad leaves are popular in raw green salads. Romaine is much more nutritious than Iceberg Lettuce.
[see: Produce]

Glossary

rosemary — Rosemary is the leaf of an evergreen shrub native to the Mediterranean region. Rosemary belongs to the mint family and is used in cooking as an herb in stews, sautés, broiled and grilled foods. Use fresh or dry.
[see: Herb, Spice, Seasonings]

roulade — In Vegan cuisine a roulade is a shank of gluten steak stuffed with vegetables, rolled up and sautéed. Alternatives to the gluten flank steak would be bean curd wrap, nut and bean mash or just about anything that will work such as wide noodles.

rue — A rue is a lightly fried mixture of wheat flour and oil. Seasoning may be added to the rue. The rue then becomes the base for thickened gravies and sauces.

rye — Another ancient grain belonging to the Gramineae family of grasses. Rye is an important grain used in bread-making.
[see: Beans, Nuts, Seeds & Grains]

saffron — The dried stigmas of the purple autumn crocus, saffron is a yellow food dye used in Indian cooking.

[see: Herb, Spice, Seasonings]

sage

Sage is a small bush herb and member of the mint family. Sage is used sparingly in soups and stews for its mildly aromatic flavor, especially in American cuisine.
[see: Herb, Spice, Seasonings]

sauté, to

Pan cooking a group of mixed foods together, through the stages of pan frying or searing, to steaming and finally simmering with a sauce.

savory

A mild annual herb used in soups and salads.

[see: Herb, Spice, Seasonings]

scald, to

To heat moist food up to a temperature of 185 degrees Fahrenheit without ever boiling.

searing

Searing foods is the act of browning the sides of the food in a medium hot pan of light oil. This is done to seal in the flavor and to preserve food shape.

seitan

A wheat gluten based veggie 'meat, high in protein. Seitan is usually a mixture of wheat flour and gluten flour. Seitan has been consumed in the Orient for thousands of years.
[see Vegan Meats chapter]
[see: Baking Mixes, Flours, Pastas & Cereals]

Glossary

semolina flour

Semolina flour is a cream colored wheat flour used to make pastas. Its high gluten content keep pasta from falling apart.
[see: Baking Mixes, Flours, Pastas & Cereals]

sesame seeds

The seeds from an annual plant grown in the tropics. These seeds are prized for their distinctive, nutty flavored oil used in cooking as well as the seed as a food stuff. In the Middle East and Eastern Mediterranean region these seeds are ground into a butter and used to make Tahini.
[see: Beans, Nuts, Seeds & Grains]

shortening

Vegetable Shortening is vegetable oil that has been hydrogenated, a process which transforms the free fatty acids by binding them with hydrogen. This partially solidifies the oil making it more useful in baking.
[see: Oils & Butters]

simmer, to

Simmering is to cook moist foods at a temperature of between 130 and 185 degrees Fahrenheit. Simmering usually occurs after the food is brought to a boil.

soy beans

Soy beans are the source of a great many food and industrial products. Green picked soy beans are a delicacy steamed, tofu and tofu products come from soy beans, textured and

isolated soy bean proteins are used to create meat analogs, delicious and nutritious soy milk is made from soy beans, soy flour for baking and soy oil excellent for cooking, also come from the soy bean. Many industrial products such as glues, pharmaceutical drugs, paints, fertilizer, insect repellants and pet food are also created from the soy bean plant. Belonging to the Pea family of plants, soy beans originally grew wild in eastern Asia and have been cultivated by the Chinese for thousands of years. Since antiquity, the Chinese have considered the soybean to be their most important crop. In the 17th century soy beans were tried as crops in Europe and England but never reached large scale production. In 1804 the soybean was introduced to the United States, which now is the world's largest producer of soybeans. [see Vegan Meats chapter]
[see: Beans, Nuts, Seeds & Grains]

spinach

A green garden vegetable that is consumed cooked or raw. Spinach is high in vitamins A, B and C. Native to southwest Asia it has been cultivated in Europe since the 16th century AD. Spinach was grown in gardens by the first American settlers. Spinach is a member of the Goosefoot family of plants.

[see: Produce]

Glossary

squash Belonging to the gourd family of vine plants, squashes come in a wide variety. There are three main categories of squash: summer squashes, autumn squashes and winter squashes. Summer squashes can be steamed, stewed or sautéed with edible skins while autumn and winter varieties have tough skins and should be baked. Autumn and winter squashes are starchy vegetables with tuber like properties.

[see: Produce]

steam, to Steaming is the cooking process whereby foods cooked entirely by steam heat from a source of boiling liquid located beneath the food. Steaming retains most of the vitamins and enzymes that may be destroyed in other cooking processes.

steep To steep is to allow a tea or food to soak in hot water.

stew A slow cooked food mixture with less liquid than a soup and thickened with starch.

stock In Vegan cuisine, stock is a liquid flavoring agent. Stock is made by cooking down a large volume of vegetable matter in water and then straining off the broth for use as stock.
[see **Vegetable Stock** recipe]

string beans Garden vegetable, pole or bush variety, with edible pod and seeds. Eaten raw or lightly cooked. Also called green beans, they are related to wax beans.

[see: Produce]

stuffing A moist, baked mixture of vegetables, breads and or grains.

 Sucanat An acronym for Sugar Cane Natural, which is an excellent substitute for honey or cane sugar.

[see: Sweeteners & Baking Agents]

sucrose Sucrose is the simplest form of carbohydrate. Obtained from plants, especially the sugar cane and sugar beet, sucrose is the energy created for plants by plants, through photosynthesis.

 sugar The world's most popular food sweetener, sugar, is the crystallized sucrose of the sugar cane plant. Sugar is made by milling, baking, boiling, filtering and refiltering the cane until all the molasses syrup is removed. Sugar is marketed in various forms such as white sugar, raw sugar, evaporated cane juice, dark to light brown sugar and molasses. Sugar cane is native to India and cultivated in Europe by the end of the first millen-

nium. Columbus brought cuttings to the West Indies and Cortez established plantations in Mexico. From this beginning sugar spread throughout the southern hemisphere. Products other than sugar cane described as sugar include beet sugar, fruit sugar or fructose and maple sugar.
[see: Sweeteners & Baking Agents]

---

sweet potato

A tropical climbing plant, with thick edible roots (tubers), whose meat can be yellow, red, or white in appearance, and very sweet to the taste. Though not the same in taste or size, the sweet potato is commonly referred to as a yam.
[see: Produce]

---

tahini

A butter made from ground sesame seeds. Tahini sauce is a light blend of tahini butter lemon, water and salt.

[see: Oils & Butters]

---

tamale

Corn husks, banana or tea leaves used to encase a spiced, mashed stuffing that is slow steamed. Tamales are usually corn husks filled with cheese and sweetened sour cream.
[see: Misc Grocer]

---

tamari

An aged soy sauce containing no sugars. Tamari sauce is a generic term for a blend of soy sauce, sesame oil and rice vinegar. [see *Tamari* sauce]

[see: Misc Grocer]

---

tamarind The sweet flesh of the seed pod of the St. Johns Bread tree. Used in Indian and Southeast Asian cuisine for flavoring sauces and drinks. Flour from the ground seed or bean, called carob, is used in baking.

[see: Baking Mixes, Flours, Pastas & Cereals]

---

taro A plant that is an important food source to peoples of the Pacific and in South America, where it is known as the Malanga. In America it is known mostly as the ornamental 'elephant' plant because of its leaves. The green leaves of the taro can be eaten if boiled for about an hour, because of the high oxalic acid content they are poisonous if eaten raw. The root is boiled and used in many applications such as the Hawaiian Poi.

[see: Produce]

---

tarragon A leafy herb considered most sublime by the French. Tarragon's licorice like flavor is almost identical to anise, and is used fresh and dry.

[see: Herb, Spice, Seasonings]

---

tempeh A high protein food, rich in B vitamins including B12, made from cultured soy beans. Sometimes other grains are added and fermented with the

soy beans. Tempeh has been produced and consumed in the Orient
for thousands of years.[see Vegan
Meats chapter]

[see: Soy Products]

thyme

One of the great garden herbs, thyme
comes in several varieties with different bouquets and flavors. Used for
stews, sauces, soups, and sautés
thyme deepens the flavor of food.
Thyme belongs to the mint family.

[see: Herb, Spice, Seasonings]

tofu

The pressed curd of soy milk made
from the soy bean. Tofu is easily
digestible and high in protein. A good
source of B vitamins and calcium, tofu
has been a staple protein food in the
Orient for thousands of years and in
the United States, only a few decades
of use has made tofu a well known
food. Tofu comes in several forms:
soft, firm and extra firm tofu, silken
tofu in soft, firm and extra firm, dehydrated tofu and tofu powder. [see
Vegan Meats chapter]

[see: Soy Products]

tomato

The tomato is probably the most popular and most used of all garden vegetables. Tomatoes are one of the best
sources of vitamin C and A of any
vegetable or fruit. Tomatoes are
canned more than any other single
vegetable in the United States. Originating in Central America, the tomato

was eaten by American colonists before it was a staple of sauce making in Italy. Tomato belongs to the night shade family of plants.

[see: Produce]

---

truffle   A fungus prized for its flavor is one of the world's most expensive foods. Truffles defy cultivation and only grow underground near oak trees. The black French truffles have the best flavor and can only be foraged by trained pigs. Truffles have a very strong aroma and flavor and should be used sparingly. Shavings are usually sufficient when added to a dish at the end of the cooking period.

[see: Misc Grocer]

---

tuber   An enlarged section of a plant's stem that is buried and close to the root of the plant. Many plants produce edible tubers such as the potato, taro and yam. Edible tubers are usually starchy vegetables.

[see: Produce]

TVP   TVP (Textured Vegetable Protein) is a fibrous soy protein product that resembles animal flesh. Generally TVP is sold in granular, chunked or in various mixes with other vegetable sourced ingredients. An extensive line of cold cuts made with TVP, i.e. bacon, ham, turkey etc., are available on the market as well.

[see Vegan Meats chapter]
[see: TVP Products]

TVP burger blend

A dehydrated blend of isolated soy and wheat proteins, with vegetables and spices, which are reconstituted into a ground meat analogue.
[see Vegan Meats chapter]
[see: TVP Products]

---

vanilla

Produced from a bean that grows from a vine belonging to the orchid family, vanilla is a flavoring extract that is used in desserts and confections. Native to the tropics, vanilla was first cultivated in Mexico.
[see: Herb, Spice, Seasonings]

---

vinaigrette

A salad dressing made with herbs, optional flavorings and a 3:1 ratio of oil to vinegar.

---

vinegar

The product of fermented wine, fruit juice or cereals, vinegar is a sour liquid substance used in salad dressings and pickled foods. Vinegar is made by oxidizing the alcohol away from the fermented liquid.
[see: Misc Grocer]

---

vital wheat gluten

The essential protein derived from wheat. A natural water extraction process produces a fine powder of

isolated proteins, known commercially as Vital Wheat Gluten.
[see: Baking Mixes, Flours, Pastas & Cereals]

vitamins A group of complex compounds found in living matter that are essential for maintaining human health. Vitamins are identified as A, B complex, C, D, E and K and can all be obtained from vegetable sourced foods. Vitamin B-12 can be obtained from some fermented foods and yeast.

walnut A popular edible nut that is native to the North America and southern Europe with the U.S. the world's chief producer. Walnuts are high in protein, oil and B vitamins.
[see: Beans, Nuts, Seeds & Grains]

wild rice A small reed like rice that grows wild in the great lakes region of the U.S. and Canada. A staple food of the Indians native to that region it is high in B vitamins, starch and protein. Popular a pilaf grain.
[see: Beans, Nuts, Seeds & Grains]

won ton A stuffed Chinese wheat pastry or dumpling cooked in soup or liquid. Usually made with eggs, won tons can be made vegan.
[see: Misc Grocer]

Glossary

xanthum gum

A vegetable starch binding agent used in baking and other applications for thickening moist foods.

[see: Sweeteners & Baking Agents]

xylitol

A sugar derived from birch tree sap, it is a more complex carbohydrate than sugar and metabolized slower. Xylitol contains half the calories than contained in the same amount of white sugar.

[see: Sweeteners & Baking Agents]

yam

A member of the sweet potato family, this edible starchy tuber of a tropical climbing plant is orange-red in appearance. Though not as sweet, and much larger in average size, this tuber can be used as a substitute for sweet potatoes.

[see: Produce]

zucchini

A member of the squash family, also call Italian squash. Zucchini is a soft summer squash.

[see: Produce]

Appendix

Herb/Spice Table

We've included the following chart to assist in the procurement of herbs and spices that are needed for a particular cuisine. This table should help reduce excess pantry stock.

Country Codes

[A] African
[B] North American
[C] Continental
[D] Italian
[E] Indian
[F] Middle Eastern
[G] Mexican
[H] Oriental
[I] Pacific
[J] South American

Table 8: World Herb / Spice Table

HERB/SPICE	A	B	C	D	E	F	G	H	I	J
allspice	X	X	X		X	X			X	X
anise clove		X	X	X		X		X		
basil		X	X	X						
bay leaves		X	X	X	X					
cajun spice blend	X	X								X
caraway seeds		X	X	X						
cardamom	X	X	X		X	X				
cayenne	X	X	X	X	X	X	X			X
celery seeds		X	X		X	X				
chili powder	X	X					X	X		X
cilantro			X		X		X	X	X	
HERB/SPICE	A	B	C	D	E	F	G	H	I	J

Appendix

Table 8: World Herb / Spice Table

Country Codes

[A] African
[B] North American
[C] Continental
[D] Italian
[E] Indian
[F] Middle Eastern
[G] Mexican
[H] Oriental
[I] Pacific
[J] South American

HERB/SPICE	A	B	C	D	E	F	G	H	I	J
cinnamon	X	X	X		X	X			X	X
clove	X	X	X		X			X	X	X
coriander	X	X	X		X	X		X		
cumin		X			X	X	X			X
curry powder					X				X	
dill		X	X			X				
ginger					X			X	X	
mace		X	X	X	X				X	X
marjoram		X	X	X						
mint	X	X	X	X	X	X	X	X	X	X
mustard		X	X	X	X			X	X	X
nutmeg	X	X	X		X					X
onion powder		X	X	X		X	X	X		X
oregano				X			X			X
paprika		X	X			X				
parsley	X	X	X	X	X	X	X	X		X
rosemary	X	X	X	X		X				
sage		X	X	X			X			
savory		X	X	X						
tarragon		X	X	X		X				
thyme	X	X	X	X	X	X				
HERB/SPICE	A	B	C	D	E	F	G	H	I	J

Herb Application Chart

There are times when you need to substitute an ingredient, or vary a recipe's flavor. The following two charts are designed to assist in that process.

Application
Codes

[A] SALAD
[B] SOUP
[C] SAUCES
[D] SAUTES
[E] CASSEROLE
[F] BREADS
[G] DESSERTS
[H] MISC.

Table 9: Herb Application Chart

HERB	A	B	C	D	E	F	G	H
basil	X	X	X	X	X			
bay leaves		X	X					
cilantro	X	X	X	X	X			
dill	X	X	X	X	X	X		X
marjoram	X	X	X	X	X	X		
mint	X	X	X	X	X	X	X	X
oregano	X	X	X	X	X	X		
parsley	X	X	X	X	X			
rosemary		X	X	X	X	X		
sage		X	X	X	X	X		
savory	X	X	X	X	X			
tarragon			X	X				
thyme	X	X	X	X	X	X		
HERB	A	B	C	D	E	F	G	H

Spice Application Chart

Application
Codes

[A] SALAD
[B] SOUP
[C] SAUCES
[D] SAUTES
[E] CASSEROLE
[F] BREADS
[G] DESSERTS
[H] MISC.

Table 10: Spice Application Chart

SPICE	A	B	C	D	E	F	G	H
allspice	X	X	X	X	X	X	X	X
anise clove		X	X	X			X	X
SPICE	A	B	C	D	E	F	G	H

Table 10: Spice Application Chart

Application
Codes

[A] SALAD
[B] SOUP
[C] SAUCES
[D] SAUTES
[E] CASSEROLE
[F] BREADS
[G] DESSERTS
[H] MISC.

SPICE	A	B	C	D	E	F	G	H
cajun spice blend	X	X	X	X	X			
caraway seed	X					X		
cardamom		X	X	X	X		X	
cayenne	X	X	X	X	X		X	X
celery seeds	X	X				X		X
chili powder		X	X	X	X			X
cinnamon		X	X	X	X	X	X	X
clove		X	X				X	X
coriander	X	X	X	X	X		X	
cumin	X	X	X	X	X			
curry paste			X	X				
curry powder	X	X	X	X	X			
dill seed	X					X		
fenugreek	X	X			X			
file powder		X	X	X				
garlic powder	X	X	X		X	X		X
ginger	X	X	X	X		X	X	X
mace		X	X				X	X
mustard	X	X	X	X	X			
nutmeg		X	X	X			X	X
onion powder	X	X	X		X	X		X
paprika	X	X	X	X	X			
SPICE	A	B	C	D	E	F	G	H

Appendix

Cooking-Time Table

Baked root vegetables and squashes are tasty and healthy ways to eat these foods. The following is a cooking chart for baking:

Table 11: Cooking-Time Table

VEGETABLE	OVEN TEMP	COOKING TIME
acorn, butternut squash	450°F	45-60 Min
baking potatoes	450°F	45-60 Min
sweet potato / yam	450°F	45-60 Min
onion	400°F	30-45 Min
garlic clove	450°F	20-25 Min
tomato	450°F	20-25 Min
eggplant	450°F	30-45 Min
zucchini, summer squash	400°F	35-45 Min

For other unusual tubers or squashes, baking time depends on size and hardness of vegetable. When baking whole vegetable, simple place in a hot oven. Thin skinned squashes and potatoes should be wrapped in aluminum foil or otherwise covered. If vegetables are cut in half and stuffed, be sure to baste and keep loosely covered for at least first half of baking time.

Hot Pepper Chart

One of the most critical aspects of professional cooking, is knowing when enough is enough! When it comes to adjusting how "hot" a recipe should be, use this guide:

Table 12: Hot Pepper Chart

PEPPER NAME (CONDITION)	HEAT SCALE
Demre (fresh)	1
Sante Fe Grande (fresh)	2
Serrano (fresh) Banana Peppers (fresh)	3
Mexican Negro (fresh)	4
Yellow Peter (fresh) Jalapeno (fresh) Long Hot Finger (fresh)	5
Bermuda (fresh) Turkish (fresh)	6
Aji Yellow (dried) Pueblo (dried)	7
Thai Sun (dried) Giant Serrano (dried) Hot Lemon (dried)	8
Scotch Bonnet (dried) Brown Congo (dried) Red Chili (fresh)	9
Habenero (dried) Tabasco (fresh)	10
PEPPER NAME (CONDITION)	HEAT SCALE

Note: The above chart indicates the range of spice-heat supplied by individual peppers. Combinations of different peppers, used in different quantities, can supply the necessary 'heat' as desired in a dish. Increasing the amount of peppers used in a food's preparation will increase the spice heat of the food. How-

Appendix

ever, peppers rated lower on the heat scale cannot increase the spice heat of a dish beyond the upper middle range of numbers. Only the hottest of peppers govern the highest numbers on the Hot Pepper Chart.

Food Pyramid
I've included a food pyramid to illustrate the optimum daily food requirements for a vegan diet. These suggestions are based on an adult of average size and weight, and can be adjusted to compensate for individual life-styles.

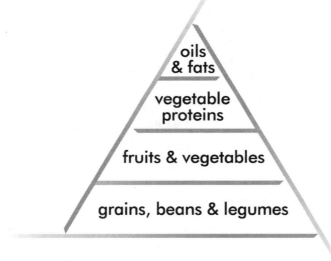

Table 13: Optimum Daily Food Requirements

WHOLE GRAINS	1/2 - 1 LB	40%	1000 CALORIES
VEGETABLES & FRUITS	1 - 2 LB	30%	700 - 1000 CALORIES
VEGETABLE PROTEINS	50 - 65 GRAMS	20%	350 - 500 CALORIES
OILS & FATS	2 - 5 OZ	10%	200 - 400 CALORIES

Measurement Conversion Table

Table 14: Measurement Conversion Table

tsp	=	60 drops
teaspoon	=	1/3 Tbsp [Tablespoon]
pinch	=	1/8 tsp [teaspoon]
Tbsp	=	3 tsp [teaspoons]
oz	=	2 Tbsp [Tablespoons]
4 Tablespoons	=	1/4 cup
8 Tablespoons	=	1/2 cup
16 Tablespoons	=	1 cup
cup	=	8 oz [ounces]
pt	=	2 cups
ounce [oz]	=	28 g [grams]
qt	=	2 pt [pints]
2 quarts	=	1/2 gal [gallon]
gal	=	128 oz [ounces]
lb	=	16 oz [ounces]
kilogram	=	2.2 lb [pounds]
peck	=	8 qt [quarts]
bushel	=	4 pecks

Appendix

Table 15: Metric to Standard Table

Liquid Quantities		Dry Quantities	
5ml =	1 teaspoon	14 grams =	1/2 ounce
20ml =	1 Tablespoon	28 grams =	1 ounce
30ml =	1 fluid ounce	244 grams =	8 ounces
250ml =	8 fluid ounces	488 grams =	1 pound

Metric Conversion Terms

g = gram
kg = kilogram
m = meter
cm = centimeter
mm = millimeter
km = kilometer
l = liter
ml = milliliter

Resource Directory

Introduction

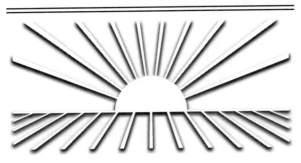

This resource directory is a guide and reference, for the purchasing of vegan ingredients. Included are the names of companies and distributors of food products, which are used at Veggie Works.

Vegan cuisine is based upon quality and innovation. As such, we welcome your suggestions and recommendations! Based on personal experience, I know you'll develop your own approaches to my processes. Fell free to share them! Veggie Works is a successful business, due to our belief that shared experience leads to refinement. So again, when you come across products and techniques, that will improve the joy of cooking, we'd love receive your suggestions!

In the case of fresh produce, many of these sources have to be geographically accessible. We recommend that you make every attempt to purchase from local farms, and try adjusting recipes to utilize geographically seasonable produce. When purchasing from large grocers, influence the produce department's manager to use local sources! This practice will not only contribute to your communities local economy, but will also go a long way towards returning agriculture to a environmentally benign industry.

Baking Mixes, Flours, Pastas & Cereals

Veggie Works, Inc.
(vegan meats, tvp, wheat gluten, seitan)
817 Belmar Shopping Plaza
Belmar, NJ 07719
888.950.7576
www.veggieworksworld.com

Arrowhead Mills, Inc.
(grains, cereals)
Box 2059
Hereford, TX 79045

Athens Pastries & Frozen Foods, Inc.
(puff pastry, filo dough)
Cleveland, OH 44142-2596

Eden Foods, Inc.
(soy & grain products, cereals)
Clinton, MI 49236
www.edenfoods.com

Millinas Organic Pasta
(rice pasta)
(Arrowhead Mills)
PO Box 550 Aptos, CA 95001-0550

DeBoles Organic Pastas
(pasta)
(Arrowhead Mills)
1-800-749-0730

King Arthur Flour
(unbleached white flour)
Norwich, VT
1-800-777-4434

General Mills, Inc.
(grains, cereals)
Minneapolis, MN 55440

S.B. Thomas
(grains, cereals)
(affiliate of Best Foods, Inc.)
PO Box 535
Totowah, NJ 07511-0535

Hodgeson Mill, Inc.
(grains, cereals)
1203 Niccum Ave.,
Effingham, IL 62401
1-800-5250177, ext 31

Natural Foods, Inc.
Milwaukie, OR 97222

Resource Directory

Jaclyn's Food Products, Inc.   Cherry Hill, NJ 08034

Annie Chun's Gourmet Foods, Inc.   P.O. Box 2418
San Rafael, CA 94901
455-479-8272
www.anniechun.com

Produce

A&P   (organic produce, misc health food products)
2 Paragon Drive
Montvale, NJ 07645
201.573.9700
www.aptca.com

Foodtown   (organic produce, misc health food products)
www.shopfoodtown.com

Wild Oats   (organic produce, misc health food products)
1.800.494.WILD
www.wildoat.com

Fresh Fields   (organic produce, misc health food products)
632.936.1960
917.810.1667

Soy Products

EdenSoy
(soy milk, soy products)
Eden Foods, Inc.
701 Tecumseh Road,
Clinton, MI 49236
1-888-769-6455

Silk
(soy milk, soy products)
White Wave, Inc.
Boulder, CO 80301
1-800-488-9283

Vitasoy USA Inc.
(soy milk, soy products)
PO Box 2012,
South San Francisco, CA 94083
1-800-VITASOY (848-2769)
www.vitasoy-usa.com

Mori-Nu Tofu
(tofu, silken)
PO Box 6160,
Torrance, CA 90504
(Dist.: Morinaga Nutritional Foods)
(2050 W. 190th St., #110)
(Torrance, CA 90404)
1-800-669-8638

Fresh Tofu, Inc.
(tofu, tempeh, tvp, ect.)
1101 Harrison St.
Allentown, PA 18103

Kikkoman Foods, Inc.
(soy sauce)
Walworth, WI 53184

Tree of Life, Inc.
dist.: Soy Kaas
(soy cheeses, tofu)
St. Augustine, FL 32085-0410
1-800-238-3947
treeoflife.com

Resource Directory

Naysoya, Inc.   (soy cheeses, tofu)
Ayer, MA 01432
1-800-229-TOFU

WholeSoy Co.   (soy cream, yogurt)
49 Stevenson St. #1075
San Francisco CA 94105
415-495-2870
www.wholesoy.com

Smoke & Fire   (tofu & tempeh - smoked)
Natural Foods, Inc.   P.O. Box 743
Gt. Barrington, MA 01230
413-528-6891
www.smokeandfire.com

Tofutti Brands, Inc.   (soy cheeses, ice creams, ect.)
Cranford, NJ 07016
www.tofuttibrandsinc.com
www.tofutti@nac.net

TVP Products

Veggie Works, Inc.   (vegan meats, tvp, wheat gluten, seitan)
817 Belmar Shopping Plaza
Belmar, NJ 07719
888.950.7576
www.veggieworksworld.com

White Wave, Inc.   1-800-488-9283
whitewave.com

Herb, Spice, Seasonings

McCormack & Co., Inc.
(herbs & spices)
Hunt Valley, MD 21031-1100
1-800-632-5847

Magic Seasonings Blends, Inc.
(cajun seasoning blends)
824 distributors Row
Harahan, LA 70123
1-800-457-2857

Frontier Natural Products CO-OP
(herbs & spices)
Norway, IA 52318
1-800-669-3275
www.frontiercorp.com

C.V. Finer Foods, Inc.
PO Box 88, Winthrop, ME 04364
1-800-355-6221

Knor Foods, Inc.
(dehydrated soups, boullions, spices)
CPC Food Service
Dist. CPC International Inc.
Englewood Cliffs, NJ 07632-9976

Lewis Laboratories International, Ltd.
49 Richmondwille Row
Westport, CT 06880

Resource Directory

Beans, Nuts, Seeds & Grains

Frontier Herbs, Inc. (bulk nuts, seeds)
www.frontiercoop.com

Goya Foods, Inc. (oils, beans, spice blends)
Secaucus, NJ 07096
1-888-298-0849

**Thep Padung Porn
Coconut Co.** (coconut milk, flakes)
Bangkok, Thailand

Woodstock Farms, Inc. (bulk grains, nuts, seeds)
1-800-526-4349

Sweeteners & Baking Agents

Cloud Nine Distributors Hoboken, NJ 07030

Now Foods, Inc. Bloomingdale, IL 60108

Ener-G Foods, Inc. (egg replacement substitute)
P.O.Box 84487
Seattle, WA 98124-5787
www.ener-g.com
1-800-331-5222

413

Cumberland Baking Co.   Brooklyn, NY 11205

Tree of Life, Inc.   (natural foods distributor, baking agents)
St. Augustine, FL 32085-0410
1-800-238-3947
treeoflife.com

Chatfield's Chocolate Chips   (vegan chocolate chips)
American Natural Snacks
St. Augustine, FL

Sunspire, Inc.   (chocolate chips)
2114 Adams Ave.
San Leandro, CA94577
510-569-9731

Misc Grocer

A&P   (organic produce, misc health food products)
2 Paragon Drive
Montvale, NJ 07645
201.573.9700
www.aptca.com

Foodtown   (organic produce, misc health food products)
www.shopfoodtown.com

Wild Oats   (organic produce, misc health food products)
1.800.494.WILD
www.wildoat.com

Resource Directory

Fresh Fields   (organic produce, misc health food products)
632.936.1960
917.810.1667

Live Food Products   (Bragg's Liquid Aminos)
Santa Barbara, CA 93102
1-800-446-1990

Vegan Meats

Veggie Works, Inc.   (vegan meats, tvp, wheat gluten, seitan)
817 Belmar Shopping Plaza
Belmar, NJ 07719
888.950.7576
www.veggieworksworld.com

Smart Deli Lightlife Foods, Inc.   (vegan deli meats)
153 Industrial Blvd.
Turners Falls, MA 01376
1-800-SOY EASY M-F 9-5 EST
www.Lightlife.com

Yves Fine Foods, Inc.   (meat analogs, vegan deli meats)
Yves Veggie cuisine, Inc.
Delta (Vancouver), BC Canada
www.yvesveggie.com

Vegi-Deli   (sliced vegan deli meats)
Green Options, Inc.
P.O. Box 881781
1-888-473-3667
www.vegideli.com

Oils & Butters

Crazy Richard's Peanut Butter
(peanut butter)
PO Box 715
Dublin, OH 43017
www. crazyrichards.com

Barlean's Organic Oils
(flax oil)
4936 Lake Terrel Rd.,
Ferndale, WA 98248
1-800-445-3529

Spectrum Natural Foods, Inc.
(olive oil, balsamic vinegar, etc.)
www.spectrumnaturals.com
1-800-995-2705

The Hain Food Group, Inc.
(oils, condiments, etc.)
Uniondale, NY 11553
1-800-434-4246

California Olive Oil Corp.
(imported olive oil)
134 Canal St.
Salem, MA 01970
www.olive-oil.com

Joyva Corp.
(sesame butter)
Brooklyn, NY 11237

Goya Foods, Inc.
(oils, beans, spice blends)
Secaucus, NJ 07096

Kadoya Sesame Mills, Inc.
Japan

Homespun Recipes

Introduction

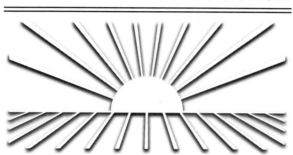

Recipes are not written in stone! There are factors, such as available ingredients and desired serving size, which can influence the final results of any recipe. We recognize that you are going to adjust many of this book's recipes, to suit your personal needs...and taste! For this reason, a special chapter is devoted to your creative genius. Most important, you should recognize that cooking is also a statement of ones' personal beliefs; that it is a heritage, passed down through the generations; from father to daughter, mother to grandmother! For this reason, the reader should document their experience with vegan cuisine, not just for friends and family, but for future generations as well.

With this philosophy in mind, the following pages include ten recipe templates. These blank templates include space for your recipe's introductory statement, twenty rows for ingredient listings, and two and one-half pages for instructions. Before you do any writing in them, make sure you've read the following guidelines:

First, document all of your steps on separate scratch paper. (You can always photocopy the templates, for use as scratch paper.) When you've streamlined your recipe, only then should you enter this information into the following template pages. You should enter a recipe title, short description, projected serving portions, your name and (for historical reasons) the date you entered the recipe. All ingredients are entered into the ingredients table in the same order they're called for in the actual cooking instructions. The cooking instructions should include preparatory steps in the opening paragraphs. Next, the cooking steps themselves, and finally, any suggested presentation tips.

This protocol will reinforce discipline, and help you to avoid any chance that you've omitted relevant ingredients and instructional steps. Most published recipes demonstrate this formal process. To the uninitiated, this procedure may seem a bit extraneous. Just remind yourself whenever you find yourself tempted to cut corners, future generations will salute you for insight and good taste!

TITLE:_____

DESCRIPTION:_____

_____

_____

_____

_____

_____

_____

_____

_____

_____

PORTIONS:_____

AUTHOR:_____**DATE:**___/___/___

MEASURE	INGREDIENT

Homespun Recipes

MEASURE	INGREDIENT

INSTRUCTIONS:_____

_____

_____

_____

_____

_____

_____

_____

_____

_____

_____

_____

_____

Homespun Recipes

TITLE:_____

DESCRIPTION:_____

_____

_____

_____

_____

_____

_____

_____

_____

_____

_____

PORTIONS:_____

AUTHOR:_____**DATE:**___/___/___

MEASURE	INGREDIENT

Homespun Recipes

MEASURE	INGREDIENT

INSTRUCTIONS:_____

423

Homespun Recipes

TITLE:_____

DESCRIPTION:_____

_____

_____

_____

_____

_____

_____

_____

_____

_____

PORTIONS:_____

AUTHOR:_____**DATE:**__/__/__

MEASURE	INGREDIENT

Homespun Recipes

MEASURE	INGREDIENT

INSTRUCTIONS:

Homespun Recipes

TITLE:_____

DESCRIPTION:_____

_____

_____

_____

_____

_____

_____

_____

_____

_____

_____

PORTIONS:_____

AUTHOR:_____**DATE:**__/__/__

MEASURE	INGREDIENT

Homespun Recipes

MEASURE	INGREDIENT

INSTRUCTIONS:

Homespun Recipes

TITLE:_____

DESCRIPTION:_____

_____

_____

_____

_____

_____

_____

_____

_____

_____

PORTIONS:_____

AUTHOR:_____**DATE:**__/__/__

MEASURE	INGREDIENT

Homespun Recipes

MEASURE	INGREDIENT

INSTRUCTIONS:_____

_____

_____

_____

_____

_____

_____

_____

_____

_____

_____

_____

Homespun Recipes

TITLE:_____

DESCRIPTION:_____

_____

_____

_____

_____

_____

_____

_____

_____

PORTIONS:_____

AUTHOR:_____**DATE:**__/__/__

MEASURE	INGREDIENT

Homespun Recipes

MEASURE	INGREDIENT

INSTRUCTIONS:

Homespun Recipes

TITLE:_____

DESCRIPTION:_____

_____

_____

_____

_____

_____

_____

_____

_____

_____

PORTIONS:_____

AUTHOR:_____**DATE:**__/__/__

MEASURE	INGREDIENT

Homespun Recipes

MEASURE	INGREDIENT

INSTRUCTIONS:_____

_____

_____

_____

_____

_____

_____

_____

_____

_____

_____

_____

_____

Homespun Recipes

TITLE:_____

DESCRIPTION:_____

_____

_____

_____

_____

_____

_____

_____

_____

_____

PORTIONS:_____

AUTHOR:_____**DATE:**__/__/__

MEASURE	INGREDIENT

Homespun Recipes

MEASURE	INGREDIENT

INSTRUCTIONS:

Homespun Recipes

TITLE:_____

DESCRIPTION:_____

_____

_____

_____

_____

_____

_____

_____

_____

_____

PORTIONS:_____

AUTHOR:_____**DATE:**__/__/__

MEASURE	INGREDIENT

Homespun Recipes

MEASURE	INGREDIENT

INSTRUCTIONS:_____

_____

_____

_____

_____

_____

_____

_____

_____

_____

_____

_____

_____

_____

Homespun Recipes

TITLE:_____

DESCRIPTION:_____

_____

_____

_____

_____

_____

_____

_____

_____

_____

PORTIONS:_____

AUTHOR:_____**DATE:**___/___/___

MEASURE	INGREDIENT

Homespun Recipes

MEASURE	INGREDIENT

INSTRUCTIONS:_____

_____

_____

_____

_____

_____

_____

_____

_____

_____

_____

_____

_____

Homespun Recipes

Index

The following is an extended index of the Veggie Works Vegan Cookbook. Recipe titles are bold-italicized. Other entries are glossary references, with the balance going to relevant chapters and subjects of interest.

Every effort has been expended to ensure the integrity this index. If errors are discovered, we'd genuinely appreciate knowing about them; so please email your flags to: <lgbrossa@hotmail.com>, with "Index Error" in the subject header.

A

A Introduction 1
A-1 sauce 242, 339
acorn squash 12, 401
active dry yeast 245, 247, 248, 255, 257, 265, 266, 267
agar agar 10, 343
aldente 144
alfalfa sprouts 80
Alfredo Sauce 99
All American Barbecue - theme 338
allspice 10, 343, 397, 399
almond 344
almond extract 324
almonds 310
aluminum foil 304
ambrosia 31
American diet 3, 185, 243
American Stew 200
American Sunday Picnic - theme 338
American White Bean Soup 42

amino acids 285, 287
animal products 2
anise 10, 344, 397, 399
Appendix Chapter 397
apple 16, 296, 300, 313
apple cider vinegar 10
apple juice 313
Apple Pie 297
apple sauce 296, 341
Apple Sauce Doughnuts 296
arrowroot 344
arrowroot powder 103, 114, 205
artichoke 126, 149, 345
artichoke hearts 153
Artichokes Italian Style 126
asafetida 9, 345
Asian 204
asparagus 12, 48, 162, 181, 207, 210, 220, 223, 224, 225, 227, 230, 238, 242, 329
au gratin 345
Au Gratin Vegetables 125
Author 5
Autumn Moon Soup 41
avocado 31, 33, 34, 36, 37, 79, 80, 345
Avocado & Hummus Sandwich 79
Avocado & Soy Cheese Sandwich 80

B

Babaganouj 13
baby carrots 148
Baby Food Chapter 325
Baby's 'Jello' 327
Baby's Fruit 326
Baby's Grains 326
Baby's Nut-Seed Milk 327
Baby's Pudding 328
Baby's Salad 328
Baby's Soy Milk 329
Baby's Steamed Vegetables 329
bacon 81, 284
bacon bits 284
Bacon Lettuce & Tomato Sandwich 81
bake 345
Baked Beans 127

Index

Index

Index

Index

Index

Index

Index

X

Y

Z